S0-BYI-745

THE PERFECTLY CONTENTED MEAT-EATER'S GUIDE TO VEGETARIANISM

WESTFIELD PUBLIC LIBRARY
333 West Hoover Street
Westfield, IN 46074

"It's hard to believe, but there's some good information in this book. What makes the book distinctive is its sense of humor. Far from detracting from the issues, the use of humor often cuts to the heart of a problem sooner than a lot of more serious discussion. For anyone interested in food, this book is not to be missed."–**Keith Akers**, author of *Vegetarian Sourcebook*

"Closely reasoned, witty, and wry. Imagine a stand-up comic convincing an audience of omnivores to "Go Vegetarian."– **Kristin Aronson**, author of *To Eat Flesh They Are Willing, Are Their Spirits Weak?*

"Mark Reinhardt uses his zany humor to prove that meat is no laughing matter. Here's the perfect book to investigate the vegetarian lifestyle and come up smiling.. A user-friendly almanac of facts and information that should impress even the most dedicated meat-eater."–**Henry Spira**, animal activist

"Reinhardt's book is informative without being pedantic. It's entertaining without being frivolous. I can't wait to buy a copy for my meat-eating friends."–**Rynn Berry**, author of *Famous Vegetarians and Their Favorite Recipes*

"If *The Perfectly Contented Meat-Eater's Guide to Vegetarianism* had been around when I became a vegetarian, my parents might have laughed instead of cried. It's light, it's witty, and it makes very good sense."–**Jennifer Raymond**, vegetarian cook

"There are probably millions of nice, normal, sane vegetarians, but Mark Reinhardt isn't one of them. He's a wise-cracking, straight-shooting former carnivore who gave up meat (which had to be especially difficult for an attorney) and lived to tell about it. With a refreshingly light hand, he clearly defines the issues facing all of us who consume food as well as the conflicting beliefs within the vegetarian community. Reinhardt is that rarest and most persuasive of advocates: he takes his beliefs, but not himself, very seriously. Regardless of your own beliefs, you'll enjoy the book."– **Kenn Amdahl**, author of *There Are No Electrons: Electronics for Earthlings*

THE PERFECTLY CONTENTED MEAT-EATER'S GUIDE TO VEGETARIANISM

A Book for Those Who *Really* Don't
Want to be Hassled about Their Diet

Mark Warren Reinhardt

Illustrated by Joy Reinhardt

Continuum • New York

WESTFIELD PUBLIC LIBRARY
333 West Hoover Street
Westfield, IN 46074

1998

The Continuum Publishing Company
370 Lexington Avenue
New York, NY 10017

Copyright © 1998 by Mark Warren Reinhardt

All rights reserved. No part of this book may be reproduced, stored in a retrieval system, or transmitted, in any form or by any means, electronic, mechanical, photocopying, recording, or otherwise, without the written permission of The Continuum Publishing Company.

Printed in the United States of America

Library of Congress Cataloging-in-Publication Data

Reinhardt, Mark Warren.
  The perfectly contented meat-eater's guide to vegetarianism: a book for those who really don't want to be hassled about their diet / Mark Warren Reinhardt
     p.   cm.
  Includes bibliographical references. 249
  ISBN 0-8264-1082-0 (pbk. : alk. paper)
  1. Vegetarianism. 2. Nutrition.   I. Title.
TX392.R45   1998
613.2'62–dc21   97-41023
                                                          CIP

to Fritz and Joy

Acknowledgments

There are lots of wonderful people I want to acknowledge for their help with this book. My heartfelt thanks

...to *Jennie Collura, Brian Graff* and the *North American Vegetarian Society* for originally pushing me into this project, and for their help along the way,

...to *Kristin Aronson, Ph.D.* for her intellectual inspiration, and for her many practical suggestions,

...to *Keith Akers, Kate Lawrence*, and the fine folks at the Vegetarian Society of Colorado for putting up with my writing over the years, and for originally publishing some of the ideas I've refined and brought together in this book,

...to *Susan Zimmerman*, the most ethical vegetarian I know, for all her great ideas,

...to my mother, *Joy Reinhardt*, for the wonderful artwork,

...and to *Martin Rowe*, for believing in the project and making it a reality.

Finally, I want to acknowledge the vegetarians of this world. (You know who you are!) Thank you all for being role models, for your inspiration and support, and for sharing a way of life that, over the years, has given me so much happiness.

Contents

The First Part

Why the heck would anyone be a vegetarian?

The Second Part
Okay, maybe I'll think about vegetarianism.
But tell me...what the heck would I eat?

The Third Part
So, if I actually decide to become a vegetarian, just what can I expect? or... leading the vegetarian life

Preface

To the meat-eater

All right, I know what you're thinking. You need a book on vegetarianism about as much as you need the latest popular venereal disease. You don't even cook. Cooking is a lot of trouble and is best left to eccentric people like Julia Child and experts like Mrs. Paul, Mrs. Field, Mrs. Butterworth, and Mrs. Smith.

Anyway, you don't want to hear about vegetarianism. Vegetarians are very strange folks. They're into fanatical causes like animal rights and all those weird religions from exotic places like Mongolia and San Francisco.

Even if vegetarianism might be healthy and good for the Earth, you don't have to worry about that. You do your part for the environment by carpooling with your bowling team and mowing the lawn. And as for health...well, your diet's healthy enough. You don't eat much red meat anyway—mostly "chicken" and "fish"—and it's been months since you had any really serious diseases.

But even though you don't really need this book, maybe it will help you understand that lunatic-fringe vegetarian kid of yours. Better yet, why not buy a copy for your Uncle Louie—the one who's had two bypass operations and always has grease dripping down his chin. Yeah, Uncle Louie could use some enlightenment.

Before you give it to him, though, read this book yourself. You might find that **"chicken" and "fish" aren't as groovy as you thought**. But you'll discover all kinds of new foods that are. (We're talking low fat, zero cholesterol, tasty, and best of all, cheap!) You'll also pick up some **pointers on barbecuing**, and you'll get lots of **foolproof dieting tips**, including some that have nothing at all to do with what you eat. (I promise.)

Invite Uncle Louie to dinner. Pretend you're Julia Child and whip him up a fast gourmet vegetarian dinner. Give his heart one night's reprieve from the constant onslaught of animal fat. He just might like it, and he might not have to go in for that third bypass operation. You'll be proud of yourself.

To the vegetarian

Okay, so you probably feel a little silly standing there in the bookstore reading the Preface of a book meant for meat-eaters. Don't worry. Just tell yourself that you're considering this book as a present for all those meat-eaters out there who just can't seem to understand your weird diet.

There's your overweight cousin Irene for example. After all, if she reads this book and actually becomes a vegetarian, she'll slim down and feel gorgeous for the first time. Good for her! She'll probably be so grateful she'll give you her car.

So buy this book for Cousin Irene. But before you give it to her, it will be perfectly proper to read it yourself. When you do you'll learn what the *worst* **vegetarian foods** are, you'll get tips on how to **score big on your date** with that perfect person (or so you think) you met at the office watercooler, and you'll get to see those great **nude photographs** we slipped in between pages 121 and 122. You might even decide to keep this book around for a while, just to make sure it's right for Irene. Take your time—you don't want to rush into anything.

Remember, this book is meant for meat-eaters, not vegetarians. So tell the woman at the cash register it's a gift for someone else. Then keep it hidden in a drawer in your kitchen. No one but you has to know the truth.

*put on your name tag
and get out the handshake buzzer,
we've got...*

a bunch of introductions...

A question of definition (p. 23)

Introduction #1

You're a meat-eater. You love your steaks and bacon and salmon mousse and moose. You even like those "chicken nugget" things with the special secret sauce. And you've never seriously thought about vegetarianism. *You don't want to think about vegetarianism.* The whole concept is about as welcome in your life as nuclear war or tape worms. No, it's worse than that. You'd probably put vegetarianism in that special category you reserve for *really* scary things—things like root canal work, insurance salesmen, and the Home Shopping Network.

If you think the whole point of this book is to tear the cheeseburger out of your hand and plop you down in a Tibetan monastery to survive on sprouts and carrot juice for the rest of your life, relax...The monastery is really in Nepal. (Just kidding!)

No, the philosophy here is that vegetarianism should *add* to your life, not subtract from it. The aim is not to get you to give up anything, but rather to introduce you to some new ideas that have added immeasurably to the lives of millions of people around the world. If, in the process, you leap up and scream "Alleluia! I'm enlightened now!" and decide that eating meat is not for you, that would be extremely groovy. But if you just get a new appreciation for what vegetarianism is all about, that's great too. At the very least you'll have a few hours away from the dentist, and I promise not to try to sell you insurance.

Introduction #2

Bob, a case study

Let's imagine the typical reader I'm trying to entice here. I don't want to offend any female readers, but let's just say his name is Bob (a good palindrome). He's forty-something, he once lived in Texas, and, shucks ma'am, he does like "down-home" cooking. Indeed, all his life Bob's been a "meat and potatoes" kind of guy—the kind of guy who wouldn't have been caught dead reading a stupid book like this one.

The trouble is, a couple of things have happened lately to make Bob rethink his priorities. The first is that he's contracted Dunlop's Disease. (For non-medical readers, this is a condition not uncommon in middle-aged men. It occurs when the belly "done lops" over the belt buckle.) More importantly, Bob just got back from his annual physical. His blood cholesterol level was somewhere in excess of 250 mg./dl., and the doctor told him if he didn't make some changes fast he was headed straight to "Bypass City". Since Bob's paid a lot of money into the government's Social Security program and wants to live to get some of it back, he's taking this advice seriously.

Bob opens this book with the best of intentions. Maybe there are some quick tips in here, he thinks. Something that will lower his cholesterol a hundred points or so before the big game on Sunday. After all, Ted and Susan are doing steaks for the tailgate party.

Bob's dilemma, of course, is that he doesn't want to change his lifestyle. More specifically, he doesn't want to give up meat. After all, Bob's been eating meat for forty-something years. It's an old friend. He loves the stuff. Sure, he's had those little pangs of guilt about killing brown-eyed cows from time to time, but he puts those out of his mind. Anyway, Bob knows about the "V" word, and it's not for him. The "V" word, of course, is "vegetarianism", and Bob knows that all vegetarians are weird. Eating meat is natural, he reasons. Even if he has to visit Bypass City every few years, he's not giving up his meat.

Perhaps you're a little bit like Bob. Most people are. Even most of us vegetarians are converts, and we craved meat at one point in our lives. The fact is that meat can be powerfully addicting—kind of like chocolate, or maybe even *Days of Our Lives.* So we vegetarians understand if you meat-eaters break into a cold sweat at the thought of someone locking you out of the local McDonald's, or telling you that you can never bite into chickens' legs again.

> **Don't worry! The number one rule of this book is that everyone should be able to eat anything they want and as much as they want!**

So, what's the point? Bob might say (and you might agree with him). *Life's been bad enough since I gave up smoking, cybersex and martinis at lunch. I'm not ready for any more sacrifices. Anyway, I have no willpower, and I'm always going to love meat. So I'm a lost cause. I'm never going to become a vegetarian!*

It's funny, though, how things can change when you just change your point of view. There are millions of vegetarians out there. We don't have any more willpower than Bob. We don't need it. We're very happy with our diets, thank you, and wouldn't go back to eating meat for anything. Sacrifice? Hardly.

From our vegetarian point of view we feel sorry for Bob. It's terrible that he has to worry about cholesterol and saturated fat and Dunlop's Disease. It's terrible that he might have to visit Bypass City. It's even terrible that he can't look a cow in the eye. Life is too short for all of that—we're busy enjoying dinner. Mostly, though, we feel sorry for Bob because of what he eats. Don't take offense, but we don't even like to be in the same room with that stuff, much less put it in our mouths.

In **Part 1** of this book we'll talk a little bit about vegetarianism, and I'll try to show Bob what things look like from this side of the fence. I think if Bob can experience the vegetarian point of view, he's going to have a great big hankering to change his life for the better— wild horses couldn't keep him from changing his life for the better.

In **Part 2** I'll show Bob how he can make these changes. More specifically, since he doesn't have a clue what vegetarians eat, I'll give him lots of ideas, and introduce him to some funky new foods.

While he's enjoying all these new foods, Bob will want to hang around for **Part 3** (which by coincidence immediately follows Part 2). That's where we'll explore that extra-strange interface where the strange world of vegetarianism meets the strange world of meat-eating. If Bob is going to try vegetarianism he'll need some advice on meeting women, getting along with his relatives and buying a refrigerator. We vegetarians can help with all that.

You should feel free to read over Bob's shoulder. And be sure to take notes. There are going to be tests all along the way.

Still *another* Introduction

Getting the terms straight

People don't really understand vegetarians or the unusual way they choose to eat. Given the general level of confusion about what vegetarianism really is, it seems prudent to define the terms I'll be

WESTFIELD PUBLIC LIBRARY
333 West Hoover Street
Westfield, IN 46074

using throughout this book. As the saying goes, you can't tell the players without a scorecard, and it's especially tough here since vegetarians usually don't wear numbers on their backs. Here are some handy definitions:

> **Vegetarians**—People who consistently choose not to eat the flesh of animals.

Vegetarians, though, are a large and diverse group of folks. There are two general kinds of vegetarians:

1. Ovo-Lacto Vegetarians—These are vegetarians who eat dairy products ("lacto") and chickens' eggs ("ovo"). The Latin is just thrown in to add an air of mystery. Are there vegetarians who are only "lacto", or only "ovo"? Certainly there are, but keeping track of them with Latin terms seems unnecessarily complicated.

2. Vegans (pronounced "vee-guns")—These folks choose not to eat *any* animal products, including dairy, eggs and (usually) honey. They may also be referred to as "strict vegetarians" (because they're all good disciplinarians?) or "pure vegetarians". (No doubt, because they're all so pure at heart!)

There were no vegetarians before 1842!

You history buffs will be happy to know that the term "vegetarian" was coined sometime around 1842 by the folks who would soon found The Vegetarian Society of the United Kingdom. It's derived from the Latin word "vegetus", meaning "whole, sound, fresh, or lively". This is appropriate, because vegetarianism has to do with a lot more than just vegetables. The term "vegan" wasn't used until 1944 when the Vegan Society was founded in England.

Despite these rather recent origins, I must humbly point out that, of course, the vegan style of eating goes way back to the Garden of Eden.

But wait! Some vegetarians eat "chicken" and "fish"!

Or so they say. Go into most restaurants and ask what vegetarian items are being served and the waitperson is sure to point out a few "fish" items on the menu, and maybe even a dish or two with chickens in them. It's a popular misconception that keeps us vegetarians

Just who are vegetarians, anyway?

To answer this question, our intrepid interviewer has crossed the U.S. of A., shamelessly soliciting real made-up people for their thoughts about vegetarians. Here are some of the answers:

Carol Menloe, Media Consultant, Hollywood, CA: *Are there still vegetarians? I thought all that was passé.*

Ed and Ralph Poplawski (they're brothers!), Steelworkers, Pittsburgh, PA: **Ed:** *A vegetarian? Yeah, that's one of those people like a communist or a hippie, isn't it? I don't have much use for those kind of people.* **Ralph:** *Wasn't that Charles Manson guy a vegetarian?*

Dale Rice, Health Nut, Berkeley, CA: *Vegetarians are great, as long as they don't cook their food, eat only sea vegetables before noon, and properly balance their intake of grain hulls and fruit seeds according to the phases of the moon.*

Cynthia Brooks, Animal Rights Activist, Rochester, NY: *A vegetarian, of course, doesn't use antibiotics. It's not ethical to kill germs.*

David Andrews, Businessman, Chicago, IL: *Chicken and fish are fine, I suppose, but I need a good steak once in a while.*

Susan and Gene Webb, "Yuppies", Greenwich, CT: *We used to be vegetarians in college. That was fine for us then, but we all have to mature. Now we're into entertaining the right people and finding quality time for our two talented and lovely children. The future belongs to those who properly manage their assets.*

Ed Jackson, Rancher, Laramie, WY: *Vegetarians? You've got to be kidding! If I had one here I'd brand him, castrate him, wire a tag to his ear and put him out in the field. Say,* **you're** *not a vegetarian, are you?*

Billy Bob Johnson, Redneck, Waco, TX: *Vegetarians are all fruits and nuts. Get it—'Fruits and Nuts'? What do you mean you've heard that before?*

Sandra Wilmer, Store Clerk, Springfield, MO: *I took my dog in to one for shots, and he seemed nice.*

Mom, Sweet Old Lady, Anytown, USA: *Eat your beef now sonny, and don't think about that any more.*

explaining our diet over and over. (That's okay, it's a subject we like to talk about!) This misconception has also led to a joke popular among vegetarians:

> *"You know, sharks are vegetarian."*
> *"Sharks!?"*
> *"Yeah, they only eat fish!"*

Let's get it straight right now: Vegetarians don't eat "chicken" or "fish". Therefore, if you eat "chicken" or "fish" you're *not* a vegetarian.

It's funny though. Even when they know their definitions, it's amazing how many people want to be associated with the "V" word, and think of themselves as vegetarian when they really aren't. They bend the rules just a little, and make up their own silly terms like **"pesce-vegetarian"** and **"pollo-vegetarian"**. Now, we don't want to be old sticks-in-the-mud, but you're soon going to see that there are some **very good reasons why we vegetarians don't eat chickens or fishes.** We'd rather not go tampering with vegetarianism to include these things.

So, what should we do about this? If you've given up red meat, but continue to eat birds and fishes, you're not technically a vegetarian yet. (This means you don't get the souvenir certificate suitable for framing, and you don't get to learn the secret handshake.) But don't give up. Just because you don't meet the definition of vegetarian doesn't mean you aren't on the right track! We're going to give you a new name (something without a "V" in it, please), pat you on the back, and acknowledge how far you've come. Then I hope you'll read the rest of this book and learn what real vegetarianism is all about. (As a matter of fact, the very next one of these boring introductions is written just for you!) Who knows, by the time you reach those really boring chapters later in this book we might be scheduling your secret swearing-in ceremony!

Chicken or chickens, fish or fishes, those are the questions

Chickens and fishes are animals, of course, and each one is an individual. When we kill them and put them on our dinner plates, though, we lump them all together under the misnomer "chicken" or "fish". This doesn't seem right. In this book I'll call them chickens and fishes (or at least "chicken" and "fish" with quotes) regardless of where they are located or what the state of their health is. Hopefully this will remind us that each one is (or was) an individual and deserves to be recognized as such.

...and cows and pigs, there's another question

It's the same way for cows and pigs. When we kill them for food we strip them of their individual status and keep ourselves from thinking of them as living beings by using euphemistic terms like "beef", "pork", and "veal". This isn't right either. When I have to use these terms in this book I'll put them in quotes, just so nobody forgets the animals these "foods" came from.

---

speaking of names...

What do you call a guy who eats rice?

A vegetarian friend of mine was eating lunch in his company cafeteria. He didn't have much food in the house the night before, so he'd brought in a simple lunch of plain brown rice. A co-worker looked at what he was eating and said: "Hey, I bet you're one of those microbiologists."

Yet another silly Introduction

Wait, I don't need this book!
I'm practically a vegetarian already!

See if this sounds familiar:
- You're concerned about your health.
- You've been trying to cut back on fat and eat a healthier diet.
- You've been trying to get more exercise.
- You've *just about* given up "red" meat.
- You've been eating more "chicken" and "fish".
- You're practically a vegetarian already!

If the above describes you, congratulations. You seem to be moving toward a healthier lifestyle. Now, we certainly don't want to discourage you in your efforts or risk offending you, but there are just a few things that we gung-ho, rabid vegetarians feel obliged to point out:

1. Everybody is "almost a vegetarian".

Yes, it's true. Whenever we vegetarians get around to discussing our favorite topic, virtually everyone we talk to professes to be darned near to being a vegetarian already. Everyone seems to have cut way back on the dreaded "red" meat in favor of the quintessentially healthy "chicken" and "fish". Now, we don't question the sincerity of these folks, but it *does* make us wonder. Just how do those hamburger joints stay in business?

2. Chickens and fishes may not be as healthy as you think.

Here's the conventional wisdom:
- Chickens and fishes are high protein foods with less fat than "beef";
- Fat is bad;
- *Ergo*, chickens and fishes are good for you.

Well, just because the first two of these propositions may be true, doesn't necessarily justify the conclusion. Indeed, chickens and fishes have some problems of their own, at least when they're used for human food:
- Chickens and fishes are generally lower in fat than "beef", but much *higher* in cholesterol.
- Sure, they have lots of protein. In fact, they have *too much* protein, and that makes them *bad* for your health, not good for it.
- Finally, both of these "foods" have some serious contamination problems. Chickens are often laced with salmonella and other bacteria. And as for fishes, well they're the universal repository for virtually every contaminant on the planet (mercury, PCBs, chlordane, dioxin, DDT, etc.). The U.S. Environmental Protection Agency issues "fish" consumption advisories by the thousands for these contaminants. And if that isn't enough, *Consumer Reports* magazine found 44% of the supermarket "fish" samples they tested to be substantially contaminated with E. coli (fecal) bacteria. If you're eating chickens and fishes you'd better wash your hands *after* you fix dinner as well as before.

We'll talk more about all of this later. The important thing to know now is that while chickens and fishes *might* be healthier to eat than "beef", that's not saying much, and it misses the point. The point is, they aren't *nearly* as healthy as the things you *should* be eating.

3. If you're a "chicken" and "fish" person, you're missing scads of important environmental and ethical issues.

Okay, so maybe you'd rather not think of the environmental and ethical ramifications of your food choices. I know it's tough. But as we go through this book I'll encourage you to look at things from a *new perspective*. Instead of denying the truth, why not use it to your *advantage*? Once you understand the environmental and ethical issues (as outlined in detail in the breathtakingly exciting upcoming chapters) it will be much, *much* easier to stick to the healthy diet you know you want to have. That's because **good health for you and good health for the world around you naturally go together**. Bear with me a little longer. This is all going to be very easy!

Question authority #1

A wise man (or maybe he was just a wiseguy) once said that if you don't have the facts to back up what you're saying, you only have an opinion—just like everybody else. With this in mind I've tried to back up what I've said in this book with facts. I've made every effort to acquire data from the most conservative and accurate sources I could find, and verify that data wherever possible, with the intent that this book should be as reliable as anything in print. (You can find many of these sources in the Resources section at the end of the book.)

Does that mean we innocent readers should believe everything we read in this book?

Not on your life!

People lie with statistics all the time, and you can find published data to support any position. I invite you—no, I *urge* you—to question everything in this book. Get involved. Go to the library, call the American Meat Institute to get their facts/opinions, and then reach your own conclusions.

> **Vegetarianism isn't a religion—we vegetarians don't ask you to take anything on faith.**

Interest in vegetarianism is thriving, and the whole concept of vegetarianism will eventually prevail in our society, because it is supported by two simple things: the truth and human reason. That's why we love your scrutiny!

So, don't take a vegetarian's word for anything. Use your brain. Put us to the test.

The meat-eating life? (p. 29)

The First Part

Why the heck would anyone be a vegetarian?

We'll look at the reasons for eating meat and the reasons for being vegetarian, and let you figure it out for yourself. Then we'll look at some vegetarian-related issues like feminism and your waistline. Finally, we'll tie it all together and let you make your own choices, keeping in mind your willpower (low) and the available excuses (plentiful). (Hey, we're all human!)

The benefits of fiber (p. 57)

Chapter 1

Why we all do what we do...
The Great Reasons

Why be a vegetarian?

T hat's the weighty, philosophical question this book attempts to address. While the answer is fairly simple, maybe the question is wrong. Maybe the question should be:

Why eat meat?

A fter all, meat-eating is a more active endeavor than *not* eating meat. If you just sit around watching old episodes of *Bonanza* you're not eating meat. Meat-eating, on the other hand, takes work. You've got to raise an animal, grow crops to feed it, care for it, lug it around, kill it, skin it, clean it, lug it around some more, chop it up, take it home and cook it (or some variation of that sequence). That's a *lot* more work than watching *Bonanza*, and a lot more work than simply eating the corn or the soybeans that you grew to feed the animal in the first place.

So why go to all that trouble just to have something to eat with your green beans and baked potato and Sara Lee pound cake? Why not just throw an extra potato in the oven and a few more beans in the pot? Better yet, why not have an extra piece of pound cake?

Reasons to eat meat

Y ou can probably come up with lots of reasons why you eat meat, but—now don't be offended by this—most of them aren't true. Unless you're genetically different from 99.99% of the rest of meat-eaters on Earth (maybe you have scales and an extra toe), you eat meat because of one fact:

> **You eat meat because you grew up being taught that it was the thing to do, and you've never had to seriously question that fact.**

Now, isn't that true?

So, what happens if you do question it? If you do question your meat-eating ways, you'll find two (and only two) very good, very rational reasons to support your behavior.

The Two Great Reasons to eat meat:

1. It tastes good.

2. It's convenient.

Let's look at the **Two Great Reasons** a little closer.

Taste...

Who can deny that, once they get used to it, humans love the taste of animals? Most people eat the flesh of the same few types of creatures two or three times a day, literally every day of their lives. That's a lot of eating the same old thing. People wouldn't do that unless they really, *really* liked it, would they? Most meat is fairly high in fat and calories. People like foods high in fat and calories. They have what food scientists call "mouth appeal", and they make us want to lean back in our Lazy-Boys and fall asleep. We like that.

Question: *If people like meat so much, isn't that evidence that it is our natural food?*
Answer #1: The average zoo elephant will eat Hostess Twinkies out of your hand until you get tired of feeding him.
Answer #2: The sign says: "Please don't feed Hostess Twinkies to the elephants—it makes them sick."

...and convenience.

What about convenience? Ninety-nine percent of the folks in the Western World (to find it, go to the Eastern World and turn left) eat meat, give or take a few guys in Des Moines. That means that virtually every restaurant you go into will have a plethora of meat dishes on the menu. Lots of choices. And if you're eating dinner at a friend's house, on an airplane, at the ballpark, or even out of your friendly neighborhood grocer's freezer case, the odds are overwhelming that meat will be on the menu. It's just this simple.

Simple truth #1

If most people eat meat, it's easier to go along with the crowd. It's always less convenient to be an individualist.

Of course, like most simple truths, this one leads to a great irony:

Great irony of life #1

Meat-eating is inherently much more complicated than vegetarianism (feeding animals, building slaughterhouses, hosing out pig pens, etc., etc.), but for the *individual* in our society meat-eating is much easier.

Question: *If 99% of the people in our society eat meat, it must be the right thing to do, huh? After all, a billion steak eaters can't be wrong!*
Answer #1: If a billion steak eaters decided to jump off a cliff, etc., etc.
Answer #2: Yeah, and we've got too many lawyers, too.

---

*Wait, you say. What about vitamins? What about protein?? What about the "beef" ads on television??? What about all the big, strong football players who have their pre-game steak dinners and then belch when someone's helmet hits them in the stomach???? And what about Mom, who in 1977 **very distinctly** said we need to finish our liver to get enough iron?????*

With all due deference to Mom, she was wrong. As we'll see later in this book, the *overwhelming* weight of scientific evidence (as confirmed by many millions of healthy vegetarians around the world) is that **you don't need animal products to live, and indeed you're much, *much* healthier without them.**

It tastes good, and it's convenient. If you want to support eating meat, those are your arguments.

Reasons to be a vegetarian

In contrast to the **Two Great Reasons to eat meat**, there are three great reasons to be a vegetarian. (Obviously, since three is greater than two, this must be the way to go.) Here they are.

The Three Great Reasons to be a vegetarian:

1. It's better for you.
Unless you plan on being hit by a bus sometime soon, a vegetarian diet will make you healthier, and you'll live longer.

2. It's better for the Earth.
Switching to a vegetarian diet just may be the best thing you can do in your personal life to help the environment.

3. It's kind.
Every time you eat a vegetarian meal, rather than one centered around animal products, you are reducing the pain and suffering in this world.

Now, as a meat-eater, there are two ways you might react to this news. You might say, "Hey, none of that matters to me. What matters to me are the **Two Great Reasons to eat meat.**" If that's the case, you might want to skip right to the semi-funny joke on page 115, and then donate this book to charity on your way out to buy "pork" chops. Thanks for bearing with me this far anyway.

My guess, though, is that you won't have that reaction. My guess is that you'll say to yourself, "Okay, tell me more about the **Three Great Reasons to be a vegetarian**, and I'll think about it. Of course, I'm not promising anything, because the **Two Great Reasons to eat meat** are pretty darn good reasons."

If that's your reaction, that's fair enough. We'll just move on through some of the exciting chapters coming up. Don't go away, but if you want to have a *Bonanza* rerun or two tuned in while you read, be my guest.

Other reasons to eat meat...Or not

All right, if you insist, there may be a few other reasons to eat meat or not to eat meat:

Could image be a reason?

Maybe you've decided that you want that Western demeanor— you know, riding, roping, branding, etc. What better way to enhance the look than by hanging around the old chuckwagon, gnawing on a T-bone? Just wipe your greasy hands on your jeans and wave to the Marlboro Man in the distance.

Even we vegetarians have to admit that meat can be an important part of the American cowboy, tough-guy image. Yup, you'll be as rugged as an old piece of galvanized steel, cruder than cheap toilet paper. And the image isn't limited to cowboys either. The private eye, infantry sergeant, and occasional litigation attorney can also benefit. In our world, image is everything. Just remember: things can never be bad as long as you're looking good!

How about money?

Don't forget, vegetarianism is cheaper than eating meat, and for some folks that may be a terrific reason to be a vegetarian. Vegetarians make cheap dates, too!

...or religion?

Religion, of course, has always been a great reason for people to do or not do almost everything. Many of the world's great religions, including Hinduism, Buddhism, Judaism, and Christianity have advocated abstention from meat to one degree or another. But it can work the other way, too.

A number of years ago I went to lunch at a bagel restaurant. The clerk behind the counter (let's just call him Jimmy) couldn't understand why I wanted a vegetarian lunch. It seems that Jimmy was heavily involved with some kind of fundamentalist church, and he believed it was a sin *not* to eat meat.

I told Jimmy that I found it hard to believe that God would insist on us being violent towards our fellow creatures, and indeed maybe He/She was the god of those creatures as well. Of course Jimmy would have none of this, and he begged me in vain to let him put a little "ham" or roast "beef" on my plate to insure my salvation. Jimmy snarled at me when I left. He probably still thinks I'm the world's greatest sinner.

Can religion be used as a reason to be a vegetarian? You bet. Can it be used as a reason to eat meat? Sure, why not?

Chapter 2

The First Great Reason to be a vegetarian is your health

*(...Because if you wreck your body,
where are you going to live?)*

Sure, you've got to die of something, but you don't necessarily have to die of all those *other* things.

The two largest killers of human beings in "developed" countries are heart disease and cancer. Thousands of scientific studies have linked these diseases to diet. If you have a television or read the newspaper you hear about new ones every week. So that leads to a question...

> **What are you doing in your personal life to promote your long term health? What are you doing to minimize the chance that you're going to be one of the "statistics" of these dreadful diseases?**

I conducted a massive, scientifically valid poll to determine the public's answers to these questions. Well, actually, I just surveyed a few of my friends. Here are the answers I got:

Greg: Skips breakfast and lunch.

Dennis: Cuts back on coffee and alcohol.

Gloria: Buys "healthy" frozen dinners.

Blake: Drinks lots of milk. Worries about sugar.

Rita: Takes calcium supplements.

Almost Everyone: Eats more chickens and fishes.

As this survey demonstrates, one of the problems with trying to modify our lifestyles and eat right for good health is the conflicting sources of information about what we should be doing. We live in a strange society where few allopathic doctors are adequately trained in nutrition, and where most of the data consumers have on the subject come from the advertising media. If you listen to those advertisements, then you know that *any one* of the following criteria absolutely insures a healthy product: high in polyunsaturates, low in saturated fat, high in calcium, low in sodium, high in protein, low in sugar, high in carbohydrates, low in carbohydrates, high in "fish" oil, low in "fish" oil, etc. It's a moving target, and keep in mind that a lot of really good foods (grapes, barley, lima beans from Peru, several brands of really nice 30-year-old Scotch, etc.) don't exactly have big advertising budgets.

All of this gets even more confusing when the scientific community comes out with conflicting information all the time about whether particular foods (1) are the greatest benefits to public health since Ted Bundy was arrested, or (2) will kill you instantly on contact.

So, what's a body to do???

Simple. A body's to become a vegetarian!

Nobody can follow all the advice in all those diet and health studies that come out daily, that's for sure. But in the twenty-odd years that I've been a vegetarian (actually, I've been a vegetarian in the even years as well), I can say that the vast, vast majority of the recommendations of the studies that I've heard about is supported by a vegetarian diet—automatically!

The world seems to be catching on to this, too. There's now tons of information out there showing that **vegetarians have *significantly* lower rates of heart disease, cancer, strokes, hypertension, Type II diabetes, obesity, and lots of other bad things than meat-eaters.** (It isn't just flaky vegetarian groups telling us this, either. Read, for example, the American Dietetic Association's Position Paper on Vegetarianism, or look at the dramatic results from the China-Cornell-Oxford Project on Nutrition, Health and Environment at Cornell University, probably the largest and most comprehensive study of the relationship between diet and disease ever undertaken.)

Of course, it's no coincidence that fruits and vegetables are so often featured in the "medical breakthrough of the day" reports, and that vegetarians are healthier than meat-eaters. There are some inherent, scientifically measurable qualities in plant-based foods that make them better for us than animal-based foods. For example, they contain no cholesterol, are naturally **low in fat**, and are **our only sources of fiber**. And that's just the beginning!

Sure, you're probably thinking at this point, *I already know vegetables and fruits and grains and beans are good for me. I eat all those things anyway. But who's to say meat doesn't have some things I need too? Anyway, **what about protein and vitamins and minerals?? How do you vegetarians ever get enough of all those things we invented the four basic food groups to make sure we get enough of???***

These are good questions, and to answer them we'll spend this chapter taking an imaginary journey through the wonderful world of food. We'll look at the things we need from our diets, and see how plant-based foods and animal-based foods compare. Then you can draw your own conclusions about what you should be eating. First, though, we need to take a little lesson in thermodynamics.

Before we talk about food, let's talk about energy

I don't want to get sacrilegious here and offend half of this book's readership (or any of the members of her family), but let's just imagine what might have happened if Moses had had a distant cousin named Abner. Abner might have gone up to the mountaintop to spend a few days at his summer place, and in the course of doing so he just might have achieved enlightenment in the art of calculating the nutritional value of foods. And after he got back he might have gathered his loyal following of Bacolytes around him to pass on his enlightenment.

If all this had actually happened, he would have given them...

The First Commandment of Food Calculations: Thou shalt measure everything by calories.

To understand why the First Commandment of Food Calculations is so darned important we need an example. Here's a nutritional analysis similar to those you might find in a typical magazine displayed at your grocer's check out aisle (right next to the new pictures of Elvis). It compares the nutritive value of eight ounce servings of some common food items:

Food	Quantity	Thiamin
T-bone Steak	8 oz.	.23 mg.
Broccoli	8 oz.	.15 mg.

Food	Quantity	Vitamin E
Flounders or Soles	8 oz.	4.29 ATE
Broccoli	8 oz.	3.76 ATE

Food	Quantity	Vitamin B-6
Porterhouse Steak	8 oz.	.84 mg.
Broccoli	8 oz.	.36 mg.

Food	Quantity	Riboflavin
Cows' Milk	8 oz.	4.74 mg.
Broccoli	8 oz.	2.00 mg.

Aha! you say. *Viva Burger King! Viva Dairy Queen! Viva Jack-In-The-Box!* All those ads on television for meat and milk were right on the money. Just get a load of those vitamins! No wonder football players are so healthy. And by contrast, pity that poor, pathetic broccoli. It looks pretty skimpy in the old vitamin department. No wonder it's eschewed (as opposed to *chewed*) by presidents and school kids and bowling teams.

The problem with this comparison, though, is that the human body has no nutritional need to get a certain number of "eight ounce servings" of food every day. What it does have a need for is calories. Calories are a measurement of stored energy, of course, and we all have to eat a certain number of them every day to have enough strength to play soccer, write symphonies and push the buttons on our TV remote controls. As a very rough estimate, your average burly male needs about 2700 Calories a day. Your average demure female gets by with about 2000. (See pages 113 and 114 for lots more fascinating information about Calories and calories.)

If we don't get enough calories our stomachs are like that man-eating plant in *The Little Shop of Horrors*. ("Feed me!") After a while we die. If we get too many calories our stomachs say, "I can't believe you ate the whole thing." After a while we notice our heads starting to look like small olives on big mounds of tuna fish. (See the exciting chapter on dieting later in this book for exotic details.) As long as our stomachs get the right number of calories they rarely say, "Hey, you ate an extra *three ounces* of food today," or "We need one more 'serving' down here before bedtime!"

Once you look at your body's requirements on a calorie basis, nutrition becomes a fairly easy game. Suppose, for example, you need 2500 Calories a day to give you adequate energy to push those remote control buttons. Consider those 2500 Calories as spending money, with which you can "buy" up to 2500 Calories worth of food each day. Some foods are more calorie-dense than others and will cost you more of your imaginary calorie money. If you want to buy a hot fudge sundae, for example, it might cost you 1000 Calories, leaving you with only 1500 left for the rest of the day's food. On the other hand, a radish goes cheap—costing less than 1 Calorie.

You win the nutrition game by spending your calorie money on a combination of foods that will provide you with all the nutrients you need for that day, and not give you too much of the stuff you don't want (fat, sodium, etc.). Pretty simple, huh?

To see how this works in practice, let's go back to the list of foods above. Suppose instead of eating an eight ounce serving of these foods, you decide that you'll spend your whole 2500 Calories on each one. Here's what you'll get:

Food	Quantity	Thiamin
Broccoli	2500 C	5.80 mg.
T-bone Steak	2500 C	1.05 mg.

Food	Quantity	Vitamin E
Broccoli	2500 C	148.21 ATE
Flounders or Soles	2500 C	51.92 ATE

Food	Quantity	Vitamin B-6
Broccoli	2500 C	14.20 mg.
Porterhouse Steak	2500 C	3.58 mg.

Food	Quantity	Riboflavin
Broccoli	2500 C	10.62 mg.
Cows' Milk	2500 C	6.6 mg.

Kind of a different story, isn't it? The stuff that looked so great when we measured by "ounces" looks pretty anemic when we measure by a day's worth of calories, and vice versa.

As a general rule meat and dairy products are very calorie-dense. Eating an eight ounce serving of them will probably give you more of some vitamins and minerals than eating eight ounces of vegetables. The drawback is that you'll have to spend lots and lots of your calorie dollars, which won't leave you with many left over for other foods. On the other hand, if you look at the return you get *for each calorie dollar spent,* you'll find that plant-based foods give you *much* more for your money. Let's say it another way:

> **If calories are land and vitamins and minerals (and other good stuff) are people, then vegetables are like Manhattan. Meat is more like...well, Wyoming. (Now there's an appropriate analogy!)**

We'll talk a lot more about this throughout the book when we compare the benefits and drawbacks of various foods. Right now here's what you need to know:

> **You only get to eat a limited number of calories. (Alas!) You want to make the most of each one of those little suckers!**

Now that we know about calories, we have the tools to analyze what we eat and make our decisions with a little more scientific accuracy than we get from the meat and dairy ads. And that's just what we're going to do.

Caution, danger, beware!

*The numbers you read in this book
(and everywhere else) aren't accurate!*

We all want to know what vitamins and minerals and protein and calories and other cool things are in the food we eat. But this is not easy information to supply. Consider that there are thousands of different foods out there. Add on top of that the fact that individual samples of these foods may vary depending on where and how they are produced, how they are transported, the time elapsed before they are eaten, etc. (For example, some people claim that organically grown produce has significantly more vitamins and minerals than non-organic produce, but I'll bet the pesticide companies would dispute this.) Next, be aware that cooking a food, and the method used for cooking, can significantly change its composition. And all of this doesn't even consider the human body's absorption and retention of those vitamins and minerals and other neat-o things.

What's a person to do when looking for reliable nutritional information?

Well, there are lots of sources of it out there, most significantly the friendly and helpful government of the good old United States of America. The Department of Agriculture (USDA), Agricultural Research Service, Nutrient Data Laboratory (does all that fit on a business card?) is charged with meeting the daunting task of telling us what's in our food. They do the analyses and report more information than you'd ever care to know about thousands and thousands of foods. This information is published in several printed forms, and is available for searching and downloading off the Internet.

That sounds great! So what's the problem?

The problem, which I discovered when I was doing research for this book, is that the information isn't accurate! Even though the government reports its numbers to a precision of three decimal places, even a cursory look at the publications will tell you that the numbers themselves can vary wildly depending on when and where they are reported. How wildly? The reported quantities of the *very first* mineral in the *very first* food I looked at showed a variation of *several hundred percent* between two publications from the same government office! Privately published books purportedly based on the government information showed still different numbers.

If the U.S. government's official information is this bad, one can only guess as to how accurate the food companies may be in generating the nutrition data you read on the boxes and cans your favorite foods come in. For example, let's say you're a consumer who loves tomatoes but who's worried about fat intake. Do you believe the information on the label of a can of your favorite brand of tomatoes (0% of calories from fat) or the government's information (14% of calories from fat!)? It's a real problem!

So, what's a body to do?

Unless otherwise noted, the food composition information in this book is based on data for raw foods from the USDA Nutrient Database for Standard Reference, Release 11, and interim amendments thereto. This was the most complete and up-to-date government database available at the time of publication. Is this information accurate? No, but it's probably the best I can do. Certainly it is accurate enough to support the basic concepts of vegetarian vs. non-vegetarian nutrition that are presented in these pages.

Food composition data seems to be more of an art than a science, but even if that wasn't true, remember: It's easy to manipulate data. It's easy to lie with statistics. As I've said once before, don't believe *anything* you read, whether it's here or in the magazine ads for "beef", where they give you data on meat that's had the fat surgically removed. Take the time to investigate. Your health is worth it.

Things we eat #1: Protein

There are three energy-containing nutrients (okay, four if you count alcohol) in the foods we eat—protein, fat and carbohydrates. We're going to look at all of them, but there's a reason I'm starting with protein. The absolute number one question that meat-eaters ask vegetarians is:

Where do you get your protein?

We get asked this question **a lot!** Meat-eaters worry that we aren't getting enough protein on a vegetarian diet. It's nice that they're so concerned, but they really needn't be. Because, as we'll see below...

> **It's impossible to design a reasonably varied
> vegetarian diet that *doesn't* supply enough protein!**

Instead of meat-eaters worrying about vegetarians with respect to this protein business, we should be worried about them. A much more important question is...

> **If you're going to eat meat and fish and dairy prod-
> ucts, how will you keep from getting *too much*
> protein???..**

Let's venture into the wonderful world of protein and find out why this might be a problem.

So, what is this stuff, and how much do we need?

Proteins form a class of chemical compounds made up of dozens, and sometimes hundreds, of molecules called amino acids. What all these amino acids (and therefore proteins too!) have in common is that they're made up of carbon and hydrogen and oxygen (just like carbohydrates and fats), but with the significant addition of *nitrogen*. (Write this down—we'll come back to it later!) There are about twenty amino acids that are considered important to human nutrition, and of these eight (or nine or ten, depending on what you read!) are considered *essential*. These essential amino acids cannot be synthesized by the human body, and therefore must be supplied *as is* in our diets. (We'll get back to this, too.)

There is no doubt that human beings need protein in their diets to avoid death and other unpleasant things. Protein is used by our bodies to digest food and to build muscle.

The U.S. Recommended Dietary Allowance for protein is 0.8 grams per kilogram of ideal (lean) body weight per day.

The government conveniently translates this for us as 44 grams per day for the basic 120 lb. (55 kg.) female, or 56 grams per day for the basic 156 lb. (64 kg.) male. Since **each gram of protein provides us with about four Calories of energy**, your trusty notebook computer will tell you that this means that about 8.8% and 8.3% of the calories your basic female and male consume on their respective 2000 and 2700 Calorie diets should be supplied by protein. Yes, football players and weight lifters and other people interested in building triceps on top of their biceps might need more protein, but only a *little* more. Say 10-25% more than the rest of us need. Even they shouldn't need more than 10-11% of their calories from protein.

So, how's a body supposed to get this stuff on one of those silly vegetarian diets?

We vegetarians get protein from just about everything we eat. Okay, fruits have precious little protein (although they have lots of other good stuff) and alcohol has none. So if we fashioned a diet from just those things (call it the piña colada diet!) we could have serious problems with protein if something else like starvation, cirrhosis of the liver, or hangovers didn't get us first. But with the exception of fruits and alcohol, almost everything else we vegetarians eat has protein *in abundance*, so it's easy to meet our protein requirements from vegetables and grains.

Here's the protein content of eight ounce servings of some common foods:

Food	Quantity	Protein (g)
Soybeans	8 oz.	82.76
T-bone Steak	8 oz.	42.57
Chickens	8 oz.	42.18
Cod Fishes	8 oz.	40.39
Whole Wheat Bread	8 oz.	22.00
Skim Milk	8 oz.	7.73
Potatoes	8 oz.	4.70
Green Beans	8 oz.	4.13
Apples	8 oz.	.43

Hey, you threw in soybeans as a ringer!

Yes, I did! Soybeans and the products made from them, along with lots of other legumes, happen to be terrific sources of protein for vegetarians. But forget soybeans for a moment. Look at the other foods here and you won't see any surprises. Just like your great-aunt Minnie always said, meat is a terrific source of protein. And just like Mr. Fudd, your high school football coach, warned you, those vegetarian foods look pretty wimpy in comparison. But we all know that any scientifically valid comparison of foods must be done on a *calorie* basis. So, let's rewrite our list and compare the protein content of 100 Calories of these same foods:

Food	Quantity	Protein (g)	% of C from Protein
Cod fishes	100 C	21.72	86.88
Skim milk	100 C	9.77	39.07
Soybeans	100 C	8.77	35.09
Chickens	100 C	8.65	34.60
T-bone Steak	100 C	8.65	31.55
Green Beans	100 C	5.87	23.48
Whole Wheat Bread	100 C	3.94	15.77
Potatoes	100 C	2.15	10.48
Apples	100 C	.32	1.29

Well, when we make a *scientifically valid* comparison based on calories, the infamous soybeans fall back in the pack and vegetarian foods *still* don't look as good as the meat and dairy products, much less "fish".

The important thing, though, is to look at the last column of our list—the percentage of calories in these foods supplied by protein. **Remember, if we eat a diet that averages more than the 8.3-8.8% requirement (okay, 11% for you weight lifters), and if we eat enough calories (not a problem for most of us) we can't *help* but get enough protein.**

Now, look at the vegetarian items on this list. Almost all vegetables, grains and legumes get more than 10% of their calories from protein. If we eat a variety of these foods, we vegetarians are *easily* going to beat out the 8.3-8.8% requirement, even if our diet includes a lot of relatively low protein fruits and the occasional no-protein (except for the olive) martini. And if we want to be weightlifting vegetarians (and there have been many!) we're *still* not going to have any problem at all getting enough protein.

But wait a second. Aren't some proteins better than others? Isn't good old-fashioned meat protein better than that vegetarian stuff???

Many people have the idea that meat protein has something magical that vegetarian food can't provide. The idea gets back to those "essential" amino acids we mentioned earlier. Meat provides all of the essential amino acids in roughly the right percentages that our bodies need. (When you think about it, this kind of figures, since meat is flesh itself.) Plant-based foods, on the other hand, have these essential amino acids present in differing proportions.

The essential amino acid present in the smallest amount is referred to as the "limiting" amino acid, because it is thought to limit the practical value of the protein. (The idea is that no matter how many engines you may have, if you only have four windshields you can only build four cars.) Back in the 1970s when we weren't hanging out in discos, we vegetarians were told to "combine" proteins by eating plant foods with different limiting amino acids so as to basically create "whole" proteins in our stomachs. The original edition of Frances Moore Lappé's landmark book *Diet for a Small Planet* was based on this idea.

The whole idea of combining proteins was an interesting concept, but one that has since been proven totally unnecessary. First, it's been found that your body is smart enough to tally up the amino acids in foods even if they aren't eaten at the same time. Even more important, science has shown us that while plant foods may have differing proportions of the essential amino acids, they almost invariably have all essential and nonessential amino acids in sufficient quantity to meet human nutritional requirements. That being true, let's say it again for emphasis:

> No one—not even the experts at the American Meat Institute—can design a reasonably varied vegetarian diet of sufficient Calories that *won't* give you adequate protein and essential amino acids.

So, it's clear that we will not only get enough protein by eating plants, but we'll also get enough of all the amino acids as well. Does this mean that plant protein is just as good as animal protein? No, as we'll see later, it's *better!*

But wait. Even if plants can provide enough protein, meat supplies even more. You can't have too much of a good thing, can you?

Most people don't know it, but in the case of protein you definitely *can!* To understand why let's take an imaginary trip down into your innermost parts (yuck!) and see what happens when you ingest food. What happens is that your body wants to burn that food as fuel. In the case of carbohydrates, made up of carbon and hydrogen and oxygen, your body can quickly convert them to the end-products of aerobic decomposition (carbon dioxide and water), releasing energy in the process. (Okay, I realize this is a gross oversimplification, but if you really wanted to learn the intricacies of biochemistry you wouldn't be reading a book like this one, would you?)

When your body digests proteins, though, it has more of a problem. Remember? I said they also contain nitrogen. Well, that nitrogen has to be removed before the proteins can be burned as fuel. Your body does that in two not-so-convenient steps. First, the amino group is broken off in a process called deamination, and the nitrogen enters the liver as plain old ammonia (NH_3). Your liver (which also does windows) converts this ammonia to a slightly less toxic compound called urea, and (just like a good bureaucrat) sends the problem on to some-body else. In this case it is the kidneys. It is their job to put the urea into urine for eventual excretion. This step requires taking a bit of cal-cium from the blood, which eventually must be replaced by calcium from the bone. (If you can't guess where this is going, read the breath-taking chapter on calcium, coming up shortly!)

It's no secret that these steps in digesting protein are hard on your liver and kidneys. Think about the high-protein diet Cousin Irene found in that women's magazine. Remember that the magazine cau-tioned Irene to drink lots of water with that diet, to kind of "flush out" those internal organs? It's important to have lots of water in your diet to digest proteins, because one of the ways your liver and kidneys deal with getting rid of this stuff is to dilute it. How ironic that meat, which requires more water to digest than plant-based foods, naturally contains *less* water (55-60% vs. 85-95%) than plant-based foods.

Not only is too much protein a problem generally, but **animal pro-tein is particularly onerous.** The protein in meat is especially high in sulfur-containing amino acids, and depletes calcium from the body more readily than plant protein. Studies have also shown links with high blood pressure and some cancers, with the speculation that over-consumption of animal proteins can affect the immune system.

Even more serious are the data of the China-Cornell-Oxford Project, which show a positive correlation between the consumption of animal protein and high total cholesterol and LDL ("bad" choles-terol) blood levels. That's right—*they found the consumption of ani-mal protein to be a major factor in clogging up your arteries.* And just the opposite was true for plant protein!

All of this is still very preliminary. Keep tuned to your local news outlet. This is an important area of study, and in the future you're going to be hearing a *lot* about the effects of animal protein on your body.

But I don't think I eat too much protein.

Nobody does. But the fact remains that animal-based foods are inherently high in fat and protein. Meat gets *all* its calories from fat and protein. Therefore, if you take the fat out of animal products (skim milk), or if you eat "low-fat" animal products (skinless chickens, some kinds of fishes) what you're left with is *very concentrated ani-mal protein.*

People in the United States and Western Europe consume *way more protein than they need*—typically about 100 g. a day rather than the 50 g. or so that the government recommends. That extra animal protein will take its toll on your liver and kidneys and bones, and maybe your immune system, arteries and heart as well.

If protein has all these problems, how come it's got such a great reputation?

High protein foods (*i.e.*, animal-based foods) are also high-money foods. They require large, capital-intensive infrastructures, and often rely on massive government subsidies. They also have large advertising budgets that allow them to command a premium price in the supermarket. Unfortunately for the folks in these industries, meat and dairy products have precious little going for them nutritionally. One of the things they *do* have, though, is protein in abundance. Since protein is something our bodies need, the promoters of animal-based foods have pushed the protein benefits of their products. This is easy to do, because people associate protein's competitors—carbohydrates and fats—with heavy Italian meals and rich desserts. Everybody thinks those things will make them fat (unjustly, in the case of carbohydrates), and protein looks good in comparison.

After so many years of meat and dairy advertisements, people have come to think of protein as health food. To a point it is. But in this case it's awfully easy to get too much of a good thing. In the last few years the science of nutrition has begun to discover what too much protein—particularly animal protein—can do to our bodies. It isn't a pretty sight.

Still not convinced you can get enough protein on a vegetarian diet?

Try these handy exercises.

Some people find the whole idea of science and numbers to be somewhat daunting. They'd rather listen to Mom or their high school football coach, or maybe even their family doctor who tells them they'd better be careful about protein if they want to try a vegetarian diet. If you're one of those people, we understand. Here are some things you might try to satisfy yourself that you'll get all the protein you need on a vegetarian (or even better, a *vegan*) diet:

• Go visit the local vegetarian society in your area (it's almost certain that there is one). Ask the people you meet how long they've been vegetarian and whether they're suffering from any serious diseases—protein deficiencies or otherwise.

● Now, figure out how many vegetarians there must be in the world (hint: millions in the U.S. and western Europe, hundreds of millions around the globe). If a vegetarian diet didn't supply enough of something as basic and important as protein, wouldn't there be an awful lot of people in *big* trouble? Where are all these folks???

● Visit your local medical library (or simply ask your doctor) and see how many cases you can find of *real* people who have had protein deficiencies, and who (1) were getting enough calories, and (2) weren't alcoholics. Were you able to find *any* of these cases? If so, how many of them were vegetarians?

This doesn't have to be overly complicated. The many millions of humans who live long healthy lives on plant-based diets should be enough to convince anyone that getting enough protein is not a problem vegetarians should *ever* have to worry about.

Things we eat #2: Fat

F at tastes better than fat-free or low-fat. Fat is a way to treat yourself, and remind yourself of all those good things Mom made for you to eat when you were young and thin and could eat those things without feeling guilty.

But life isn't that simple anymore. Unless you've just come back to town from an extended vacation in one of the more remote areas of Neptune, you've heard enough preaching about the fat in your diet over the last few years to—using an animal rights term—choke a horse. If you're sick of hearing about how bad fat is for you, I'll be brief. If you're sick of having to worry about how much fat is in every single bite of lasagna or mince meat pie, *boy have I got a diet for you.* Guess what it is?

Fat in our diet does a lot of crummy things to our bodies. It raises our blood cholesterol levels and, starting at a *very early age*, contributes to the buildup of fatty plaque in our arteries that eventually leads to heart disease and strokes. And if that isn't enough, there's also lots of evidence linking the consumption of fat with breast, colon, prostate, and other forms of cancer.

> **Isn't it just typical that something that tastes so good would do all this? Isn't that the way your whole day has been going so far?**

Fat comes in two exciting flavors. First, there's thick, gloppy, *saturated* fat, in which the little miniature carbon atoms are holding hands with all the little miniature hydrogen atoms they can safely take to the prom. Closely linked to this group are hydrogenated "trans" fats like margarine and shortening.

Then there are liquid, less gloppy, *unsaturated* fats, where the carbon atoms have hands free for one (*mono-unsaturated fats*) or more (*poly-unsaturated fats*) pairs of new hydrogen atoms. Of these two brands of fat, saturated fat is by far the worst kind. (It just makes sense that we shouldn't want to eat any fat that is going to be solid at body temperature, doesn't it?)

The medical expert powers-that-be tell us that 30% or fewer of our calories should come from fat. Even this number is pretty high. Doctors who have been successful in reversing the effects of heart disease with diet have had their patients eat a diet with less than 10% fat.

You probably don't have to be told the relative merits of plant-based foods vs. animal-based foods on the old fat scale. But, just to refresh your memory, here's the percentage of calories as fat in some common plant and animal-based foods:

Food	% of C from Fat	% of Fat that's Saturated
"Bacon"	93	37
Ground "Beef"	77	41
Cheddar Cheese	74	64
Chickens	63	29
Chickens' Eggs	61	31
Salmon	52	24
Cows' Milk	49	62
Soybeans	43	14
Flounders or Soles	12	24
Broccoli	11	15
Strawberries	8	5
Brown Rice	7	20
Potatoes	1	26

If you want to stay away from fat in your diet, it should be pretty clear what sections of the grocery store you should be avoiding (that's right, all those refrigerated shelves below the pictures of the smiling animals). Plant-based foods are not only dramatically lower in fat than meat and dairy products, but the fat they do have tends to be unsaturated, which is much easier on your body than the saturated fats prevalent in those unmentionable products.

But what about cholesterol?

I'm so glad you asked! Cholesterol is standing right next to fat in the police lineup of dietary thugs just waiting to get their greasy little hands on your body. If you want to limit your cholesterol intake (which you should), your dietary choices are easy. Plants don't contain reportable amounts of cholesterol.

Not even potato chips?

Not even potato chips.

All the cholesterol in your diet comes from animal products.

The U.S. Government recommends a daily cholesterol intake of less than 300 mg. Here's the amount you'll get if you take in all of your 2500 Calories for a day from these foods:

Food	Quantity	Cholesterol Content
Chickens' Eggs	2500 C	7131 mg.
Cow's Liver	2500 C	6189 mg.
Flounders or Soles	2500 C	1319 mg.
Chickens	2500 C	872 mg.
Ground "Beef"	2500 C	685 mg.
T-bone Steak	2500 C	651 mg.
Cows' Milk	2500 C	553 mg.
Anything from the Vegetable Kingdom	2500 C	0 mg.

Fishes and chickens don't look very good on this chart, do they? **Fishes and chickens have *more* cholesterol than "beef".** Animal products in general don't look very good. But remember—*you don't ever have to worry about these numbers again.* **If you eat a vegan diet your cholesterol intake will automatically be zero!**

The whole issue of fat and cholesterol in your food should be fairly straightforward. But here are just a few things to remember to keep you out of the woods:

● **Fat plants?** Almost all plant-based foods are low in fat, but there are exceptions. Olives and avocados are very high in fat, as are most nuts and as are peanuts (which, of course, are actually legumes). Even though the fats in these foods are largely unsaturated, you'll probably want to go easy on them. Too much vegetable fat isn't good for you either.

> **Question:** *What's the only nut that's low in fat?*
> **Answer:** The chestnut! (About 8% of calories from fat. And it's very tasty, too!)

● **Fats are light.** Just as with everything else, always calculate the fat in foods on a *calorie* basis. Fat tends to be lighter than the other components of the foods we eat, including water. (Remember how the grease always floated to the top of your mother's spaghetti sauce with ground "beef"?) This allows unscrupulous producers of both animal-based foods and (sadly) plant-based foods as well to misrepresent their products as lower in fat by reporting fat content by *weight* rather than by *calories*. This kind of blatant lie should be illegal, but heck, that would undo several hundred years of tradition in the advertising profession. Just be sure that you aren't suckered in, never believe the fat claims on the front label of a product. Always go to the fine print and compare the fat (and everything else) in the foods you eat on a calorie basis.

● **Skinny animals?** For people concerned with their fat intake there are lots of "low-fat" or "reduced fat" meat and dairy products to choose from out there. Sure most of them are boring and tasteless, but people line up to eat them anyway. Beware, however.

(1) First of all, they **may not really be low in fat at all.** Be sure to calculate the *percentage of calories from fat*.

(2) Next, think about what kind of **processing** went into making a naturally high-fat product into a low-fat one. We have to do a lot of monkeying with our food to make a vegetarian diet high in fat, or a diet based on animal products low in fat. Do you really want to eat food that has been monkeyed with?

(3) Remember that if the fat *isn't* there, it must be replaced by something else. If the food producer has lied, and is calculating fat content on weight rather than calories, that something else is probably *water*. If the food truly is low-fat, **as the fat content goes down, the protein content is certainly going up.** (Remember, meat is all fat and protein and water.) That may sound good at first, but as we learned in the last segment on protein, concentrated animal protein is *very* hard on the old body.

Hmmm...lots of fat and/or lots of protein. With animal products you can't really win either way.

Deciphering the food labels

With the nutrition labels required on most food products in the United States it's easy to calculate the fat content. The label gives you total Calories and also gives you Calories from fat.

To get the fat content as the percentage of calories from fat, divide "Calories from fat" by "total Calories".

This calculation is the correct one. If it doesn't agree with the "low fat" claims on the front of the package, you know the producer has lied, and is trying to sell his or her product as low-fat based on a weight calculation, which is scientifically invalid.

Wouldn't it be easier if food producers did the calculation for you and reported "percentage of calories from fat" on the label? Sure it would, but then it would be harder for them to lie on the front of the package.

In those cases where you don't have the "Calories from fat" number, you can still calculate the fat content of the food, because you know that **every gram of fat has about nine Calories.** Therefore:

Percentage of calories from fat = 9 x grams of fat ÷ total Calories

Pretty easy, huh?

Hey, how come "2%" milk is really 35% fat???

It depends on how you define the fat content. The dairy industry will proudly tell you that this milk has only 2% fat *by weight.* In this book, though, we always look at *percentage of calories from fat.* I'll tell you that 2% milk gets 35% of its calories from fat.

So which is better?

As the **First Commandment of Food Calculations** tells us, only calculations based on calories have any real meaning. Measuring the weight of the fat as a percentage of the total weight of the food tells us nothing.

If you're not convinced, try this great Mr. Wizard-type of experiment. Put a glass half full of "2%" milk on your kitchen table. Good. Now, with the help of an adult, fill the glass the rest of the way up with water. Okay, by my calculations you didn't change the nutritional value of the milk by diluting it. It still gets 35% of its calories from fat. By the dairy industry's calculations though, you've just turned the "2%" milk into milk that has only "1%" fat, because you've doubled its total weight while keeping the weight of the fat constant. Amazing! By that thinking, if you drink enough water with your meals you can get the fat content of not only milk, but also the richest ice cream, pure butter, or anything else for that matter, down to almost zero.

I might say the "2%" label on milk is mere marketing hype designed to mislead the public into thinking this is a low-fat food, but I don't want to get sued so I won't say that. You can figure it out for yourself.

Things we eat #3: Carbohydrates

If we cut down on protein and fat, what's left to eat?

*...or, why it's okay to stuff yourself on
spaghetti and pancakes*

Sure, you need some fat in your diet, but you don't want to get too much. Sure, you need some protein. But we've also seen that too much of that can be disastrous as well. But you've got to get your calories somewhere, so what are you going to eat? Well, there are only two other kinds of foods that your body can digest:

1. Alcohol, and
2. Carbohydrates

Now, I don't want to spoil any good parties here, but even though your body can get calories from alcohol (about six Calories per gram, actually) this stuff may be a bit too toxic to be a good source for *a lot* of your calories. No, as you just might have guessed, carbohydrates are probably a better choice.

But you're talking about pasta and potatoes.
That stuff will make me fat!

Nonsense! Weighing in at a scant **four Calories per gram**, it's not the carbohydrates in potatoes and pasta that make you fat—it's the sour cream and butter and Alfredo sauce and other fat stuff (at nine Calories per gram) that you put on top of them. You already know all this.

So, what's so great about these carbohydrate things?

Carbohydrates are simply **the most efficient fuel you can put in your body.** (That's why athletes are wise to load up on carbohydrates instead of steak before the big game.) As a matter of fact, if you eat anything else, your body has to change it into carbohydrates before it can be burned. Carbohydrates are basic fuel. What could be better?

How much of this stuff do I need?

Experts tell us that we should get 60% of our calories from carbohydrates. An ideal diet might have as much as 80% carbohydrates (10-20% fats, 10-12% protein). Of course, the other thing to remember is that if you eat whole foods you'll get *complex* carbohydrates, which will be a lot better for you than their refined counterparts. (Because you're such a *complex* person!)

Where do I get them?

You'll get lots of carbohydrates from all plant foods—fruits, vegetables, and grains—and even from dairy products. Where you *shouldn't* look for carbohydrates is in meat (or chickens, or fishes), because they have **none.**

Let's say it again for emphasis:

> *Most* of your diet should be comprised of carbohydrates—clean-burning fuel that will satisfy your hunger and give you the energy to beat your brother Tom in the sack race. But meat doesn't give you *any* carbohydrates at all!

Doesn't it seem odd, then, that most people in our society base their diets on meat?

things we need but don't seem to get enough of...

Things we eat #4: Dietary fiber

(It's not something you can weave a shirt out of,
but then again, you don't have to iron it either.)

Everybody knows about fiber. It's that stuff you get from "adult" cereals and laxatives with strange names. It's good for you too. Everybody knows that there are a zillion studies that show how important fiber is in decreasing your risk of everything from colon cancer (bad stuff—you'd rather die of something else) to hemorrhoids (a/k/a "George Brett's Disease").

"Fiber" is the name we give to indigestible carbohydrates in our diet. It's made up of stuff like cellulose (*i.e.*, wood chips) that most people can't get very excited about eating. But we should. Fiber is calorie-free (since we can't digest it), and it comes in two flavors: soluble and insoluble. That's good news, but even better news is the wonderful stuff it does for you as it makes its way through your body.

• **Insoluble fiber in your diet cleans things out.** (*Subtitled: "We don't want you to be like your accountant and have to work it out with a pencil."*) All those wood chips cruising through the old intestines scrape along the walls and clean things out. It sounds painful, but it isn't.

Think about your intestines for a minute. When was the last time you did any serious vacuuming or dusting down there? They could use some work, especially if you've been eating meat and there are a bunch of dead animals rotting away inside your body.

Here's the deal. The body's waste matter contains many carcinogens. Fiber (1) decreases the amount of time this bad stuff remains in the intestine, making everything as regular as Old Faithful, (2) increases bulk, thereby decreasing the concentration of carcinogens, and (3) changes the bacterial composition of the intestinal lining making it less vulnerable to cancer. It's been estimated that if everyone in the good old U.S. of A. started eating a diet rich in fruits and vegetables, cancer deaths could be cut by a third in 10 years.

• **Soluble fiber in your diet lowers your blood cholesterol levels.** Yes, the people who know about these things tell us that we can reduce our blood cholesterol levels by eating at least three grams of soluble fiber a day and, of course, keeping our saturated fat and cholesterol intake low.

• **Fiber helps maintain that trim, chiseled body of yours.** They make sponges out of cellulose. When fiber hits your stomach it absorbs water and fills you up. You stop eating before you go back for that all-important fifth helping. Conversely, when fiber is taken out of food you can eat it faster (there's nothing to chew!), and you end up eating more of it before you feel full.

> **Question:** *So I get full faster. Big deal. Won't I be hungry again an hour later?*
> **Answer:** Maybe. But by that time you'll be out on the golf course—away from all temptation.

Think about it. Something that fills us up, but doesn't add calories. Such a deal!

• **Fiber tastes good.** When people get used to eating whole foods, the refined counterparts of those same foods seem dull and tasteless in comparison. Brown rice tastes better than white rice, whole wheat flour tastes better than white flour, potatoes taste better with the skins left on them. Life is too short to eat food that tastes like wallpaper paste (or maybe even the wall itself)!

But I like wallpaper paste. I started eating paste in elementary school, and now I'm hooked on Wonder bread!

Everything depends on what you're used to, and there are lots of folks who may have to ease their way into a diet rich in fiber. They'll be happy once they get there though.

How do I know if I'm getting enough fiber?

The U.S. Government recommends that we get 25 grams of fiber a day in our diets (11.5 g. per 1000C), but the average American, setting a bad example for the world as usual, gets only half of that. There's an easy way to get an indication of whether you're getting enough fiber in your diet. If your "stools" (this is a family book, so I always look for the least offensive euphemisms possible) float like sea otters you're *probably* getting enough fiber. But if they look like, have the texture of, and sink like rocks (*i.e.,* if you spend enough time in the bathroom every morning to read the entire *New York Times—including all the classified ads*) you're probably not getting enough fiber.

Where do I get fiber?

You already know where to get fiber. Your cousin Rita gave you that weird recipe for oat bran muffins, and you've already sat through thirty hours of television commercials for fiber laxatives on the evening news. But it doesn't have to be that complicated. The important thing is to eat a variety of fruits and vegetables and whole grains, and skip all that refined and processed stuff in your diet. Here's a tip—try to avoid eating anything that's white. (That's right—look for foods where you can actually see the wood chips.)

There's one place where you won't get fiber in your diet, and that's from animal products. Because **meat and dairy products don't have any fiber. Nada. Zippo. And that goes for chickens and fishes, too!** So, if you're a meat-eater you might want to consider partaking of the cardboard tray your steak came on when the grocery store sold it to you. (*What? They don't make those trays out of cardboard anymore???*) Otherwise, that steak is going to take up *lots* of your daily calorie allowance and give you **no fiber whatsoever** in return. And that means you're going to have to eat *even more* fiber in the rest of your diet to make up the difference.

Example: If half of your daily calories come from meat and dairy products (not unlikely, since these foods are so calorie-dense) the rest of your diet will have to contain *twice* as much fiber as that of your vegetarian counterpart.

Remember, if you don't get enough fiber that steak you ate is just going to sit there in your intestines rotting out (yuck!), and the next morning you're going to spend another hour in the bathroom.

Wow, it's tough to be a meat-eater! No wonder they sell those laxatives on the evening news.

Let's sum up.

F iber **shouldn't even be an issue** in your life. And it should be of **no concern** to you if you just do two simple things:

1. Become a vegetarian.

2. Get used to eating those great-tasting whole foods. *Whole wheat, brown rice, unpeeled vegetables and fruits* (well, maybe not unpeeled bananas), etc.

There's lots of exciting and entertaining stuff happening in this world. So, get your fiber. You've got better things to think about than your intestines.

things we need in our diet,
but didn't think we could get from rabbit food #1...

The calculus of getting enough calcium

H ere's what you hear about calcium all the time, and it's **very true**: *Calcium is an essential dietary mineral, necessary for strong bones and good teeth!*

Here's something else you hear all the time, and it isn't true at all: *To make sure you get enough calcium, be sure to drink your milk and eat lots of dairy products!* (Bring up the patriotic music and the pictures of healthy, smiling people with milk mustaches.)

In the United States, people eat dairy products like crazy, yet the U.S. Centers for Disease Control estimates that 75% of American females over the age of 35 are suffering from some degree of osteoporosis (loss of bone density). Moreover, looking around the world, there is a *positive* correlation between the amount of dairy products a country consumes and the amount of osteoporosis in that country— lots of osteoporosis in the United States and northern Europe, not much at all in Asia and Africa.

What's wrong with this picture?

Doesn't cows' milk have lots of calcium in it?

Sure it does!

So, are humans just the victims of shoddy body construction by the Almighty? Do some of us just have inferior bones?

Not at all!

Here's what's wrong with the picture:

> The more meat (including fishes and chickens)
> humans eat, the more problems they'll have in main-
> taining bone density.

There are many reasons for this:

1. Meat has very little calcium. It just makes sense that the calcium in an animal goes into the bones, and there isn't much left in the flesh. Since most human meat-eaters (as opposed to most *natural* carnivores) don't eat the bones of the animals they consume, they miss out.

In fact, **meat has *so little calcium*, that if you *only* ate meat, you'd be lucky to get even 10% of the calcium you need** (I'll give you some numbers later on). Similarly, if a big portion of the calories in your diet comes from calcium-poor meat, you'll need *that much more* calcium from the other things you eat to make up the difference.

2. Meat is high in protein. *Isn't that good???* No! The protein in animal flesh is even *worse* news for your bones than its lack of calcium. As explained in that certain section on protein earlier on, excess protein does all kinds of nasty things to you. One of those nasty things is that it leaches calcium out of your body when you digest it. That's bad. You'd much rather have calcium in your bones than in your urine.

3. Meat is high in phosphorus and sulfur, and forms an acidic condition in your blood. So, who cares? Your bones care! The folks at the central control room in your body have a notice on the wall which requires them to maintain your blood pH level at all costs. "Beef" and fishes and chickens, unlike foods of vegetable origin, lower your blood pH, and that acid has to be buffered by alkaline calcium that comes straight from your bones. Just imagine what happens to limestone when it's doused with phosphoric and sulfuric acid.

What's the end result of all of this? The amount of calcium humans need keeps magically changing as we eat more meat and our osteoporosis problem keeps getting worse. Health authorities around the world have recommended everything from 350 mg./day on up. The recommended daily dietary allowance (RDA) of calcium in the meat-ridden U.S. is now 800 mg./day (1200 mg./day for teenagers), and some "authorities" recommend as much as 1400 mg./day.

Massive doses of calcium won't solve our problems. But even if they could, looking to dairy products is not the answer.

Dairy products are lousy sources of dietary calcium.

A cup of milk has 291 milligrams of calcium in it. Three ounces of cheddar cheese have over 600. *Wow, this stuff sounds great! Let's just drink a glass of milk and eat some cheese every day, and we'll never have to worry about calcium again!*

Of course it doesn't work that way. (If it did, 75% of American women wouldn't have to worry about osteoporosis, would they?) In actuality there are some real problems with trying to meet our calcium needs from dairy products. First, while dairy products do indeed have lots of calcium, they also have a lot of calories. As we'll see below, that means they aren't as calcium-rich as they might first appear. More importantly, though, they are very high in protein, just like meat. So at the same time dairy products are putting calcium into your body, they are contributing to it being leached out.

As of the time this book was written (mid-afternoon on a Monday) there were lots of conflicting results from studies made on this phenomenon. Some suggest that dairy products may have some positive effect on your overall calcium balance, while others suggest the overall effect is negative.

Be that as it may, there is no question that **dairy products are no panacea for the problem of osteoporosis.** Balancing the pluses and minuses, you're probably just going to break even. (Get it? "Break" even!) *At best* dairy products account for lots of calories in your diet, with very limited calcium benefit. Those calories could be better spent on foods that will *for sure* meet your calcium needs, and, even more importantly, won't dissolve your bones in the process. I bet by now you can guess what those foods are.

What's a body to eat?

(How about dark green, leafy vegetables!?)

Here's the calcium content of some common foods:

Common Food	Quantity	Calcium Content
Cows' Milk	1 cup	291 mg.
Mustard Greens	1 cup	58 mg.
Collard Greens	1 cup	52 mg.
Ground "Beef"	4 oz.	9 mg.

Well, there are no surprises here, are there? We knew that cows' milk contains a lot of calcium (as opposed to being a good *dietary source* of calcium), and we expected meat to be very low in calcium.

But we learned earlier that only silly people (and government agencies, food marketers, etc.) compare the nutritive value of *volumes or weights* of foods. To be meaningful, you have to compare foods on a *calorie* basis. So, what happens if we compare the calcium content of 100 Calories worth of each of these foods?

Common Food	Quantity	Calcium Content
Collard Greens	100 C	468 mg.
Mustard Greens	100 C	396 mg.
Cows' Milk	100 C	194 mg.
Ground "Beef"	100 C	3 mg.

Holy Smokes! When we make a *real* comparison of these foods the picture really changes. Meat practically drops out of sight, and, *lo and behold*, we find that **dark green, leafy vegetables have way more calcium than cows' milk!** More importantly, because these foods don't have the high protein content that plagues dairy products, this calcium can be used by your body to turn those ping pong ball bones of yours into golf balls.

Wait a minute, these foods are ringers! Nobody's going to live on collard and mustard greens!

Okay, I have to admit that dark green, leafy vegetables like mustard greens and collards (and many others) are the *very best* dietary sources of calcium there are. Other vegetarian foods may not have *this much* calcium, but they *do* have quite a bit. Here are the foods we dealt with above, together with a random sampling of some other foods, and the amount of the dietary calcium you'd theoretically get if you lived on each one for a day:

Common Food	Quantity	Calcium Content
Collard Greens	2500 C	11,694 mg.
Mustard Greens	2500 C	9904 mg.
Cows' Milk*	2500 C	4858 mg.
Broccoli	2500 C	4286 mg.
Iceberg Lettuce	2500 C	3958 mg.
Oranges	2500 C	2128 mg.
Strawberries	2500 C	1167 mg.
Whole Wheat Bread	2500 C	732 mg.
Flounders or Soles*	2500 C	495 mg.
Apples	2500 C	297 mg.
Potatoes	2500 C	222 mg.
Chickens*	2500 C	128 mg.
Ground "Beef"*	2500 C	64 mg.

(* Ignores the calcium depleting qualities of these "foods")

Looking at these numbers a couple of things should be clear, even to us intellectual lightweights:

First, it's no wonder that people who consume meat have problems with calcium. *Even if it didn't pull calcium out of their bodies, meat has way too little of the stuff to live on.*

Second, it won't be hard to get enough calcium from a diet of mixed fruits, vegetables and grains, even using the generous American RDA designed for folks who eat a lot of protein.

Remember though, getting enough calcium in our diets isn't the real problem for us humans trying to keep our bones strong. The *real problem* is not with calcium intake at all. The *real problem* is with eating foods high in *animal protein* which deplete calcium from the body by way of the kidneys, leading to weakened bones and osteoporosis.

Should *calcium be of concern for vegetarians?* Yes. We should be concerned for our meat-eating friends.

Still not convinced? Consider this...

Calcium is a mineral. It can't be produced by the body, but rather must be ingested. If one can't get enough calcium from plant-based foods, then where does the dairy cow get all that calcium to put into her milk?

---

*things we need in our diet, but didn't think we
could get from rabbit food #2...*

Iron

Vegetarian: *It's cold in this room. Can we turn the heat up?*
Meat-eater: *If you'd eat red meat and get some iron in your blood, you wouldn't be cold all the time. Anyway, it's warm in here.*
Vegetarian: *How come I can see my breath?*

Iron plays a key role in helping your blood move oxygen from your lungs to your muscles, your brain, and other important places. It's by far the most macho of the dietary minerals. Everyone knows they need iron in their diets, and they figure that eating something rugged like a piece of undercooked red meat is the way to get it. The perception is that vegetables are too wimpy to supply a powerful mineral like iron.

Well, let's just see.

The recommended daily allowance for iron is 18 mg. for women and teenagers, and 10 mg. for men. Here's how much we can find in some of our favorite foods:

Food	Quantity	Iron
Liver	8 oz.	13.64 mg.
Spinach	8 oz.	6.15 mg.
T-bone Steak	8 oz.	4.74 mg.
Chickens	8 oz.	2.04 mg.
Broccoli	8 oz.	2.00 mg.
Potatoes	8 oz.	1.72 mg.
Iceberg Lettuce	8 oz.	1.13 mg.
Flounders or Soles	8 oz.	.82 mg.
Apples	8 oz.	.41 mg.
Cows' Milk	8 oz.	.11 mg.

Well, this isn't any too surprising, is it? Just as the "beef" industry has been telling us, steak weighs in with lots of iron, and liver has even more. Vegetables are okay, but nothing to write home about. Fruits and dairy products look pretty anemic. (That's a pun.)

But as we've already learned, the above chart is meaningless, *because the human body doesn't have a metabolic requirement for "ounces" of food.* No, our bodies have requirements for *calories,* and only nutritional comparisons made on the basis of equal calories have any meaning. So let's see how these same foods look if we compare 100 Calories of each:

Food	Quantity	Iron
Spinach	100 C	12.32 mg.
Liver	100 C	4.77 mg.
Iceberg Lettuce	100 C	4.17 mg.
Broccoli	100 C	3.14 mg.
Potatoes	100 C	.96 mg.
T-bone Steak	100 C	.88 mg.
Chickens	100 C	.42 mg.
Flounders or Soles	100 C	.40 mg.
Apples	100 C	.30 mg.
Cows' Milk	100 C	.08 mg.

Well, that certainly changes things! Steak is a good source of iron all right, but it isn't as good as broccoli or potatoes. Liver is an even better source, but it's far from the best. Just look at spinach! Fourteen times the iron of steak??‼ No wonder Popeye could beat up the bad guys!

Suppose you're a woman and you're concerned about your iron intake. What would happen if you got *all* of your daily requirement of 2000 Calories from the above foods?

Food	Quantity	Iron
Spinach	2000 C	246 mg.
Liver	2000 C	95 mg.
Iceberg Lettuce	2000 C	83 mg.
Broccoli	2000 C	63 mg.
Potatoes	2000 C	19 mg.
T-bone Steak	2000 C	18 mg.
Chickens	2000 C	8 mg.
Flounders or Soles	2000 C	8 mg.
Apples	2000 C	6 mg.
Cows' Milk	2000 C	2 mg.

It's clear that a woman won't have any problem getting her required 18 mg./day of iron if she lives on lots of "beef". But it's just as clear that she can also get plenty of iron on a vegetarian diet that includes lots of green, leafy vegetables. (Where have we heard about *them* before?) The other thing that's pretty darned obvious from seeing cows' milk at the bottom of this table is that **dairy products are** *terrible* **dietary sources of iron.** So if you get a good portion of your daily calories from dairy products, you'll need even more iron from everything else you eat to make up the difference.

But isn't it easier for our bodies to absorb iron from animal flesh?

Perhaps, but the difference isn't likely to be too significant. The iron in animal flesh is about 40% "heme" iron, which is absorbed at a higher rate than the "non-heme" type. On the other hand, ascorbic acid (vitamin C), which is *virtually non-existent in meat and dairy products*, enhances non-heme iron absorption. It's even possible that the high ascorbic acid content of a diet rich in fruits and vegetables may render iron more absorbable than the iron in a meat-centered diet. Go figure.

Can a person get too much iron?

As if there wasn't already enough to worry about in life, the answer is probably yes. Excess iron, a concern for men as they age and women after menopause, encourages the formation of free radicals that can promote heart attacks and do damage to your body. (In the next section we'll talk more about these nasty free radical dudes, and see how a vegetarian diet can give you some protection there, too.)

So, how come the world thinks vegetarians are apt to become anemic???

People are all different, and it's certainly possible for an individual eating even the healthiest diet to become anemic. If that person happens to be a vegetarian, it's easy for people to jump to conclusions and wrongly blame the vegetarian diet.

Nevertheless, despite the fact that food from the plant kingdom provides more than enough iron for human needs, it certainly *is* possible for new vegetarians to become anemic when they change diets.

Here's a typical scenario: Julia is all excited about her new vegetarian diet. Instead of hamburgers she's eating grilled cheese sandwiches; instead of steaks she's having quiche, and instead of spaghetti with meatballs she orders the fettucine Alfredo. Julia becomes anemic. How come?

Here's the problem: Julia is making the same mistake that unfortunately plagues many new vegetarians. She's substituting dairy products for the meat in her diet. With a substantial number of her calories now coming from a food source that is notoriously low in iron, it should be no surprise that she's running a risk of anemia.

Here's the solution: Instead of eating more dairy products, Julia should be replacing her meat calories with foods from the plant kingdom. That way she'll continue to get lots of iron. She'll also get all the other groovy benefits of a plant-based diet (low fat, no cholesterol, high calcium, high vitamins, high fiber, etc.).

Meat or dairy—you just can't win

Meat is high in iron, but *horribly low* in calcium. Dairy products are high in calcium (although not a good *dietary source* of calcium), but *horribly low* in iron. You just can't win with either one. Vegetables, on the other hand, are high in *both* of these things, just as they are in lots of other vitamins and minerals you need. They don't have the other unsavory drawbacks of meat and dairy products either (high fat, high cholesterol, no fiber, excess protein your body must somehow deal with, etc.).

Here's an experiment you can try at home: try substituting broccoli (or something else green) for that hot dog or glass of milk. Feel better?

other things that are very nice in our diets #1...

Antioxidants

In a family book like this one, I hate to be *anti*-anything. On the other hand, there seems to be a whole barrel-full of scientific evidence that these little fellows can do us some good.

Antioxidants—vitamins C and E and beta-carotene—work against something called "free radicals" in your body. "Free radicals" sound dangerous (like maybe guys in army jackets with machine guns) and they are. They're molecules that carry an unpaired electron, and what they cause (and what antioxidants prevent) is oxygen damage to your body's cells. (You know the damage oxygen can do. Just remember your neighbor Ralph who was always trying to sell you that "classic" Triumph sports car he had parked behind his garage. Remember how its body finally rusted into nothing? Well, by way of loose analogy—*very* loose—oxygen can do a number on your body, too.)

Antioxidants are wonderful things. They can protect you against heart disease, cancer, arthritis, and early aging. And guess what? They're found in abundance in vegetarian foods!

So, how much do I need, and where do I get them?

Here's a little table to cut out and paste to your refrigerator:

Antioxidant	Recommended Daily Allowance	Food Sources
Vitamin C	60 mg.	Citrus fruits, strawberries, peppers, tomatoes, broccoli, potatoes
Vitamin E	5-10 mg.	Seeds, nuts, vegetable oils, wheat germ

| Beta-carotene | Nothing official, but USDA says 5-6 mg. | Carrots, squash, broccoli, yams, cantaloupe, Swiss chard, kale, spinach, peaches, strawberries |

How come I can't just take some pills?

Life is never that simple. Studies so far suggest that taking these compounds in vitamin pills doesn't do the same thing, and can actually have *negative* effects. There's more going on here than modern science, or even your mother, understands. You're going to have to eat your vegetables.

other things that are very nice in our diets #2...

Phytochemicals

*(Maybe you do need to put a few more chemicals
into your body.)*

In addition to antioxidants, plant foods contain a number of other substances that play an important role in both the prevention and treatment of disease. Sometimes lumped together under the name "phytochemicals" (*phyto* = plant; *chemicals* = chemicals) or "functional foods", these very handy compounds are found in most fruits and vegetables, and they fight (or "phyt") cancer and other chronic diseases like diabetes, cardiovascular disease, hypertension, osteoporosis, and arthritis.

It's going to be a long time before the experts identify all the beneficial chemicals in all the different plant foods and figure out exactly why they are good for us. What we know for sure is that these compounds all have long, complicated names, and they appear to work in complicated ways.

Some phytochemicals, such as carotenoids and flavonoids (I'll test you on these names later), are widespread in the vegetable kingdom and can serve as antioxidants. Other phytochemicals in fruits bind nitrates preventing them from converting to cancer-causing nitrosamines. Perhaps most important, though, phytochemicals appear to stimulate the manufacture of enzymes in your body that can enhance immune function, help in the excretion of carcinogens, prevent the formation of tumors, etc.

Of course, how these plant chemicals work in preventing and treating disease isn't nearly as important as the fact that indeed they *do* work. Here's a list of just some of the discoveries so far:

● High levels of cancer-fighting compounds have been identified in **broccoli** (indoles, isothiocyanates, and sulforaphane), **tomatoes** (lycopene, p-coumaric acid and chlorogenic acid), **onions and garlic** (allylic sulfides), and **citrus fruits** (limonoids—the stuff that tastes bitter).

● **Soy products** have been found to have phytochemicals that play roles in preventing breast cancer (genistein) and reducing serum cholesterol levels (isoflavonoids).

● Another phytochemical named phenethylisothiocyanate (easy for me to say) may block the effects of carcinogens in cigarette smoke as well. (Tell your cousin Oliver with the four-pack-a-day habit to eat his veggies!) And big surprise...**dark green vegetables** are a particularly good source of isothiocyanates.

Of course, this is just the beginning. Pay attention to the "medical breakthrough of the day" column of your local paper for new discoveries. In the meantime, eat a variety of fruits and vegetables to make sure you're getting a variety of phytochemicals in your diet. Who knows what great vegetarian foods will be next on the list!?

So, there you go. There are at least two important lessons to be learned here:

1. Broccoli's reputation as an anti-cancer food is well deserved.

2. When choosing a healthy diet from the names of various European countries, opt for *Belgian endive* rather than *cheese Danish,* and *Swiss chard* rather than *Swiss cheese.*

other things that are very nice in our diets #3...

B₁₂ (no, it's not the Pentagon's latest bomber!)

You probably think this is the place I tell you about all the great vegetarian foods that are terrific sources of vitamin B_{12}. Well, I'm not going to do that, and for one simple reason. Other than vitamin D (which our bodies happily make from sunlight), plant-based foods are great sources of all the nutrients we need *except* vitamin B_{12}. They're *not* reliable sources of B_{12}!

Huh?

That's right, for practical purposes there's no vitamin B_{12} in plant-based foods. It is naturally present in foods of animal origin only.

(Okay, for you techno-geeks let the record show that vitamin B_{12} has been reported in certain fermented foods like tempeh, beer, soy sauce, and miso, and other studies have shown that it can be absorbed by plants from organically fertilized soils, but you can't rely on these sources.)

But wait, isn't B_{12} good stuff to have? Don't humans need B_{12} to survive??

That's right too.

So, if humans need vitamin B_{12} to survive, but it's only found in animal-based foods, that means we need to eat food from animals! That means humans are supposed *to eat food from animals! (Hallelujah, and pass the corn dogs!)*

Well, not exactly. What it really means is that our hygiene habits have changed faster than the evolution of our bodies. Let me explain.

Vitamin B_{12} (cobalamin) is a cobalt-containing compound that controls blood formation and neural development and function. It is produced by dozens of microorganisms in our environment and in our own bodies. We only need tiny amounts of it, and back in the old days when Yul Brynner had hair and our forefathers scrounged the forests and dug up roots to survive, they got lots of vitamin B_{12} from the microorganisms in the dirt they ingested.

The problem now is that we wash everything we eat. We're just too darned clean! (*"You want pesticides on that apple?" "Yeah, fine— but not one speck of dirt!"*) Meat-eaters don't have to worry about all this cleanliness because their foods are loaded with microorganisms (that's an understatement!), and ovo-lacto vegetarians shouldn't give B_{12} a second thought either. Actually, since we need such a small amount (at most only 6 mcg./day) and our bodies produce the stuff, even most vegans shouldn't ever have a problem. But some will.

If you're a human or a vegan (or both) and you need some vitamin B_{12} in your diet, don't despair. Many processed foods have B_{12} added. (The numbers should increase as more people decide to forego animal products.)

When it comes to vitamin B_{12}, you've got four choices:

1. Roll your vegetables around in the back yard before eating to replace the dirt you're missing.
2. Attack a cow and eat her.
3. Use a cow as a wet nurse.
4. Look for foods with B_{12} added, and/or take a B_{12} supplement once in a while.

I'll let you figure out what seems natural and what doesn't.

things that aren't very nice in our diets...

Pesticides and other non-tasty tidbits

In our overcrowded, overproducing society, the products and by-products of modern chemistry are everywhere. It seems like every time we turn our backs pesticides and other contaminants (PCBs, heavy metals, etc.) are trying to make their way into our bodies. Sure, lots of talented people are working diligently to keep our food supply safe, but it's a daunting task, and most of us don't have the level of comfort about the whole process that we would like. Fortunately there's something easy that can be done about this, and (you guessed it!) that something is vegetarianism.

A lot has been said about the benefits of "eating low on the food chain," and it's good advice. Many pesticides and other chemicals aren't water soluble, and they tend to accumulate in the tissue of animals. So, if we eat a cow or a pig or a chicken, we may end up ingesting much of the chemical residue from all the plants that cow or pig or chicken ate during his or her lifetime.

The problem is even worse with fishes. Not only do they live in a polluted environment in the first place (everything always seems to end up in the water), but many of the fishes humans consume are carnivorous, so the bioaccumulation process has already taken place two or more times even before we even get them home from the market and under the broiler.

The U.S. Environmental Protection Agency estimates that 90-95% of the pesticide residues in our diet come from meat, fishes and dairy products. We can avoid all this by eating "low on the food chain"—that is, eating vegetarian.

Other exciting health issues

Smoking or meat?

They say that cigarette smoking is the #1 preventable cause of death in our society. But sometimes it isn't so easy to isolate the contribution any one factor makes in causing disease. The overwhelming majority of people who die from smoking-related diseases are also meat-eaters.

> • *If someone dies from lung cancer, would they also have died if they'd spent their life eating a cancer-fighting vegetarian diet rather than one centered on cancer-inducing animal products?*
>
> • *If someone dies because smoking constricts arteries of the heart that are already clogged with fatty deposits from years of eating animal fats, is the heart disease "caused" by smoking, or by diet?*

Who knows? Cigarette smoking is a terrible public health problem, to be sure. But then so is eating meat and dairy products. If you engage in either practice, you can expect, as a gross estimate, to lose about seven years of your life. But quality of life is important too, and animal products are implicated with *even more* diseases and chronic

A quick comparison of cigarette smoking and meat-eating

	Smoking	Meat-Eating
Highly enjoyable for the folks who do it	✓	✓
...Repugnant to those who don't	✓	✓
Implicated in a million studies as being absolutely terrible for your health	✓	✓
• Heart Disease	✓	✓
• Cancer	✓	✓
• Halitosis	✓	✓
• Causes disease when used as directed	✓	✓
Addictive	✓	?
Expensive	✓	✓
Harms other creatures	✓	✓
Big time environmental destruction	?	✓

health problems than cigarettes. Furthermore, *many* more people eat meat than smoke. **Are cigarettes the #1 preventable cause of death, or is perhaps diet?**

Is meat addictive?

V egetarians could argue with the meat industry forever about this one. Clearly meat doesn't generate the strong physical addiction of heroin or other drugs. But what about psychological addiction?

Let's suppose that meat *isn't* addictive. How, then, does one explain the presence of meat—at least *some* meat—in almost every dish on almost every restaurant menu in every one of the wealthier countries on Earth? How does one explain the presence of meat in almost every meal, in almost every home in these countries? Sure, this could be explained by the **First Great Reason for eating meat**—that people like its taste. But people like the taste of chocolate too, and you don't see it in every dessert. Isn't it just possible that meat-eaters have to have their "fix" two or three times a day?

If this sounds absurd (and it probably will to most meat-eaters) try a little experiment. Take a confirmed meat-eater (yourself maybe) out to dinner, and suggest that he or she try the vegetarian dish on the menu (there will probably be one—and *only* one). The odds are that you won't get a very favorable reaction. Indeed, the reaction may be downright hostile. This is *only one meal*. Is this addiction?

If you are a meat-eater, think about how often you eat meat. Be honest now. When was the last time you had lunch or dinner that *didn't* include any meat? Okay, now think about having to go the *rest of your life* without eating meat. Is there just a little feeling of panic? Is this addiction?

A society addicted to litigation

I n the United States we have a national sport of suing cigarette companies over the health problems their products cause. But no one sues the meat and dairy industry for these *very same reasons*, even though their products carry *no warning labels*, and even though their products are often *misrepresented* as being "healthy". How come? Could it be that none of the potential plaintiffs (sick people, public health officials) can stay off meat long enough to file the papers?

Bad habits and children

As a society we castigate the cigarette companies whenever we find the slightest evidence that they may be luring our children into the unhealthy practice of smoking. On the other hand, we don't mind a bit when fast food companies use clowns and playgrounds and toy promotions to blatantly entice our kids into the lifetime practice (dare I say *habit*?) of eating equally unhealthy fast-food burgers and chickens. How come? Could it be because all those kids' parents have the "habit", too?

But I've had a meat "habit" for 72 years...
If I were to suddenly become a vegetarian it would kill me!

Nonsense. Since a vegetarian diet is wonderfully good for the body, the vast majority of people can go right from being big time meat-eaters to being vegetarians or vegans without ever missing a beat. They'll feel great and never look back. A few people though (maybe 5%) might encounter some rebellion from deep within.

The human body is an amazing machine that can make accommodation for almost anything. But after years of getting their daily two or three doses of animal fat and making the best of it, it's possible your intestines will be surprised if they suddenly see a big wallop of millet and kale coming down the tube. They may start screaming. *What the XX*@X is going on up there???!!*

Actually, given the human experience with alcohol, tobacco, and derivatives of the poppy plant, it's amazing more people *don't* have physical withdrawal symptoms when they go off meat. If you're one of those rare people who does, though, remember three things:

1. Take it easy. You can ease into vegetarianism as your body adjusts—and it *will* adjust. (Most people ease into vegetarianism anyway!)

2. Remember, the human body has **no** metabolic requirement for animal products. Alcoholics feel bad when they go off booze, too.

3. This is *not* your body telling you you're doing the wrong thing. Rather, it's telling you about all the wrong things you did in the past.

The "system"

*(...because we all like to kvetch about
the government!)*

*[Warning: This section contains semi-political views
that will probably be offensive to almost everyone,
except those who like to believe that big government
conspiracies are the source of all their troubles.]*

Vegetarians are often plagued with those traits that start with the letter "s". We tend to be sarcastic, skeptical, suspicious, cynical—things like that. One of the things we direct all these "s" traits toward is the close relationship between the meat and dairy industries and our own United States Government. (I know that I personally worry that maybe Ronald McDonald has secretly become a member of our President's cabinet.) For lack of a better phrase, and with the unashamed intent of making it sound as ominous as possible, let's refer to this relationship as "the System". (*Note:* If you are reading this book in a country other than the United States, feel free to substitute your country's meat and dairy industries and your country's government. Odds are, things are pretty much the same wherever you are.)

To understand how "the System" works, consider the tobacco example. Our government spends lots of money on subsidies to encourage farmers to grow tobacco, and lots more money by allowing the tobacco industry a tax deduction on its annual advertising budget. Then, once the cigarettes are lining the store shelves we spend more money attacking the industry and the advertising we've just subsidized by, among other things, getting the Surgeon General to declare war on "Joe" the smoking camel. Finally, we shell out huge bucks through Medicare, etc. to take care of all the people who are harmed by cigarette smoke. Makes sense, huh?

Multiply the tobacco example many times and you get some idea of what the meat and dairy industries are doing to us. Start with $4.8 billion in direct annual payments to feed grain growers. Add to that subsidized grazing leases on 270 million acres of federal land, infrastructure improvements, costs of water supply and environmental clean-up, attempts at soil conservation, meat inspection, extension services, technical and trade assistance, and on and on. Now you've got dozens of bureaucracies and hundreds of thousands of government employees helping out animal agriculture to one degree or another, and it's *still* just the beginning.

The next use of our tax dollars is to actually buy meat and dairy products. Imagine what the military must spend on these items, as just one example. How much cheaper and healthier would the vegetarian alternatives be? And consider that one in ten grocery shoppers uses food stamps. What are people buying with those taxpayer-funded stamps? What they're conditioned to buy, of course.

Here's where our story really turns grim—with a little ditty called the school lunch program. Somebody in Washington got the idea that the federal government should buy up the traditional overproduction in the dairy industry, to kind of help out the boys down on the farm. This stuff ends up in big government warehouses, and what doesn't rot gets distributed to (among other places) schools everywhere, along with lots of dairy industry propaganda. (Remember the four basic food groups when you were in school? The dairy industry printed lots of that literature.) The end result, as we all know from personal experience, is that by the age of nine virtually every child in this country has been conditioned to want, expect, and accept nothing other than a high animal fat, high protein, high cholesterol diet. It's a value system that isn't likely to change as those kids get older.

So, what have all our billions of tax dollars bought us? Disease, of course—heart disease, cancer, osteoporosis and more, because people don't know how to eat right. And our solution to that problem is to throw away more tax dollars. We create more government agencies, like the National Institutes of Health, that spend money on research. What we hope for, of course, are new miracle drugs that can wash away our sins with the pop of a pill.

The drugs we end up getting aren't nearly so exciting, but even so they are all protected by our taxpayer-funded patent system that guarantees pharmaceutical companies twenty-year monopolies on all their new inventions (along with monopoly pricing to consumers and monopoly profits for the manufacturers). This isn't to criticize the patent system, but merely to note that in the health-care industry it creates an *overwhelming* financial incentive to fund new drug research and to suppress any kind of wellness or healing that isn't drug-based. (Vitamins and broccoli, after all, are natural substances. Nobody can get rich by patenting them.)

The end result of all this madness is that we've paid countless dollars to set up a system that has led to lousy public health and a crushing $800+ billion/yr. medical bill that severely threatens our future economic prosperity. The taxpayers ultimately have to pick up most of that tab, and hey—guys that have died of heart attacks aren't going to be paying much in the way of taxes.

What can we do about all of this? Of course it would be nice to change everything overnight, and elect a President who will dine visiting heads of state at Tofu Palace, but that isn't likely to happen. Some simple steps could go a long way, though. For example, everyone agrees on many of the basics of good nutrition (fat and cholesterol are bad, fiber is good, Spam was originally part of a communist plot to overthrow the country). Why not actually teach these things to our children, and back them up with (1) school lunches that meet guidelines for good nutrition (ketchup doesn't count as a vegetable!), and (2) truthful and complete nutritional labeling on every product (including meat) in the grocery store?

Is this too much to ask of any reasonable Congressperson? How about a national health care policy that at least recognizes the concept of preventative medicine? These are small first steps; but they could take us a long way. And if they don't save us $2 (or $5, $7, or $10) for every dollar we spend, I'll eat a Big Mac on the steps of the Capitol building. [*Note:* This last statement was made for intense dramatic effect only, and should *not* be taken as a serious offer.]

If all of this works out, someday we might try something *really* radical, like actually expecting our agriculture and medical industries to compete in a capitalistic, free-market economy. But that would require our government to stop shooting itself in the foot.

It may be too much to ask. After all, Ronald McDonald has a lot in common with all those other clowns back in Washington. They all have really, really big feet.

Genes

Doesn't it just frost your shorts that no matter how healthy you try to be in life by always eating the right things, never eating, smoking or drinking the wrong things, getting plenty of exercise and—carrying it to the extreme—never having any fun at all...Doesn't it just smoke your tires that on the day you take your last, gasping breath (hopefully at an appropriately advanced age), there's going to be some schmo from your high school class who will, at the *very moment* that rigor mortis overcomes your poor helpless body, be out shooting his or her age on the golf course?

It's true, you know. It's disgusting. It's an insult! (And to make matters worse, it's probably going to be that little twit from your ninth grade gym class who threw up on your sneakers after the class had just finished the rope-climbing drill.) But, then again, that's just the way life works.

That's the way genes work, too. The mysterious codes locked in our DNA seem to control everything about us, from whether we like old Elvis Presley songs, to whether we're going to be healthy in life, to (alas!) when we're going to kick the old oaken bucket. Until we fully understand the approximately 100,000 genes in the human genome (quite a few years off, I'm afraid) there's not much we can do about it either. We're stuck with the genes we're dealt.

Okay, maybe it's not as hopeless as all that. Nobody knows for sure, and it's different for everyone, but the experts tell us that we can expect at least 80% of our good (or bad) health to be determined by our *lifestyle*, not our genes. So there are some things we can do. A good vegetarian diet and some exercise may not make you the *last* one in your high school class to putt out, and they may not even move you ahead of that little squirt from your gym class, but they'll almost assuredly put you ahead of where you would have been with *your* genes had you chosen to live life on a diet of malted milk balls and "beef" jerky.

Is life fair?

Nah.

Can we strike just a little bit of revenge?

You bet!

And speaking of genes...

Everybody's got a great Aunt Gertrude who lived life on a diet of roast "beef" and scalloped potatoes and still managed to die at 99. Sure, Gertrude had great genes. But statistics show that for every Aunt Gertrude there are quite a few Uncle Bobs and Cousin Carolines who die relatively young. They lived on a diet of roast "beef" and scalloped potatoes too, and it did them in. Speaking of genes (and even of joes) consider this article from a recent edition of *The Libbyville Times...*

Old Joe's obituary

Libbyville (AP)—Joe Johnson, Libbyville's oldest citizen, died yesterday at the age of 108. Known as "Old Joe" to his friends, Mr. Johnson recalled a more colorful time in Libbyville's past. Only last year, when reporters asked him the secret of his longevity, Old Joe Johnson replied, "I think it's all consistency. You see son, every day of my life I've smoked three packs of Chesterfields and drunk a fifth of Jim Beam." Then, laughing, he added: "Hell, that'll cure what ails ya."

Mr. Johnson died of complications from cirrhosis of the liver and lung cancer.

Body types

Look in the mouth of your cat Minnowpaws. Nice long, sharp teeth for tearing apart flesh. This is the mouth of a carnivore.

Now look in the mouth of your dog Phydeaux. More nice, long, sharp teeth—perfect for destroying your best pair of slippers.

Now look at your own teeth. Pretty different, huh? (And we're not talking about your gold crowns, either.) Human teeth are flat and dull, perfect for grinding vegetables. (Your jaw moves from side-to-side as well as up and down.) A human mouth looks a lot like that of a cow, or maybe a horse. (Remember Mr. Ed's teeth?)

Human bodies resemble those of herbivores in a lot of other respects, too. We have the ability to suck water for instance, and we sweat through our skin. Minnowpaws and Phydeaux lap their water and cool themselves through their mouths. Look at your fingers. They're perfect for peeling bananas, but not so great for pouncing on a cow and ripping it apart. More important is your intestinal tract. It's a long corrugated affair that can trap hunks of rotting tuna fishes almost forever. That's a far cry from the smooth, short intestines on carnivores that get rid of rotting meat quickly.

But humans must be omnivores. We are perfectly capable of eating animals!

That's true. It's a tough world out there, and sometimes you need to take food where you can find it. Humans were given the equipment to hunt down and digest animals, although in our natural state that would have been pretty much limited to things like grubs and bugs and worms.

Unlike Minnowpaws and Phydeaux, though, we have hell to pay when animal fat and protein become a *significant* part of our diet. And over the last few generations this is just what has happened. One might say our bodies are doing their best to adapt to our modern lifestyle, but it might be a few years yet (like maybe the next Ice Age, or the day the national debt is paid off, whichever comes first) before we physically evolve into carnivores. Until then we'll have to live with the health consequences of meat-eating.

...Or maybe try something else.

A final word about your health

Everyone is concerned with their health, and almost all of us (92%, according to a Food Marketing Institute poll) are trying to improve our diets. When the scientific evidence on meat and dairy products is *so overwhelmingly negative*, you'd think everyone would be flocking to a vegetarian diet. Yet a 1994 Roper Poll conducted for the Vegetarian Resource Group found that only between .3% and 1% of Americans are true vegetarians, and it's estimated that only 5-20% of *those* are vegans. (*So few? Heck, that's practically a negative number!*)

What's wrong with this picture?

Think about yourself. Imagine you're a Ferrari. (Oh, you sleek, racy person, you!) You keep the chrome polished and you'd never miss a regular oil change. But are you still pumping in that low octane fuel every day?

Why are you doing that??

"I do not regard flesh food as necessary to us at any stage and under any clime in which it is possible for human beings ordinarily to live. I hold flesh to be unsuited to our species."

— **Mahatma Gandhi**

"A man can live and be healthy without killing animals for food; therefore, if he eats meat, he participates in taking animal life merely for the sake of his appetite, and to act so is immoral."

— **Count Leo Tolstoy**

Chapter 3

The Second Great Reason to be a vegetarian is the environment

(...Because if we wreck the Earth,
where are we going to live?)

You could probably come up with something worse for the environment than eating animal products, but it might not be easy.

At last count—and this was several years ago—there were about 1.2 billion cows in the world. (There are probably even more today, although for the most part I imagine they are different cows.) Now, it seems that each of these animals, by belching and by various other means we cannot mention in a family book, emits about 14 cubic feet of methane gas each day. This makes cows a major source of air pollution, and a large contributor to the "greenhouse effect".

At the U.S. Government's agricultural research facility in Beltsville, Maryland they put cows in Plexiglas cages and studied the amount of methane that was produced. The idea was to alter the cow's diet and other conditions to come up with a "clean cow" that wouldn't pollute so much. This would, of course, make barns smell a whole lot better, and would make many farmers very happy. It would be a terrific use of our tax dollars. Still, there is a much simpler and more effective solution to the problem. Guess what? It starts with a "V"!

Okay, unless you work in a barn maybe you don't consider gas from cows to be the most pressing environmental issue of the decade. Maybe you'd rather hear about tuna fishermen (or is the politically correct term "fisher*persons*"?) killing dolphins, or drift nets many miles long that are lost by "fisherpersons" and then forever drift through the oceans killing everything in sight. Maybe you'd rather hear about the 80 acres of tropical rainforest being lost every minute—most of it to make way for cattle raising.

This is pretty depressing stuff. Maybe you'd rather not hear about *any* of it. The point, of course, is that our food choices have environmental repercussions, some of which we might never expect. And, of course, the choice with the biggest repercussions of all is the choice to eat animal products.

The environmental problems associated with flesh and dairy eating are simply the direct and unavoidable consequences of its inherent inefficiency. It's not anybody's fault that animal agriculture is inefficient, that's just the way it is. It's just plain physics that you have to grow and lug around a lot more food to feed to your animals than the animals in turn produce. For example:

• an acre of land used to grow oats produces 10 times the protein and 25 times the calories as the same acre used to raise "beef";

• in terms of fossil fuel energy used vs. food energy produced, plant agriculture is at least 30 times more efficient than animal agriculture.

Quite a difference, huh? Add on top of that the water needed to support those same animals, the space they take up, the waste they produce, etc. and you've got major league inefficiency.

By contrast, growing one pound of crops to make one pound of food for humans is much simpler and much less taxing on the environment.

> **Comparing the efficiency of producing plant-based human food to that of producing animal-based human food is like comparing the Swiss train system to the Three Stooges in bumper cars.**

Let's look at some of the specifics.

It takes space to raise all those animals!

Yeah, lots of space. Remember the stereotype of the Texas rancher who brags that it takes him all day just to drive across his ranch—and it's not just because his Cadillac needs a ring job? To be sure, cattle are out there tromping down the grass on the vast ranges where the buffalo used to roam in the American West. But that's just the beginning.

Almost two-thirds of the land used for raising *crops* in the United States is used for raising food for *animal* rather than human consumption. All told, more than 90% of the agricultural land in the United States, and over 36% of *all* the land in the United States is used for animal agriculture. Needless to say, **that makes the production of meat and dairy products the biggest user of American land. Not just by a little bit, but by a *whole lot.*** In Europe, where land is at a premium, animal agriculture can have an even bigger impact. In the United Kingdom, for example, nearly two-thirds of the land is used for the production of animal products.

Since the rest of the world seems to be following in the footsteps of the United States and Europe (remember those rainforests) it isn't inconceivable that one day most of the Earth's land will be used for producing meat and dairy products.

Is this how we really want to use our land?

A nimal agriculture is a big business, and like any other business it seeks to maximize its profits by making optimal use of its resources. We certainly can't blame these folks for that. Unfortunately, making optimal use of the land for producing animals isn't necessarily consistent with protecting the environment. Actually, it's pretty darned inconsistent.

Topsoil

Topsoil may not be on everybody's list of favorite after-dinner discussion topics, but it's an important concern everywhere animal agriculture is prominent. Every year, for example, the United States loses over five billion tons of soil.

How much is that?

Assuming four inches (10.16 cm) of topsoil, it's the equivalent of losing over four million acres of cropland (more than the size of Connecticut!), and at least 85% of this loss is due to animal agriculture.

Where does it go?

Consider this scenario. Cattle eat and tromp down the natural ground cover, or a tractor plows it up, allowing the land to erode. Soil is washed away. It goes downstream, spends a few days in New Orleans catching the shows in the French Quarter, and then gets pushed out into the ocean at the Mississippi delta.

Just how bad is this loss?

Who knows? But consider that the experts believe that it was animal agriculture over the last 10,000 years that transformed the Middle East, northern Africa, and much of the Sahara Desert from a lush, fertile area into what it is today. In a few hundred years our progeny may be watching a new hit action movie titled: *Lawrence of Ohio*.

Pesticides

If you're going to be maximizing the use of your land for agriculture, you don't want to be sharing this resource with other plants and animals that have no commercial value to you. Worse yet, you don't want anybody except paying customers eating your valuable plants and animals. Therefore farmers and ranchers have a strong business interest in eliminating all species of plants and animals from their land except the particular species they are growing. We can't blame them for this—it just makes good business sense.

So, if you're a farmer or a rancher what do you do to eliminate "non-commercial" species that might threaten your crops and animals?

You kill things, that's what. Over the past 40 years the use and toxicity of pesticides has increased by a factor of ten. Ranchers kill the prairie dogs and other small creatures who eat the grass and burrow in their fields. Then they kill the coyotes who, left with no natural prey, attack their animals. The government gets into the picture, too. The "Wildlife Services"(WS) is the tragically misnamed group within the U.S. Government charged with killing all those pesky native animals (over a million a year) who threaten us good citizens and our prized possessions. Not unexpectedly, most of WS's budget goes to protecting livestock.

It goes without saying that the killing won't stop until all non-commercial species are eliminated. It's simply a question of economics.

How are we doing?

Human activity has dramatically accelerated natural rates of species extinction. The American Museum of Natural History estimates that we are losing 100 animal species each day. We certainly can't blame all of this on the meat and dairy industries, but figure it out for yourself. A huge portion of the land in the United States and Europe is used for animal agriculture—to grow food for and support our bovine, porcine, etc. brethren, and the rest of the world is headed in the same direction. Animal agriculture is great if you're a rancher, an executive at McDonald's, or the shoe salesman for Imelda Marcos. But if you're a sparrow or a beetle or a gray wolf in need of a home, every new acre that the meat and dairy juggernaut consumes is truly a disaster.

Eating "organic"

Organic (or-gan-ik)— of, relating to, or arising in a bodily organ; of, relating to, or containing carbon compounds...

Are all foods organic?

From a strictly biological or chemical viewpoint, you bet they are!

Even Spam?

Absolutely!

Even Cheez Whiz?

Maybe even Cheez Whiz!

Human digestive systems are built to break down organic compounds and derive the energy and nutrients our bodies need in the process. (Not that we necessarily get these things from Spam or Cheez Whiz.)

So, how come "organic" also came to mean "produced without employment of chemically formulated fertilizers or pesticides?"

Probably because that meant fertilizers and pesticides of plant and animal origin would have to be used, and the word "organic" seemed to fit.

Does that mean that organic farming could benefit the animal agriculture industry by providing a market for animal waste?

Probably.

What will we use instead of animal waste when everyone's a vegetarian?

We'll compost our garbage.

But isn't organic produce more expensive?

Sometimes, but it wouldn't be if everyone demanded it.

Are we being too picky and obnoxious here?

Yes. Organic farming is a good idea. Support it.

It takes water to raise all those animals!

Yeah, lots of water. In California, where droughts seem to pop up even more often than espresso bars, they've passed laws restricting restaurants from serving water with meals unless a patron specifically asks for it. On the other hand, nobody has seemed to notice that two thousand gallons of water will be consumed in producing the steak that same patron orders.

Cows consume a lot of water. So do pigs and chickens. So does irrigating the soybean and corn crops grown to feed to them.

How much water?

Animal agriculture is by *far* the largest consumer of water in the United States. In fact, it accounts for more than half of all the water consumed in the United States. Okay, let's say it again for emphasis:

Most of the water we use goes, directly or indirectly, to produce meat and dairy products.

Hey, that's a lot of water! If folks in California restaurants are *really* concerned with conserving water, mayhaps they should look at what's on their plates instead of what's in their glasses.

My goodness, all these animals are messy!

If you keep a cow in your living room for a few weeks you may find that your carpets need cleaning. Now, imagine the mess all twelve billion cows on Earth must make—not to mention the billions of chickens, pigs, sheep, farmed catfish, etc. It's the old inefficiency factor again. It just figures that if we're feeding these poor creatures five or ten or twelve pounds of food and letting them inefficiently convert that to one pound of meat and dairy products, then the other four or nine or eleven pounds has to go somewhere. Where it usually goes, of course, is right into our water—right down the Mississippi to New Orleans for a night on the town with that soil we were talking about a couple of pages back.

I don't want to get indelicate here with a lot of graphic descriptions (especially since you're about to start dinner). Suffice it to say that in the United States animal agriculture produces a staggering 130 times as much...er..."waste" as the human population, and about three times the organic water pollution of all our other industries combined. Agriculture is our biggest source of water pollution, and most of that is attributable to *animal* agriculture. And this, of course, doesn't even consider the pesticide and fertilizer runoffs from all those farms (most of them!) that grow crops for animal feed.

To say that animal agriculture is a major polluter of our water is an understatement. Its effects are massive.

This sounds serious. It's probably better to eat seafood, huh?

Yeah sure, "seafood" is great. Just ignore all that stuff about the dolphins and the drift nets. And just don't count on eating it for much longer—it may not be around.

When I was a kid growing up on Chesapeake Bay, oysters were a popular food with the locals, and oystering was a big industry. The oysters are virtually gone now, a victim of overfishing and disease. And they aren't alone. Seventy percent of the world's stocks of fishes are fully exploited, overfished, depleted or rebuilding from previous overfishing. From salmon in the Pacific to the bluefin tuna in the western Atlantic, populations of hunted species of fishes and shellfish have been plummeting.

It's simply a question of supply and demand. The humans of the world kill and eat about 180 billion pounds of fishes and shellfishes a year, and nature can't replace them fast enough. There are simply too many people to be on this kind of diet in the world now, and, of course, more are coming every day.

Isn't it nice to know that vegetarians don't contribute *at all* to this problem?!

The situation is getting worse, not better

Not only is the Earth's population expanding by 80 million people a year, but the dietary habits of those people are changing too. As economies expand in Asian countries, more people are adopting a diet containing meat and dairy products, and the demand for grain to create those products is skyrocketing. Sure, we can keep chopping down forests to create new farmland for a while, but pretty soon there *won't be any forests left to chop down.*

No matter how much everyone wants to keep eating meat and dairy products, those gosh-darned laws of physics are going to keep getting in the way.

Today 35,000 people will die because of hunger, three-quarters of them children under the age of five. Shouldn't we be working to make this situation *better*, rather than focusing so much of our energy and resources on a dietary system that can only make it worse? Remember this:

> The Earth would not have the capacity to support even its current population if everyone were on a meat-eating diet. But if everyone were vegan, the Earth could easily feed 10 billion people—that's everyone we now have, and all those new folks we expect to welcome for at least the next 50 years.

What's a body to do?

A few years ago the folks at *Consumer Reports* magazine analyzed the environmental impact of a fast-food meal. They surprised a lot of people when they said the worst consequences didn't come from the plastic straw, or even the Styrofoam carton around the burger, but rather from the burger itself. They were right, of course.

A lot of us consider ourselves environmentally conscientious. We'll take the time to compost our garbage and figure out if the envelopes with the little plastic windows can be put in the recycling bin. We're proud of ourselves. But these good things are *absolutely dwarfed* by the *unnecessary* environmental destruction we'll cause if we then go out for a hamburger (or "chicken", or even "fish") dinner.

So, what's a body to do?

Dying would help enormously. So would giving up our cars and most of our material possessions. But for most of us these things would entail some pretty hefty sacrifices. It just so happens though (and it's handy as heck) that by far the *easiest* thing we can do to *massively* reduce the environmental destruction we're causing to this Earth is also something that will massively benefit our own health as well. Such a deal! And it just happens to start with the letter "V". In the words of a musical conductor I know: "One...Two...You know what to do!"

So why are you doing something else?

Hey, if eating animal products is this bad for the environment, how come environmental groups aren't working like crazy against it?

Simple—most of their members and potential members eat meat, and don't want to be told that *they* are the bad guys. So, while environmental groups may latch on to some relatively trivial animal agriculture issues (don't buy "beef" from South America! Raise those graz-ing fees!), they conveniently ignore the big picture. Too bad.

"Nothing will benefit human health and increase chances for survival of life on Earth as much as the evolution to a vegetarian diet."

—Albert Einstein

A sparrow in need of a home (p. 85)

Flossie at the dinner table (p. 96)

Chapter 4

The Third Great Reason to be a vegetarian is your high ethical standard

*(...Because if you can't live with your conscience,
where are you going to hide?)*

If you insist on eating food with a face, don't complain if someone's staring.

This is the part of the book that isn't so funny. Yes, it's hard to be overly lighthearted about subjects like death and suffering. But though you might be tempted to skip this section, please don't. I'll try not to be too grim.

People don't like to think about animal rights. And when they *do* think about it and talk about it, it's usually in the context of "Look what those *other* people are doing to the animals." When the military shoots bullets into live dogs so its doctors can practice suturing wounds, for example, it's easy for people to speak out and condemn the practice. It's almost as easy for people to condemn household products companies that feed bleach and oven cleaner to rats until they die. In these cases the ends clearly don't justify the means in most peoples' minds. More importantly though, it's easy to speak out because it's *somebody else* that's causing the problem.

It's easy for us to condemn the rich lady in the baby seal skin coat, just as long as we're not the rich lady. And those cosmetic companies that blind rabbits in testing their products are really bad all right, just as long as there's not a particular cosmetic they make that we really want to use. The point is, in animal rights, just as with any other cause, it's easy to attack *someone else*, but much harder to evaluate and challenge *our own* behavior.

That's why people don't want to hear about animal rights in a book on vegetarianism!

Here's the problem:
1. Almost everybody eats meat.
2. Eating meat is the A#1, super primo, meanest thing we do to animals.
3. People don't want to be told that they are the bad guys.

In our society we've developed an elaborate system to protect us from ever having to think about what we're doing to the animals we eat, and it is very effective. Just consider these **highly creative things we do to fool ourselves**:

● **We perpetuate a myth** that eating meat is the natural way to live. We convince ourselves that this is just the fundamental order of things and, of course, we're helpless to do anything but go along with it.

● **We reinforce that myth** by creating a mystique around the process of ranching and fishing. Rough, tough cowboys, kindly farmers and noble fishermen become colorful, larger-than-life heroes. And everybody knows that colorful, larger-than-life heroes are never wrong!

● **We draw cute caricatures** of smiling cows and chickens and pigs to adorn our fast-food restaurants and frozen food packages.

● Most important of all, we **keep the killing behind closed doors**. Indeed, most people in "developed" societies (ironically, the societies that make meat the biggest part of their diets) will *never in their lives* see a cow or pig or chicken killed for food. It's almost like that part of the process happens by magic, and nobody really has to get hurt.

Of course, the reality of eating meat isn't anything close to the fantasy we create for ourselves. In the real world the way we treat our farm animals is barbaric well beyond what most of us can imagine. And the scale on which we do it is beyond our comprehension as well. In the United States alone, over 22 million farm animals will be killed for human food today. That's 1300 lives taken in the time it takes to read this sentence. Read the sentence again and another 1300 will be gone. And the killing goes on like this 24 hours a day, 365 days a year. (366 in leap years!)

This never-ending killing is done for the enjoyment of all of us who eat meat—not to feed us, and not for our health or nutrition (all that could be *much* better done with plant agriculture), but simply for our *enjoyment*. We command it with our dollars every time we buy meat, and of course *none of it is necessary*.

The reality of eating "red" meat

Think about a steer for a moment. The real world for him is one of periodic confinement, of branding and antibiotic injections, of castration without anesthetic by men with bloody aprons wielding large steel clippers. In the real world the steer will be rounded up one day at a young age and packed tightly into a truck for the drive to the stockyards. The drive may be hundreds of miles, and under those conditions he may arrive injured or sick. If it is cold and he is unlucky, parts of his body may freeze or he may die. Once at the stockyard he will be confined in a crowded feedlot and fed a diet that, along with his inability to exercise, will add fat to his body.

Finally, he will take his place in line for the march into the slaughterhouse. He'll be terrified by the bright lights and the confusion of men and machines. As he moves closer to the front of the line, he'll be even more terrified by the smell of blood, the desperate cries of his comrades, and finally by the realization of what is going to happen to him. In the end a gun will drive a steel bolt into his skull and, if he's lucky, he'll be unconscious when the chains hoist him upside down and the butcher with a huge knife slits his throat.

The steer is luckier than other farm animals. He's the one who is treated the best.

Maybe it isn't necessarily so cruel after all...

My friend Dennis loved to kid me about my diet. Whenever we'd go out to eat and he ordered a meal that used to have a face, he'd pat me gently on the arm and say something like: "Now, don't you worry. This dish happens to be made from a very old bull who lived a satisfying and full life and who went to sleep peacefully one night but just didn't wake up."

If only Dennis was right.

But, what about chickens?

Most people don't think adult chickens or turkeys are very cute, and unfortunately that has led to their downfall in a big way. In our quest for eggs and poultry meat we humans have adopted the motto "All's fair with foul!" Just in the United States we kill 7.5 billion of them each year. (Yeah, that's billion.)

Chickens are the most abused animals on Earth. They are raised in huge buildings, fed a diet laced with antibiotics, and jammed together in filthy cages in a space smaller than a sheet of paper. The ammonia gas from their waste hangs heavy in the air. Never in their short lives will these birds be able to touch the earth, see daylight, or even stretch their wings. Under this kind of crowding and stress the animals would naturally peck at each other. The manufacturers have solved this problem by cutting off their beaks with a hot iron. (Needless to say, this is a very painful process—the equivalent of burning off a human finger without anesthetic.)

The "good" (less bad?) news is that these animals don't have long to suffer. The natural life expectancy of a chicken is about 12 years, but it's a wee bit shorter on the "farm". Laying hens are killed after 18 to 24 months, while "broiler" chickens live only eight weeks. Male chicks of laying hens aren't even that lucky (or unlucky, depending on how you look at it). They are never going to lay eggs, or grow large enough, fast enough to be of economic value to today's factory farmer. The babies are thrown into plastic bags where they are left to suffocate. Then they are ground up for animal food or fertilizer.

So, eating "chicken", or even an egg causes more cruelty than eating a steak???

Bet on it.

> You personally wouldn't treat an animal (any animal) the way chickens are treated on a factory "farm", would you? Of course you wouldn't. Then why would you want to pay someone else to do it?

But what about "free range" chickens?

Free range can mean different things to different people. Chances are the conditions are not much better at your local "organic" chicken "farm". Call and ask them how the chickens live, and how they are killed. Ask them if the "free range" is indoors or out, and if you can bring the kids over. If not, your question is answered.

"I'm not a vegetarian because I want to be healthy. I want the chickens to be healthy."

—**Isaac Bashevis Singer**

Hey, there must be better news here somewhere. What about fishes?

Fishes are cold and they have scales and they live in the water. Yuck! They aren't like us. Fishes are also silent. They don't make any cute barnyard noises we can incorporate into children's games. More importantly, they can't scream in pain. As a result, people tend to give fishes a status even lower than that of other food animals. Because they're silent it's easy for us to pretend that fishes can't feel the hooks that cut through their mouths and that they don't experience any pain when they suffocate out of the water. But of course this isn't true.

The best way to really understand fishes is to go snorkeling in the Caribbean or some other fun and warm spot. (Doesn't that sound good, *right now*?!) The beautiful, bright-colored creatures don't seem to mind much when we hulking, clumsy human beings get in the water with them. They eye us curiously but without fear, allowing us to get ever so close to them—to look, but never to touch. No one enjoying this experience can imagine that these graceful creatures are stupid.

The fishes that we hunt for food are less colorful but no less worthy. To catch them we humans use airplanes and radar and large ships that rake the water with even larger nets that trap and kill. We launch drift nets miles long that indiscriminately snare and kill everything in their path and, if lost, continue their killing forever.

Imagine the terror the fish feels when she is pulled from her home by the unseen force of a huge net or a powerful pump into an alien world where her body is suddenly burdened by gravity and she can no longer breathe. Imagine spending your last minutes of life thrashing helplessly against an unseen, deadly aggressor.

On commercial fishing boats dying fishes out of the nets are piled high, crushing those on the bottom and spilling their entrails. Antibiotics are sprayed on the pile to deal with the contamination. Below decks the fishes are gutted and frozen, and the waste ground into meal or sent back to sea with the myriad of non-target creatures who were unlucky enough to be caught in the merciless pull of the nets.

To experience the barbarity of fishing you don't have to go to sea. You need only drive down to your friendly neighborhood fishing pier. You'll find one in almost any town along the coast. Feel free to stroll around and watch the action. You'll see people threading hooks through live creatures (euphemistically known as "bait"), hoping those creatures will writhe in pain long enough before dying to attract a fish. You'll see men and women inserting plastic tongs into the stomachs of live fishes to recover swallowed hooks, and you'll see them pulling other fishes from the sea and clubbing them to death. You'll see them training their children to do the same thing.

Fishes aren't anything like us. They're cold and silent. We don't seem to be able to understand or respect them. Even on their way to becoming ethical vegetarians, most people give up eating the flesh of fishes last.

> "It isn't seafood, it's sea life." —**Linda McCartney**

Okay, so maybe eating meat and chickens and even fishes presents some ethical questions. But certainly there can't be anything wrong with eating dairy products, can there?

This is a question we vegans hear all the time. It usually comes up like this: Our dear friends have just taken their family recipe "World's Best Cheesecake" out of the refrigerator and are flabbergasted that we won't try a piece. (Ever notice that there must be at least 50,000 different "World's Best" cheesecakes?) These folks just want everybody to ooh and aah over their cooking. They certainly don't want to be confronted with the thought that anyone could have ethical problems with the old family recipe.

Our friends prefer to think that the cheese and cream and eggs that went into that tasty cheesecake came from Ma and Pa Jones' Old Tyme Farme. That's a place where all the chickens run free and happily lay their eggs for Ma and Pa with a big *cluck*, and where old Flossie the cow is so much a member of the family that she eats at the dinner table. Of course, Flossie is only happy to contribute what she can by bringing an udder full of milk in from the pasture every night after a lazy day of grazing on clover. Just like the pigs who smile when we make them into barbecue, the animals on Ma and Pa Jones' Old Tyme Farme love to please.

Of course, Ma and Pa Jones' Old Tyme Farme doesn't exist. No, the modern dairy farm is something else entirely. It's a world where young cows are artificially impregnated on a platform lovingly called the "rape rack" (to keep them lactating, cows must be kept reproducing). If the cow reproduces a female offspring that's good—it's money in the bank for the dairy farmer who has just increased his or her herd. If it's a male offspring (and, oddly, about 50% are!) the dairy farmer has a problem. This is an animal he has to get rid of. Not a big problem, mind you. The calf is allowed one night with his mother. Then he is taken away, terrified, to auction. I've heard people who have witnessed this say the mother may cry for three days.

The "veal" calf will spend the rest of his life chained in darkness, in a stall too small for him to turn around or otherwise use his muscles. He will be fed a thin gruel that will make him so anemic he will desperately seek out anything made of iron to suck on. (Remember, the milk that was meant for him goes to human truck drivers and basketball players and bankers.) All of this is good for the folks who "deal in veal", because they get a nice white cut of meat. Yeah, it's bad for the calf, but he doesn't have long to suffer. At the age of four months he will be stunned with a steel bolt and his throat will be slit open—a problem instantly transformed into more money for the dairy industry.

Meanwhile, back on the farm...the young cows are treated with growth hormones and milked on a machine that makes their bodies think several young calves must be feeding vigorously. They become walking milk factories, and they produce *lots* of milk—many times as much as they would naturally. Of course this overproduction takes a tremendous toll on their bodies. Despite the prodigious use of antibiotics and other drugs, perhaps 75% of them will live with painful mastitis. (Milk drinkers will be happy to know that there are regulations as to how much pus is allowed in the milk.) Every function of their bodies will be overstressed, and after a few years these cows will be classified as "spent".

Does that mean they can live out the rest of their lives in peace? Not hardly. At the ripe old age of four or five or six, these cows are taken to the slaughterhouse. By the time they get there they may be sick. Some of them will have broken bones because the calcium has been drained from their own bodies to go into the huge quantities of milk they produced. If necessary, they are pulled from the trucks with chains and moved with forklifts. Whatever their agony, they will be kept alive until they can be sold, because laws prohibit the sale of dead animals. [*Note:* at the time this was written a "downed" animal law was before the U.S. Congress that would also prohibit the sale of crippled animals. If we must have slaughterhouses, such a law would be a small but encouraging start.]

There is a saying that "a dairy cow never dies of old age". No, like her male calves, she dies young from the blow of the stun gun's metal bolt and a knife to the throat. She dies sick and afraid and in tremendous pain.

The smiling cows on the side of the milk carton and in the ice cream ads? Well, it must be a nice fantasy for some.

The many courageous people in the animal rights movement who have risked their personal safety to see and videotape the horrors of the factory farm and slaughterhouse tell us that the dairy industry ranks right up there with the poultry industry as the *worst* abusers of animals.

Does this mean the folks in the dairy industry are evil, wicked people? No. They are in business to maximize their profit, and they do that like all businesspeople—by exploiting to the maximum extent possible the working assets of their business. Animals are just some of those assets.

> **As long as people are willing to pay money for cows' milk, and don't care how it is obtained, nothing will change.**

Idea for a class trip #29

Go visit your local meat and dairy and poultry industries!

If the folks who bring you meat and dairy and poultry products *really* believe what they're doing is right and are proud of their efforts, they should be *delighted* to have the public come for a visit, shouldn't they? Just like any other business, they should be *delighted* to show off their facilities to your church group or your kid's Little League team. They should be *delighted* to prove that everything you've read in this book is wrong. (I wish they could!)

So why not give them the chance? Pick up the phone and call your local dairy farm, egg producer or "meat packing plant" to set up a tour. Tell them you want to see a dairy cow nursing her male offspring. Tell them you want to see chickens in the barnyard, pecking the ground with their beaks still intact. Tell them you want to witness "humane slaughter" (the oxymoron of morons).

I'm sure your local meat/dairy/poultry/etc. provider will welcome you with open arms. But just on that *off chance* that they don't, think about the reasons why. Is it because:

- Everybody wants to visit the slaughterhouse and, hey, they'd love to accommodate you, but they just don't have the room; or

 • They deal with top-secret government information, so you have to understand that for the good of the free world they can't allow visitors; or

> "But for the sake of some little mouthful of flesh we deprive a soul of the sun and light, and of that proportion of the life and time it had been born into the world to enjoy."
>
> —Plutarch

 • They have something to hide?

Do vegetarians really save lives?

Perhaps we vegetarians tend to get a little loose with our language sometimes. For example, we often congratulate ourselves on our good deeds in saving the lives of all those animals we don't eat. (Indeed, George Bernard Shaw envisioned that at his funeral the procession might include a cadre of animals who could thank his vegetarianism for their lives.) In real life, though, it isn't quite that simple.

Dr. Kristin Aronson, a philosopher and friend who writes and teaches about vegetarian and animal rights issues, argues that vegetarians don't really "save" lives at all. No farm animal is going to be spared a trip to the slaughterhouse and be allowed to live a happy and free life merely because a vegetarian, or lots of vegetarians, give up meat. Those animals are all doomed anyway. Indeed, about the best we vegetarians can hope for is to decrease the demand for meat so that fewer animals in the future are born into a life of confinement, suffering and early death. **Okay, maybe this isn't "saving lives", in the strictest sense, but it's certainly a worthy goal.**

There are at least two situations where "saving lives" might be the correct term to use. Consider "seafood", for example. Every time one of us vegetarians forgoes eating a fish or crustacean it creates a little less demand down at Frank's Friendly Fish House, which is eventually going to lead to one more fish or crustacean that can lead out its life in the sea instead of being boiled alive or crushed and suffocated on the deck of a ship. Sounds like "saving a life" to me!

And think about what might happen if *everyone* became a vegetarian tomorrow. All of the existing farm animals in captivity could be given a reprieve. Then we could let this last generation of farm animals live out their rest of their natural lives under hopefully much better conditions. (*Expensive?* Yes, but the cost would be *positively minuscule* compared to what meat costs us.) Doesn't this sound like "saving lives"? Doesn't this sound like a great idea?

A few are saved

Among the many billions of animals who meet horrible deaths at the slaughterhouse each year, a scant few have at least some measure of fortune and are saved from the butcher's knife. Sometimes chickens fall off the truck that is transporting them, or sometimes a farmer with a conscience will give a dying animal to someone with the will and the money to care for it. (As one animal rights worker put it, no businessperson is going to spend $150 on a vet bill for an animal with a market value of $10.) And then there are the dedicated, courageous, and compassionate people who defy the meat industry and look for live animals among the piles of discarded bodies of those who didn't make it to the slaughterhouse's killing floor.

If these animals are real lucky they'll eventually find their way to one of the farm sanctuaries that have been established to take care of their kind and educate the public. (These folks *do* give tours!) There they will receive love and care—two things they've never in their lives had before.

But that doesn't mean the story will end happily. Farm animals are the unfortunate products of years of selective breeding and genetic engineering. They are bred for characteristics that have nothing to do with leading long, healthy lives, and even *off* the factory farm they rarely do. Respiratory infections are common, as are a whole host of other chronic illnesses. Even on carefully monitored diets the chickens develop huge chests and the pigs become enormously fat. Their skeletal structures can't support the "meat" on their bones, and by the time they are a year or two old, most are unable to walk.

The birds that chickens once were before human domestication could fly gracefully. The boars from which pigs came were swift and sure in the wild. But, as anyone who has visited a farm animal sanctuary can attest, even the sad creatures that these animals have now become can be smart and charming and affectionate when they interact with us.

What a way to repay us humans for what we have done.

Closing credits

It seems to be in vogue that the closing credits to most movies now carry the disclaimer that "No animals were harmed in the making of this film." This is wonderful, of course. The film industry has come a long way since the days when wires were used to trip the horses in Westerns. Other industries should be so conscientious.

Still, is the disclaimer "No animals were harmed in the making of this film" really true? What exactly did the cast and film crew *eat* during those long hours of filming and editing? If they ate "ham" sandwiches, cheesesteak subs or "chicken" something-or-others, then *lots* of animals were harmed in the making of the film.

Somehow that's supposed to be okay though. It's a horrible sin if they slit a chicken's throat for dramatic impact on the screen, but perfectly okay to slit that same chicken's throat so Chuck in the cutting room (no pun intended) can have a greasy fried "chicken" lunch and throw half of it out in the trash.

Seems incongruous? Is an unhealthy lunch that will hasten Chuck's early demise more worthy of an animal's death than "dramatic impact"?

Maybe the actual fate of the animals doesn't count nearly as much as the sensitivities of the humans who may be watching.

P.S.– One of the other credits you usually see at the end of a movie (as if you cared) is the name of the caterer who worked on the film. If we believe the "no animals harmed" disclaimer, do we then surmise that these Hollywood caterers serve only vegan food? I'd love to think so, but somehow I doubt it.

P.P.S.– When you watch a movie and an animal is in danger of being killed by a hunter or in danger of going to the slaughterhouse, research lab, etc., do you root for the animal or the human aggressors? Is this consistent with whom you support with your *real dollars* in

> "I have from an early age abjured the use of meat, and the time will come when men such as I will look upon the murder of animals as they now look upon the murder of men."
>
> **–Leonardo Da Vinci**
>
> "Animals are my friends...and I don't eat my friends."
>
> **–George Bernard Shaw**

real life?

But what about plants?

So, what do vegetarians do about plants?
Don't they have feelings, too?

This is the standard question (two questions?) that somewhere between 69% and 100% of meat-eaters ask when they've been bombarded by rabid vegetarians lecturing them on animal rights and diet. Of course, this is merely big time rationalization. When meat-eaters start asking questions about "plant rights", vegetarians know they've struck a raw nerve. They know the meat-eaters are thinking: "By golly, you're trying to make me feel guilty, and you're doing such a good job of it, I'm going to find something to make you feel guilty about, too."

Fortunately, there's an easy response:

A vegetarian diet destroys far fewer plants than a diet based on animal products.

As we learned earlier in this book, animal-based agriculture is incredibly inefficient. Farmers have to grow (and destroy) five or ten or twenty times as many plants to feed meat and dairy animals as they'd have to grow if they were feeding people directly. Okay, vegetarians eat more plants *with their own teeth* than meat-eaters do. But it's meat-eaters, acting indirectly through the teeth of cows, pigs and chickens (well, maybe not chickens' *teeth*) that kill and maim lots more of our green friends.

And what about hooves?! Anyone who's ever studied a fence line in the American West knows the kind of damage that livestock can do to the natural land.

The moral of this story is that if you are concerned with the welfare of plants and want to save them from death and destruction you should stop eating altogether. If this doesn't seem entirely practical, at least become a vegetarian. In the long run you'll be doing a *big favor to lots of plants*. They'll thank you for it. (Uh oh, this means we're going to see bumper stickers that read "Love plants: eat them!")

Coincidence???

Is it just a coincidence that eating in a style that's good to other creatures is also kind to yourself? Is it merely an aberration of fate that the kinder your diet is, the healthier it is apt to be as well?

Or is there some kind of mystical linkage between the two?

Hmmmm..........

Well, if you went back to Biblical times, a guy with long hair and sandals might mention "an eye for an eye" to account for the connection. If you went back to the 1960s a very similar looking guy would explain to you how you can't have a healthy inner self when you're generating bad karma, and you definitely generate bad karma when you kill and eat others. If you only went back to the 1980s that guy would be wearing horn-rimmed glasses and driving a BMW. He'd probably shrug and say, "Hey, what goes around, comes around."

It seems like wisdom doesn't change very much through the ages.

Extreme Decadence Triple Chocolate Fudge (p. 105)

Chapter 5

*While we're appealing to your high ethical
standards, not to mention your common sense...*

Just a last word about those dairy products you eat

I magine a big bowl of your favorite ice cream. That's right, we're
talking about the stuff that costs $10 a pint at the fancy gourmet
food store where the checkers wear tuxedos and white gloves. Or
maybe you get it at that little homemade ice cream shop you swear is
scads better than any place else in town. Imagine your favorite flavor
too (Extreme Decadence Triple Chocolate Fudge, Tutti Frutti
Tangerine, Fish & Chips, Olive, etc.). It's 80% butterfat, and it goes
straight to your heart, but who cares? This stuff is so good it brings
strong men to their knees. Sex pales in comparison.

Okay, you get the idea. So, imagine there's a big bowl of this ice
cream in front of you, and you're about to take a bite. Now, imagine
that instead of being made from cows' milk they changed the recipe,
and now it's made out of *human* milk! Wouldn't that be terrific?
Wouldn't your favorite ice cream be *even better??*

It's funny, but a lot of people I've asked about this didn't think the
idea of human milk ice cream sounded too tasty. Many of them were
kind of put off by the concept. (I think the word "gross" came up a
couple of times, and they *weren't* talking about a dozen dozen.) **How
come? How come at the same time it can be "wonderfully sinful" to
consume the milk of another species, but "gross" to consume the milk
of our own species? What's wrong with this picture?**

Think about your sister, or your neighbor, or the woman who
cleans the bathrooms at work hooked up to a breast pump. Now, think
about being handed a glass of her milk—nice and fresh. If this thought
troubles you, think about the reasons why.

Familiarity breeds strange habits

Sure, we don't think of cows' milk and the products that are made from it as gross. That's because they're so familiar. They've been around all our lives, and they come from the grocery store all homogenized and pasteurized and in colorful cartons with those pictures of smiling cows on the outside. If your sister's milk were put in a nice carton with her picture on it and refrigerated, would that make it more appealing? Just remember the power of habit. **People can get used to anything! People can get used to eating maggots if they have to!**

Humans are the only animal on Earth that drinks milk past infancy and the only animal on Earth that consumes the milk of other creatures. Is this "natural"? Is this really what the higher "powers that be" had in mind, or did perhaps they intend this food for someone else? (Baby cows come to mind.)

If repeated often enough some of the strangest things can seem natural. Does that make them right?

Hey, people aren't cows!

As much as we'd all love to be baby cows when we drink our mandatory three glasses of milk a day, the real world doesn't work that way. Just because human milk is great for baby humans doesn't mean cows' milk is great for either baby or adult people. Here are just a few things to consider (yes, we've covered most of these already, but it never hurts to be repetitive, redundant, verbose and loquacious):

• Cows' milk is loaded with *fat* (49% of calories), and has *way more protein* than human milk (21% of calories, versus 6%). This is great for calves who double their body weight in less than seven weeks after birth and weigh hundreds of pounds by age one. It's not so great for humans, young or old, who don't fancy looking like cows.

• And **even if you** *do* **want to look like a cow**, you *know* all that fat (over 60% of it saturated, along with a big wallop of cholesterol) is a killer. All that protein is a killer too. And remember, if you take out the fat, not only do you get a boring product, but you make the protein problem worse. (Skim milk is 39% protein!)

• Cows' milk is the most **allergenic** food you can find, bar none. (Is somebody trying to tell us something?)

• *Most* of the people on this Earth become **lactose intolerant** (*i.e.,* they can't properly digest milk) at some point in their lives after weaning. (Somebody's *definitely* trying to tell us something!)

• Cows' milk probably **won't even make our bones and teeth stronger.** That's because the high amounts of animal protein in cow's milk leach the calcium out of our bodies as the milk puts it in.

• Cows' milk has **no fiber**, is **low in vitamins**, etc., etc. (*Yeah, yeah, we've heard this before.*)

Given these facts, how could anyone *possibly* believe this is the world's most perfect food for humans?

Who knows? People believed the planet was flat for a good long while too. But don't just get caught up in the fact that cows' milk is one of the most *unhealthy* foods you can put into your body. Keep in mind the incredible environmental destruction and animal cruelty perpetrated by the dairy industry as well.

So, what's the bottom line?

The bottom line is that if you want to do something **really weird** and **unnatural** and **bad for you**, and if you're already bored with your local heavy metal grunge band and with acting out the fantasies in *Bondage Magazine*, **have I got a deal for you!** You need look no further than your friendly neighborhood grocer's dairy case.

Sexism, dairy products, and chickens' eggs

(is Elsie the Cow really a closet feminist?)

Just because they are female we make them our slaves, and we treat them especially badly. We rape and artificially inseminate them so they are always pregnant. Every day we chain them up, violating their bodies more to take what we want. Some are mutilated and caged their whole lives. When they give birth, the female of their offspring is sold into the same captivity. We take their male babies away from them to be killed. Finally, when they are still young, but too old to produce to our standards, we kill them and take the rest of their bodies.

If these were humans this behavior would be too barbaric to even contemplate. But since they're only cows and chickens we feel justified in what we do because we want the products of their femininity—their milk and their eggs—for ourselves. We justify the rape and mutilation of the females of these species by only one thing: our pleasure.

Is this behavior sexist?

If we violate female animals to exploit what their sex produces, what kind of model is that? Isn't it incongruous for people on the one hand to talk about equality and "women's rights", but at the same time actively participate in the rape, confinement and mutilation of other females? Isn't it incongruous to demand employment rights for some females, but actively to participate in taking babies away from other females? Even if non-human animals "don't count", what kind of example does this set?

Is it consistent to simultaneously support women's rights and the production of dairy products? How so?

Stories from space

The spaceship *Free Enterprise* from a far-off galaxy is about to make its first landing on Earth. Captain Quirk turns to his right-hand man and the conversation goes something like this:

Captain Quirk: Before we land on Earth, tell me, Mr. Spook. What do Earthlings use to bind their bakery products?

Mr. Spook: Chickens' eggs, sir.

Quirk (*laughing*): Don't joke with me Mr. Spook.

Spook (*his ears pricking up*): I never joke about anything. You see, even though vegetable binders like cornstarch, potato starch and tapioca are cheaper, much healthier, readily available and just as effective, Earthlings almost universally put the reproductive matter of chickens into their cakes and cookies.

Quirk: That's kinky, Spook. Kinkier than that little dance those Martians do with the doughnuts and the oil can.

Spook: Yes sir, it is.

Quirk: Let's turn this ship around and see if we can find a planet that still believes in family values.

Chapter 6

Hips, humps, bumps, thighs and lies... vegetarianism and flab duke it out

Dieting? Who's dieting???

I know you don't have any problem at all with your weight. You, of course, have the body of Venus and/or a Greek god. (And hopefully it's even the one that's correct for your gender.) So you would never have any need for advice on dieting. But think about your cousin Irene—who has to put up with all those jokes about when her baby's due. Irene's tired of hearing that she gives literal meaning to the phrase "sit around the house", and she'd like some help. Irene knows she could use some weight loss advice, and in this chapter I won't be shy about offering it.

Here's the only diet advice you need

At this point you may get a sneaking suspicion that any diet advice you may find in this book is going to have something to do with vegetarianism. You're right. There are only three rules to follow, and here they are:

1. Don't eat animal products

If you follow this rule alone, you'll probably never have to worry about your weight again. How can I be so sure? Simple—how many fat vegetarians have you ever known? More to the point, how many fat *vegans* have you ever known? You'd have to look darned hard to find one. There just aren't any around! And for good reason. Let's face it, animal products are heavy foods, loaded with calories and fat. Just look at this totally random list of your basic animal products:

Food	Calories	Fat
Mayonnaise (1 tbs.)	57	5 g.
Egg (large)	149	10 g.
Ben & Jerry's Butter Pecan (½ cup)*	250	21 g.
"Pork" Chop	314	18 g.
Cheddar Cheese (4 oz.)	456	38 g.
McDonald's Big Mac*	530	28 g.
1/2 Chicken	989	86 g.
Porterhouse Steak (16 oz.)	1170	91 g.
Pepperoni Pizza (12")	1446	56 g.

(*product information as supplied by the companies)

Sure, you're saying. *But what about all the things that aren't on your "random" list? What about broiled skinless "chicken" breasts? What about broiled skinless "fish"? What about skim milk? Those things aren't fattening!*

True. But how exciting are those foods? And who among us has the willpower to eat *just* the low-fat things, out of all the animal products that are available? Certainly not Cousin Irene, or any of the other people in the world struggling with their weight.

A diet without animal products obviously doesn't have any of the nasty "foods" from the list above. What it *does* have is lots of fiber to fill you up, and plenty of carbohydrates, which turn off that old hunger alarm of yours *much* better than fats and proteins. But even more important, when people become vegetarian they start to think about what they eat. The result is that they reorient their diets in a healthier way. (You remember all those magazine articles you've read on dieting. Every one of them stresses the need to restructure your eating habits. Well, vegetarianism does that, almost automatically!)

2. Don't overdo the fats

Just in case you aren't reorienting your diet quite enough, I'll say it again. Sure, it's *technically possible* to be fat, even if you're a vegan, if all you're eating is potato chips and chocolate. This point number 2 is just in here to remind you there are some things that taste perfectly good, even if they aren't deep fried. Salad, for example.

3. Get some exercise

Exercise is good for you. It gets the old metabolic juices flowing, and gets you out of the house. It's hard to down large quantities of French fries while you're swimming laps. Exercise speeds up your metabolism so you'll burn more calories. It also gets those endorphins cruising around your brain, and makes you feel good about yourself.

If you follow all three of these rules, the odds are *overwhelming* that you'll never have to worry about dieting again. There are *expensive health spas* out there that use exactly this regimen and report dramatic weight loss for their clientele, even though these people are encouraged to stuff themselves with food. But you don't have to pay big bucks. You can do this at home very simply, and save your money to buy skimpy designer bathing suits.

How skinny will I...Sorry, let me restate that. How skinny will Cousin Irene be?

Well, statistics show that vegetarians have 11% less body fat than their meat-eating counterparts. Probably more (...I mean less) for vegans. If you're built like a fire hydrant, it's not likely that you're going to turn into a string bean by giving up animal products. You may still have a little flab around the edges. But you probably *will* get darn close to the ideal weight for your body type. Greek god time? Maybe not, unless you hit the weight room. The sumo wrestler's belly? Definitely gone! Your...I mean, Cousin Irene's 45-inch thighs? History!

Tell me again, what's so great about this diet?

1. It doesn't take willpower. Do it because you love animals. Do it because you want to be environmentally responsible. Do it because meat and dairy products are inherently gross. (Be honest now—wouldn't you *just love* to be grossed out by the very foods that are making you fat?) Believe me, there's all kinds of motivation here. And the longer you're away from animal products the stranger it will seem to actually think about eating someone else's flesh, or milk or eggs. Have you ever met a vegetarian who felt deprived by his or her diet? Of course you haven't, because again, there just aren't any of them around!

2. There aren't any complicated rules. You really don't want to have to think about how many portions of what size you can have from which food groups, do you? You really don't want to think about your "diet" at all. Vegetarianism is oh so simple, and it's good for you automatically.

3. You can eat as much as you want. Vegetarians eat all the time. They *love* to eat. They even eat French fries!

4. It isn't really a "diet". Life's too short to be on a "diet" all the time. "Diets" don't work because we suffer when we're on them, and none of us has the least bit of self-control. (Jackie Gleason once said that the second day of your diet will be easier than the first, because by that time you're off it.) Why deny yourself the things you love to eat, when it's so easy to love the things you really should be eating?!

> *Wait! Vegetarianism may be the simplest and most effective weight maintenance program in the history of the Universe, but it's still too complicated. Give me something that will make me skinny by this afternoon!*

Okay, maybe you only started reading here in Chapter 6, and you don't know about all the other great reasons to be a vegetarian. In that case it probably isn't realistic to think that you're going to rush out and switch to a vegetarian diet just to lose weight. Anyway, people in our society have come to expect quick and simple fixes to their problems. They want things that are fast and easy—even if they don't really work.

Let's get back to "mildly overweight" Cousin Irene who is, as we speak, taking up space (more than she'd like to) in your spare bedroom. She might be just a little hesitant to try a vegetarian diet. (Actually, Irene hasn't eaten anything that didn't come out of a Styrofoam box in years. She says she'll become a vegetarian just as soon as meatball subs are declared macrobiotic.) Irene's looking for the "quick fix" all right. She's felt compelled to try every diet and exercise product that a certain cable station from Atlanta has ever advertised, but she still feels like the Goodyear blimp in stretch pants.

Many of us can sympathize with Cousin Irene. We've done the "fat" thing. (Believe me, I know about this. I was as fat as Larry Mondello on *Leave it to Beaver* for my entire youth.) We've tried the tummy trimmers, the pills, and the diets.

I'm not really supposed to do this in a book on vegetarianism, but since I can empathize so well...okay, here goes. I'm going to offer my famous array of *non*-vegetarian diet tips. Don't tell anyone I'm doing this.

Here they are! Proven diet tips for those who want the "quick fix" and absolutely refuse to try vegetarianism!

M ake no mistake, these are not run-of-the-mill diet tips like those you might find every week in the *National Enquirer*. No sir-ee-Bob! These tips are based on established scientific principles—things like physics, chemistry, magic, incredibly wishful thinking, and the four basic food groups (to put them in order of credibility).

These diet tips are intended for you, your cousin Irene, and everyone else out there who's looking for the fast and easy route to a perfect body. Without further ado, then, here are the only *non-vegetarian* diet tips you'll ever need:

Diet Tip #1: Rinse out your mouth

We're all told that the way to lose weight is to cut down on calorie intake. In a sense this is correct. Of course, what really counts is *calorie balance*. If you burn off more calories than you take in you'll lose weight, right? Up until now, though, there have been some problems with losing weight this way. First, low calorie diets (not to be confused with vegetarian diets!) are a drag, and they can lead to nutritional imbalances. (Remember, there are substantial numbers of calories in some of the most important foods we eat—essential foods like pie and corn nuts.) And burning up calories with exercise isn't the ideal solution either. Exercise is a lot of hard work, and it's been really boring ever since that cute aerobics instructor down at the club quit. Anyway, you have to jog something like 43 miles just to burn up the calories in a pickle.

So what's the answer to this dilemma? It comes from a careful study of science. We all learned in school that a calorie is technically a measure of heat. To be precise, a calorie is the amount of heat needed to raise the temperature of one gram of water one degree Celsius. Thus, rather than cutting down on calories in our diet, it is possible to burn them up by doing such things as taking cold showers and sleeping all winter in the back yard.

If this proves inconvenient, though, just try this friendly ice water technique. Here's an example of how it works: if you drink an eight-ounce glass of ice water (228 grams of water at about 2°C) and let it heat up to your body temperature (37°C), you'll burn off about 8000 calories. Not a bad way to lose weight, huh? Forget the painful exercise. Rinse out your mouth with a few glasses of ice water and you've just burned off the calories in three cases of Hostess cupcakes!

[Editor's Note: Once again Mr. Reinhardt is shame-lessly pandering misleading information to promote his own deviant self-interest. In actuality, food Calories ("large calories"—note the capital "C") are equal to 1000 calories. This method works, but you'll need lots and lots of ice water!]

Diet Tip #2: Give blood

Most people don't realize that they can lose weight simply by giving blood. It's true though, and it's a proven technique that winos have used effectively for years. (Ever see a fat wino?)

I don't know how many calories are in a pint of blood, but it must be a bunch. (After all, it keeps vampires thriving.) Even if you eat the doughnuts they feed you, you're still going to come out way ahead. Diet conscious individuals should think of giving blood as their civic duty, kind of like voting. And Mayor Daley's old axiom about voting—"vote early, vote often"—should apply here as well. Once the Red Cross realizes they can promote blood donations as a dieting technique, people will be beating the doors down, and our blood supply will be assured for the future.

Diet Tip #3: Write to your priest

Here's a tip that can't fail, whether you're trying to lose weight, or you just want to get rid of one of those nasty little vices you picked up from your kids.

Just think of the most perverted thing you've ever done in your life. (Something even *worse* than that night in Indiana when you buttered your armpits.) Write it down on a sheet of paper, complete with every lurid detail and nuance. Sign your name legibly at the bottom and pop it into a stamped envelope addressed to your priest, mother, wife, etc. Okay, now give the envelope to your best friend (or even better, the escrow officer at your local bank) with the instruction that if you can demonstrate that you've lost 30 pounds over the next three months you'll get the letter back. Otherwise it goes in the mail.

This is the most effective technique in existence for developing instant willpower. I know what you're going to say, though—that you've never done anything you wouldn't want your priest to know about. No, of course you haven't. Well, never fear. Just put $5000 cash in the envelope, along with a nice letter of appreciation, and address it to the American Nazi Party. Enough of an incentive?

These great diet tips should work just fine for Cousin Irene. If they don't, though, you've got a real dilemma. You just might have to take the advice of this book, and suggest one more time that she could lose weight–almost *guaranteed*–just by giving up the animal products and getting some exercise. Yeah, she'll probably ignore that advice. If she doesn't, though, just think how great life could be. The springs in your couch and Volkswagon would finally have a chance to recover. Since the new vegetarian Irene would probably be on the town every night with a new suitor, there's a good chance she might marry one of them and move out. That would free up your spare bedroom to display your collection of lava lamps.

There would be one other benefit, too. Late at night when you're watching that cable station from Atlanta and the tummy trimmer ads come on, you won't have to worry about the danger of being caught sitting between Irene and the telephone.

Fat vegetarians

Okay, so there are some fat vegetarians around. Vegans even. And boy are they fat! They're called hippopotamuses. (hippopotami?)

This recalls the Johnny Carson story of the two hippopotamuses standing in a muddy pond of water in the remote jungles of Africa. The air is thick, the sun is beating down, and there's no hint of a breeze. Insects swarm around. For hours the hippopotamuses stand motionless, only their eyes sticking out of the hot, stagnant water. Finally, one hippopotamus turns to the other and says: "You know, I just can't get it through my head that it's Tuesday."

How willpower works

You're having dinner at Le Ver, the fanciest restaurant in town, and the waiter has just brought the dessert cart to your table. For the next forty minutes, in a voice any TV evangelist would love to use to describe the Lord, your waiter runs down the gustatory merits of Le Ver's fabulous desserts.

You *know* you should go with just a simple bowl of strawberries, but there, in front of your nose, is a huge slice of Le Ver's famous "World's Best Cheesecake". (Yes, one of only 50,000 so designated!) It's made just the way you like it with the chocolate chips and the sour cream frosting. Your palms are sweating as you contemplate the decision. Which thought process will make the selection easier?

The traditional willpower battle
(as practiced by non-vegetarians)

"Boy, that cheesecake looks terrific—rich, creamy, etc. But I know it's full of fat and calories. You know what they say—*a moment on the lips, forever on the hips*, and all that. I really *should* have the strawberries. Oh, gosh…[wringing of hands, gnashing of teeth]. Well, this is sort of a special occasion. After all, isn't it Joe DiMaggio's birthday or something? Everybody else is indulging. They're not worried about *their* hips. I guess it's okay to pamper myself only this once."

From the vegetarian viewpoint

"Well, let's see. We've got nice fresh berries and we've got cheesecake. I'm sure the cheesecake tastes great, but those foods seem so heavy now that I've gotten used to my new way of eating. Anyway, it's main ingredient is the bodily fluid of a large farm animal. Blah! Yukko! Gag me with an electric pitchfork! Is there really any question here?"

Chapter 7

Putting it all together!

B y now, dear meat-eater, you've patiently waded your way through six long chapters that insulted your way of life and told you way more than you ever wanted to know about eating vegetables. Perhaps you think you should finally be safe, but not so. In this final chapter of the First Part I'll do my best to try to piece together all those random and seemingly irrelevant things that came before and parlay them into other random and seemingly irrelevant things.

Wait! We've reached the last chapter of the First Part. It must be time for...

A pop quiz (for meat-eaters only!)

Y es, as if we vegetarians weren't obnoxious enough already, now here's a way to measure what you've learned or haven't learned so far. This pop quiz will test the knowledge and conviction meat-eaters have on some relevant topics of interest in the debate over meat-eating. Sharpen up those No. 2 pencils and grab a second cup of coffee. Here's your chance to show us vegetarians that everything we say is dumb—that meat-eating is still the way to go.

Rules: This is an open book test, and consultation with experts like the American Meat Institute is strictly allowed. There's no need to rush; the time limit is the rest of your life. [Hint—You can increase your time limit by switching to a vegetarian diet.]

The Natural Order of Things

1. Check all that apply:
(a)_____The sight of a cow really gets my digestive juices flowing;
(b)_____I drool over pigs;
(c)_____When I smell the inside of a barn I'm overcome with hunger.

2. It's natural for humans to be the only animal that drinks the milk of another species because:
(a)_____We're biologically identical to baby cows; or
(b)_____We never really grow up.

Your Health

1. On the following line please cite every credible scientific study showing that meat-eating is healthier than vegetarianism [you'll have plenty of room]:_____.

2. It's healthy to eat chickens and fishes because:
(a)_____Even though, calorie-for-calorie, they can have several times the cholesterol of "beef", it's "good" cholesterol;
(b)_____Modest amounts of PCBs, mercury, and salmonella bacteria in our diets actually strengthen our immune systems;
(c)_____Our kidneys and livers thrive on the workout they get from concentrated animal protein; or
(d)_____I don't know, but everybody says it is.

Animal Rights

1. Distinguishing meat-eating from hunting by saying that farm animals are "raised to be eaten" means:
(a)_____They actually enjoy being eaten;
(b)_____The chicken on your dinner table lived a much better life than the wild pheasant on your table; or
(c)_____You're supposed to hold them over your head before taking a bite.

2. What would you rather not think about regarding the meat on your plate:
(a)_____It once had a face;
(b)_____It's crawling with unknown bacteria; or
(c)_____You paid $9.00 a pound.

3. Who best exemplifies the term "animal lover":

(a)_____Marge, who spent $218 grooming Fufie at Puppy Palace;

(b)_____Ted, who gave Ducks Unlimited $1000 to protect wetlands so he can go hunting every October; or

(c)_____Sandy, who didn't spend a dime, but carried the spider she found in her kitchen outside instead of smashing it.

The Environment

1. Explain how we can find the resources (farmland, water, energy, waste disposal, etc.) to come even close to feeding the world's population on a meat-based diet. If everyone can't eat meat, how should we decide who will?

2. It's important to save dolphins from death in fishing nets, but nobody wants to save the tuna because:

(a)_____Tuna are stupid;

(b)_____Tuna have no nerves and can feel no pain or fear; or

(c)_____We all grew up watching Flipper. (Sorry, Charlie!)

3. Would you give up eating tuna fishes to save the dolphins? Would you give up eating hamburgers if it would save the rainforests?

The Meat Industry

1. "Beef gives strength" because:

(a)_____It builds muscles to lug it home from the grocery store;

(b)_____A hard artery is a strong artery;

(c)_____Your breath is strong after eating it;

(d)_____Elephants are the strongest animal on Earth, and everyone knows they love to eat cows; or

(e)_____The slogan "Builds strong bodies 12 ways" was already taken.

2. Explain why milk is a "health kick". What's healthy about it? Who does it kick?

3. They call it the "incredible edible egg" because:

(a)_____It contains an incredible 212 mg. of cholesterol;

(b)_____It causes an incredible 160,000 to 800,000 cases of salmonella poisoning in the U.S. every year;

(c)_____It's incredible anyone would consider it edible; or

(d)_____Each one comes from the chicken prepackaged in a nifty storage case.

Your Lifestyle

1. Your mother warned you not to touch dead birds when you were walking in the park. How come it was okay to put dead birds in your mouth at the dinner table? How would she have felt about Shaking and Baking the dead park pigeon? How would you have felt? Would you have eaten it if she had?

2. You eat meat because it fits with your "devil-may-care" philosophy that if you only go around once in life you may as well [check all that apply]:

(a)_____Live a little;

(b)_____Get cancer and heart disease;

(c)_____Die young.

3. If you gave up meat, which of the following would you miss the most?:

(a)_____Your self-image as a cowboy;

(b)_____The gourmet food and Continental atmosphere of the local Happy Cowboy Steak House; or

(c)_____Heartburn and constipation.

4. Vegetarians are all deprived; they just pretend to be happy with their diets: _____True or _____False.

5. Check each vegetarian food you have tried: _____tempeh; _____seitan; _____tabouleh; _____baba ghannouj; _____plantains; _____falafel; _____baigan bharta; _____nori. Perhaps you are missing something already?

Bonus Question

You fly to Phoenix to visit your old college buddy Jim. (Yeah, it's the same Jim who mooned the bridesmaids at your wedding.) Being health conscious, you order the special "low cholesterol" meal for your flight. When it comes, you notice that the guy sitting next to you in the Nehru jacket is eating the special vegetarian meal. Using your incredible deductive powers (animals contain cholesterol, plants don't) you realize his vegetarian meal has less cholesterol than your "low cholesterol" meal. What's wrong with this picture? How come the airline didn't just serve you the vegetarian meal? Would you have been upset if they had?

Special Extra Points Bonus Question

Strange beings from the planet Gronos in the fourth galaxy have come to Earth. These beings (they're called "Groans") have intelligence vastly superior to ours, and our weapons are useless against them. While their knowledge could greatly benefit our planet, they have different ideas. It seems that Groans have a voracious appetite for human flesh, and their plan is to use the Earth as a farm to supply their dinner tables back home.

Lucky you has been chosen as the representative of the human race to try to change the Groans' ideas. You are led into the huge spaceship belonging to the leader of the Groans, and into a room with two comfortable chairs in it. The leader motions for you to sit down. In an effort to put you at ease she has formed herself into a non-threatening human figure. (Actually, she looks exactly like Dr. Joyce Brothers.)

You begin by telling Dr. Brothers about the human suffering her plan will cause—the billions of innocent men, women and children who will be put to violent deaths, the tears that will be shed and the heartache that will be endured. You tell her that, while not perfect, your planet has learned a lesson from its violent past. You would expect a society as advanced as the Groans' to have mastered peaceful coexistence, and to show humanity to other civilizations.

Dr. Brothers waves you off with the back of her hand. "What is this word 'humanity'?" she asks. "On your planet humans are the only animals who commit 'inhuman' acts. Anyway, you must agree that it is the right of the strong to dominate the weak. After all, you kill and eat the other animals of Earth for *your* food, don't you?"

"Yes, of course," you answer. "But—"

Suddenly a hulking figure appears in the doorway with a large, sharp knife. You swallow hard and look back at the leader of the Groans, who now sports the self-confident smirk of a Ph.D psychologist. "You know, the people of the planet Bosco might taste just as good...," she says, "...so I'll tell you what I'll do. If you can explain to me why butchering you wouldn't have the same ethical implications, and be *exactly* like humans eating animals, I'll spare your pathetic race." She licks her lips. "On the other hand, if you can't deliver the goods, I'm anxious to try a young female of your species cooked with her mother's milk. I believe you call it a 'cheeseburger'?"

What do you tell Dr. Brothers to save the lives of yourself and your fellow human beings?

If a cow, as a representative of all cows everywhere, came and talked to you about your future plans to eat meat and dairy products, what would you tell her?

Question authority #2

When you're wondering who to believe—the guys telling you to eat meat and dairy products or the folks telling you why you shouldn't—think about one thing: Who's going to make or lose money off your decision?

Willpower revisited

or: "I just don't have the self-control to be a vegetarian!"

Here's the dinner conversation I had one night with Frank, a meat-eater. The topic of discussion turned to vegetarianism just after I ordered my meal (funny how that tends to happen!), and Frank had a thing or two to say about the subject.

"My brother's a vegetarian," he started. "No meat, no dairy, no alcohol, no coffee. The guy's healthy as all get out."

"That's great," I said.

"Yeah, I tried it once too. I was on that diet for six months. You know, I got skinny, I felt great—it was terrific!"

I looked at Frank. He wasn't thin. He didn't look so healthy. "What happened?" I asked.

He sighed. "Well, I was driving through Texas one day, and I kept seeing these big billboards every few miles for Bob's Barbecue. I just couldn't resist it. When I got there I stepped inside—just to take a look around, you understand. *No vegetables, no potatoes*, I said to myself. My stomach was growling. *Looks like I'll just have to have one of those rib sandwiches.* Frank let out a little sigh and looked embarrassed. "I guess I was ready to go back to eating meat."

Frank's story is sad beyond belief—tragedy at its most poignant. As Shakespeare would have said, paraphrasing the immortal Bob & Ray (as he often did), Frank's story is precariously close to being a bummer. Of course it does illustrate one immutable point:

Guiding principal of life #247

If you really want to be a vegetarian, (*i.e.,* if you want to be healthy and thin like Frank once was, if you want to get the certificate suitable for framing, etc., etc.), you'd best not rely on willpower!

Face it folks, Bob's Barbecue is going to be there staring you in the face for the rest of your life. There's a McDonald's, it seems, in every town in the world, and you could swear there's a "beef" jerky display by every cash register in every convenience store on Earth. If you're constantly saying to yourself, "Man, I'd really, *really* like to have one of those rib sandwiches, but I know it's going to make me fat and give me a heart attack, so I'm going to resist *even if it kills me,*" you've already lost the battle. People who like the taste of meat and rely on willpower are eventually going to be like Frank and start rationalizing. (*Hey, I'm not going to get fat and have a heart attack **today**, so why not indulge?*) Even if you're one of the few non-Frank types who can resist such temptation, **why make yourself miserable? Life is too short!**

Becoming a vegetarian in our society always takes a little self-control at the beginning. But if you want to make it easier to become a vegetarian, and certainly if you want to *stay* a vegetarian, you've got to move beyond willpower to the next level of cosmic consciousness, so to speak.

No, this isn't where I drag out the sandals and incense and play all those Ravi Shankar 8-track tapes. Rather, this is where I subtly steer all you health-oriented types over to the **Two *Other* Great Reasons to be a vegetarian**. [If you don't remember these, go back to Chapter 1, and take notes this time.] Here's the idea.

Things your mother told us about you #16

You may compromise your diet by eating something unhealthy once (or even twice) in a while, but **you don't compromise your principles.**

Once you get it into your head, then, that eating meat is wrong for you because it's an awfully nasty thing to do to the Earth and the creatures that inhabit it, you're going to be a vegetarian for life. There's no willpower involved anymore. It's now a matter of principle and, like Mom says, *You don't compromise your principles.*

Okay, maybe that sounds scary to you—"vegetarian for life". Life can be a long trip, after all—especially if you're a vegetarian. Fortunately, there's help along the way. **With vegetarianism it gets easier to live up to your principles as time goes on.**

Just so you don't forget, here's a little rehash of just a few of the changes you can expect in your life as a result of sticking to those principles (no guarantees here, but the odds are pretty good):

Lifestyle changes of the rich and vegetarian

1. You'll get **healthier** and **thinner** (at least within reason), even though you're packing away food like a squirrel on steroids.

2. Meat will become **less appetizing** and appear more like what it really is—a decaying dead animal. (Remember: why would you want to put a dead animal in your mouth?)

3. Good-for-you food like whole grains and vegetables will become **more appealing** (after all, they have texture and taste!) while bad-for-you food (cheese omelets, hash, anything covered with mayonnaise) will seem dull and gloppy in comparison. You might even find yourself waking up in the middle of the night hankering for dark, leafy green vegetables.

4. Naturally, **chocolate** may be an exception to lifestyle change #3 above.

5. You'll worry a lot less about **fat** and **cholesterol**. That will leave you more time to worry about important things like the national debt and the guy with the braided eyebrows your daughter is dating.

6. You won't feel **guilty** anymore, even when looking directly at a cow.

7. You'll **live longer**.

8. You'll wonder why your friends are **still eating meat**.

Not bad for something that doesn't take willpower, huh?

Decisions, decisions...

E ating meat is every bit as much of a conscious choice on your part as eating vegetarian. When dinner is over and you ask yourself, *why did I make that choice?*, what's your answer going to be?

Become a vegetarian—one meal at a time

Y ou don't have to make decisions for the rest of your life all at once. Down at AA they tell recovering alcoholics to take it one day at a time. Same thing here. The coaches always tell their teams to take on the tough schedule one game at a time. Same thing here, except there's no smelly locker room and you don't have to dump Gatorade on anybody's head.

Think of it this way. It's dinner time and you've got to make a decision one way or the other: is it going to be a meat or a vegetarian meal? Make it vegetarian and you can think of the six jumbo shrimps (contradiction in terms) you've just saved. They're swimming in the ocean right now, going bowling with their buddies and happily gnawing on whatever disgusting dead stuff shrimp eat. Or think of your vegetarian meal as a few more trees left standing in the rainforest, or as part of a cow left alive. (After a bunch of veggie meals you'll actually *build* a living cow—you can keep it in the back yard and take the kids for rides!)

Think of every veggie meal too as a new dose of fiber and low calorie/high nutrient heart disease- and cancer-fighting food. Not to mention a few hours when your poor beleaguered body won't have to deal with yet another dose of concentrated protein and/or high fat animal flesh.

> Remember, you've got to decide one way or the other every time you eat: meat or vegetarian? You can't avoid making this decision, even if you put down this book and go to Fiji. So you may as well think about it.

Remember too, you're not making commitments forever. Tomorrow morning at breakfast you've got to decide again.

Tired of worrying about the world's problems?

There are many problems in this world that we are helpless to do anything about. Fortunately, the extreme cruelty, wanton environmental destruction, and human disease brought on by the animal agriculture industry are *not* among them. At every meal each of us has **complete control** over whether we make these problems better or worse.

> "While we ourselves are the living graves of murdered animals, how can we expect any ideal conditions on Earth?"
>
> —George Bernard Shaw

Still unconvinced?
Decided that you'll continue to eat meat?
That's okay!

All right, so you've heard all the arguments for vegetarianism, and maybe you've decided that it's not for you, or maybe you just want to think about it for awhile. Fair enough. After all, **the decision to become a vegetarian has to come from within. It isn't something that people can be talked into. You've got to decide how you feel in your heart.**

Back at the beginning of this book I promised I wouldn't try to pressure you into anything. Anyway, there are still two more parts of this book to go. In the meantime...

...here are some convenient excuses you should feel free to borrow.

Author's Note: *I personally know all about authoring lame excuses. Back when I was a teenager the two things that were certain in life (along with death and taxes) were that the lawn needed mowing and there was homework to be done. Being the kind of kid who preferred to spend his time sleeping and listening to records, I became a master of evasion. My father would yell at me daily: "You've got more excuses than Carter's got liver pills!"*

After becoming a vegetarian and listening to meat-eaters, I know just how my father must have felt.

Take a moment to think about the reason you are choosing to continue your meat-eating ways. Now, see if that reason/excuse is given below (I bet it is!). If not, send it in, and I'll add it to the list.

Just count all these excuses. Liver pills don't even come close!

The denial/rationalization excuses (aren't they all?)

● "There's nothing wrong with eating a little meat."
● "I don't think meat-eating is as bad for [the animals, the environment, me] as they say."
● "They are raised to be eaten." (Alternative version: "If we didn't raise them for food, they never would have been born and had the chance to live.")
● "I'm an animal lover."
● "I try not to think about what I'm eating."
● "I don't take what I eat that seriously."

Blame it on somebody else

● "I think I could be a vegetarian, but my husband [kid, dog] is a real 'meat-and-potatoes' man."
● "God [Jesus, Allah, the U.S. Senate] wants us to eat meat, and the Bible [Koran, Congressional Record] tells us so."
● "My doctor insists that I eat meat."
● "It would upset [insert name here] if I didn't eat his/her pot roast."

Blame it on natural forces

● "People were intended to be carnivorous." (Alternative version: "Why do you think we have eye teeth [eyes in the front of our heads, sharp fingernails]?")
● "I tried being a vegetarian once, but my body just couldn't adjust to it."
● "I eat meat because I need extra iron [steroids, pesticides] in my diet."
● "I've just got to have a hamburger once in a while."

The "oh, poor me" excuses

● "If I gave up animal products, I don't know what I'd eat." (Alternative version: "If you don't eat animal products, what's left?")
● "I could never survive on rabbit food." (Alternative version: "I'd get too hungry.")
● "I just quit smoking, I can't give up meat too!"
● "My life is complicated enough already."

The nonsensical excuses (aren't they all?)

● "You vegetarians are all [insert insulting description here]!"
● "The animals have to die from something eventually anyway."
● "If everyone quit eating meat, what would happen to all the cows?" (Alternative version: "We'd be overrun by cows!")

The non-excuse excuses

These are the things meat-eaters say to appease us vegetarians when they just can't come up with anything else:
● "I was a vegetarian [or almost a vegetarian] for a while back in the '70s."
● "You know, you're probably right. A vegetarian diet probably is more healthy."

The excuses we vegetarians get tired of hearing

● "I'm practically a vegetarian myself." (Alternative version: "You know, I actually eat very little meat.")
● "But don't plants have feelings too?"
● "I'll think about it."

The legitimate excuses

There are, of course, some legitimate reasons for eating meat. These, though, are the excuses we vegetarians never hear:
● "I love the taste of meat so much that it's worth it to me to be cruel to animals, harm the environment and damage my own health."
● "I'm lazy [weak, spoiled, self-conscious, just like everyone else], and it's just too inconvenient for me to be a vegetarian."
● "I was raised eating meat, have eaten meat all my life, and I'm not about to start thinking for myself now."
● "Hey, I'm a kid. My parents won't let me be a vegetarian!"

Fear & loathing at the burger joint

People are terrified at the prospect of giving up meat. So terrified that they'd rather undergo bypass surgery—sometimes two or three times. So terrified that they'd rather go through life with a guilty conscience, making rationalizations (see above) for their behavior. So terrified that they'd rather be fat!

What is it about meat that holds this enormous power over people?

Why are *you* afraid to even consider giving up meat? Is meat really *that* tasty and *that* convenient that it justifies the cruelty to the animals, the environment and your own body? Have you even *tried* the vegetarian alternatives?

You haven't really thought about it with an open mind, have you? Right now you're making excuses to yourself. How come? What are you afraid of?

Does it help to know most of us vegetarians were once deathly afraid too? We agonized like crazy—many of us for years. But still, somehow, we made the decision to give up meat, completely and forever. And you know what? Once you make your mind up, the rest is easy. *Lots* easier than the agonizing. *Lots* easier than the troubles that come with meat. Really. I promise.

What are you afraid of?

The Second Part

Okay, maybe I'll think about vegetarianism. But tell me...what the heck would I eat?

It's hard to make even the most noble of decisions if you're convinced it would lead to your own imminent starvation. In this part of the book I'll try to convince you that vegetarianism isn't about starvation—it's about eating profusely! Vegetarianism isn't about eating boring foods that taste like hay and cardboard either. The upcoming chapters will tell you what we vegetarians eat, introduce you to some great new foods, and hopefully give you some ideas about how to restructure your own diet to make it more interesting and exciting. Oh boy! This is the fun part of vegetarianism!

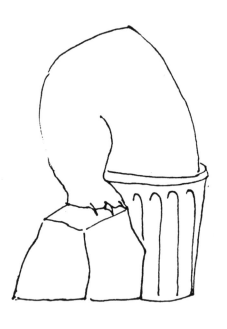

Chapter 1

What vegetarians eat

"But, what do you eat?"

That's the question meat-eaters ask vegetarians all the time. It's a good question too, because if you look at the Standard American Diet (remember, it's abbreviated "SAD") there's a lot of meat to be sure. But even among "vegetarian" foods, there aren't very many commonly eaten things that aren't dependent in some way on animal products. If something doesn't have chickens' eggs or cows' milk mixed into it, it probably has mayonnaise or butter or cheese on top of it. Tell a meat-eater you're a vegan and you don't eat any animal products and he or she will probably ask the question twice:

"But, what do you eat? What on Earth do you eat?"

Fortunately, there are some easy answers to *both* these questions:

First, many of the dishes meat-eaters already love don't need meat at all! People have become so used to throwing meat into everything, and have become so accustomed to heavy, high-fat dishes, that they've forgotten what real food tastes like. Spaghetti sauce doesn't need a bunch of ground "beef" in it to make it taste good. Soup doesn't need "chicken" broth, and stir-fry doesn't need chunks of "pork" hiding under the vegetables. Without all that meat, foods are lighter, more flavorful, and lower in calories. Best of all, you can eat more of them!

Second, you should change your eating habits! There are lots of vegetarian foods out there that you haven't tried. And with new lighter, tastier, vegetarian foods in your diet, your meals won't have to be defined by a single dish. ("Mom, what's for dinner?" "Pork chops?" "Is that all?") You can have two or three "main" dishes if you want to.

You can eat a bunch of light meals instead of one heavy one. (Your doctor will like this. The makers of Maalox won't.) You can eat at 3 o'clock in the afternoon if you like. You'll be free!

Third, you don't have to change your eating habits! Not if you don't want to, anyway. **There are vegetarian substitutes for everything!** You've heard of veggie burgers; you've heard of tofu dogs. (Don't laugh, we're going to talk more about these later.) There are great vegetarian substitutes to satisfy any animal food craving you might have—from steak to Reuben sandwiches. If you want to stuff yourself to the gills every night with a big pot roast and gravy (and a hot fudge sundae for dessert!) you can do that and *still eat a vegan diet.* I'll show you how!

All of this should point to the conclusion that vegetarians have no excuse for going hungry or being dissatisfied with their diets. In fact, we can summarize with the **First Rule of Eating Vegetarian**:

The First Rule of Eating Vegetarian

Giving up animal products should not result in one whit of sacrifice as far as tastiness of food is concerned. Every animal product has a vegan substitute that does the job with at least equal aplomb.

This all sounds too good to be true, you say? Nobody ever offered you a vegan pot roast or hot fudge sundae? Well, that's because of the **Second Rule of Eating Vegetarian**:

The Second Rule of Eating Vegetarian

Sometimes you've really got to hunt for those vegan substitutes.

"SAD" Fact #1—The Standard American Diet is pretty poor

Maybe it's no worse than the Standard British Diet, the Standard German Diet, etc., but that's not saying much. Indeed, there has been speculation that the American diet is so poor that our species has actually been extinct for the last five years. (Any indications to the contrary are said to be merely the lingering effects of food additives.)

Of course, this is not true. Indeed, several Americans are still alive, living mostly in towns that are too small and isolated to have been spotted by the marketing departments of any of the major fast food chains. (I think there's one of these towns in Alaska.)

Nevertheless, no one will argue that in a country where ketchup is a governmentally recognized official vegetable, there might be room for dietary improvement. **Let's take an average day and see what the average American (Briton, German, etc.) eats:**

● **Calories and Fat:** Enough to choke a horse, to use the popular animal rights vernacular. Yes, getting fat is pretty much assumed if you eat the Standard American Diet.

● **Vegetables:** In addition to the government-mandated ketchup, in a single day the Standard American consumes two leaves of iceberg lettuce, which are of course topped with bacon bits, cheese and Thousand Island dressing.

● **Legumes:** Huh? Oh yeah, a bowl of peanuts. These go with the liquid entries under Grains (see below).

● **Grains:** A set of Hostess Twinkies, the breading on a bucket of fried chickens, two sesame seed buns and a six pack of Bud.

● **Foods without animal products:** Three Diet Cokes and a packet of breath mints.

Okay, so maybe this is a bit of an exaggeration. But only a *bit*, mind you. What's important is that the Standard American Diet passes right by so many tasty, good-for-you foods—foods like kohlrabi, okra, kale, lentils, aduki beans, quinoa, amaranth, (*say what???*), and thousands of others.

"SAD" Fact #2—The power of habit

The "SAD" fact is that, even though we'd like to eat a better diet, we are all **creatures of habit** and, unfortunately, we've gotten into some pretty bad habits. Perhaps we can blame it on our distant predecessors who may have had few food choices available to them, and who may have had to eat whatever was handy (grubs, squirrels, deer, cattle). Somehow, though, a lot of those foods have been handed down to us, and we continue with them despite all the groovy choices we now have available to us.

Consider this. McDonald's could serve vegetarian hamburgers at much less cost and trouble than "beef" hamburgers. If we'd all grown up eating vegetarian hamburgers, we'd be just as happy with this (in fact, we'd gag at the thought of hamburgers made out of cows.) Everyone would save money and be healthier. The environment would be better off for this, and of course cows would be much better off.

So why isn't the world eating vegetarian hamburgers instead of hamburgers made out of cow flesh? Habit. It's all one big lousy habit, and bad habits are hard to break.

"SAD" Fact #3—The lure of convenience

The "SAD" fact is that, having grown up with our bad meat-eating habits, and finding ourselves in the world as we now know it, sometimes it can be a bit difficult to find vegetarian foods that meet our cravings (fast, filling, cheap, available right here and now) if not our important needs (healthy, environmentally responsible, cruelty-free). That's why we vegetarians need to get the information out there that, with a little creativity, you can put together the best diet you've ever had, and it *will* be vegetarian.

Remember this:

> Any inconvenience you may find in eating a vegetar-
> ian (or vegan) diet isn't due to an inherent problem
> with vegetarianism at all. Rather, it's due to the
> minority status of vegetarians in our society and a
> lack of accommodation on the part of flesh-eaters.

Ask Mr. Veggie-Person

I know you have lots of questions, so before we go on I've made arrangements to have an expert, Mr. Veggie-Person (formerly Mr. Potatohead), address your every concern.

Cripes, I'll starve to death! I can never fill up on salad, and an hour after eating Chinese I'm hungry again.

We're not talking about eating only bean sprouts here. You shouldn't have any problem at all getting full on a diet that includes bean and grain dishes, pasta and the aforementioned vegan pot roast, potatoes and gravy. Then, of course there's always apple pie and garlic bread. Since meat is the most calorie-dense thing that most people eat in quantity, you'll probably find yourself losing some weight, and you'll probably find yourself eating *more* than you're used to. Funny though,

Second Part: Okay, maybe I'll think about vegetarianism.
But...what the heck would I eat?

137

most people don't seem to mind either of those things.

But I love the taste of meat. How can I do without that?

You don't have to. Meat really doesn't have much taste. Think about it. For the most part the tastes people really love are the *vegetarian* flavorings that go along with their favorite meat dishes. The spices in sausage, that great carcinogenic hickory smoke off the grill, steak sauce, mustard, ketchup, mint jelly and barbecue sauce—it's all vegetarian, and you won't miss any of it. People aren't talking about Le Ver, that new gourmet restaurant that just opened in your neighborhood, because they serve chickens' breasts. No, they're talking about it because they serve chickens' breasts with tomato-ginger chutney, red wine and pistachios over a bed of arugula. It's the *non-animal* foods that have most of the flavor in this world.

All of this doesn't mean that meat can't impart a certain texture and fullness (maybe even beyond fat and calories) to a dish. As we'll see later, though, this isn't unique to animal products. There are plenty of vegetarian foods that can fill that void on your plate where the chicken's breast or the hamburger used to be.

But a vegetarian diet is so boring!

Oh, sure. And when was the last time you or any of your meat-eating buddies went more than a day without basing at least one meal around "beef", "pork", "chicken" or "fish"? It's *meat-eating* that's boring. You've been eating *the same four foods* over and over again *every single day of your life* since you learned how to chew. You just haven't realized how bored you are because you haven't been exposed to all the diversity that's out there.

Yeah, okay, *technically* meat-eaters can eat every one of the foods that vegetarians can, and then some. But in practice it doesn't work that way. You're set in your ways. To discover the millions (literally!) of exciting food items on this Earth you need something to break you away from eating the same four foods over and over again, and vegetarianism is just the tool to do it. Remember, it's the vegetarian things that are exciting on Le Ver's menu.

I'll have to learn to cook!

Yes, you will! Remember, I warned you in Chapter 1 that a vegetarian diet is less convenient than eating meat. And until the rest of society catches up to your high standards you'll have to live with a lit-tle inconvenience. (Unless, of course, you want to hit the local fast food joint's salad bar every night. But talk about *boring*!) That means you're going to have to learn to cook a few things. This can range from heating up the veggie burgers and packaged fast foods from your local health food store to preparing gourmet vegetarian meals with entrées you can't even pronounce. Think of this as expanding your horizons. (You guys out there can consider it a lesson in sensi-tivity—the women will love it.)

The 12-step plan

*O*kay, you say, *all of this is well and good, but I'm a simple per-son. Just tell me what to do, for Pete's sake!*

Since you asked, I've set forth below an incredibly simple 12-step plan (where have we heard that before?) for breaking your addiction to the Standard American Diet (wherever you live), and moving on to an incredibly exciting new vegetarian diet. It's real easy.

Step 1. Analyze what you're eating now.

Take a survey of all the foods you and your family have eaten in the last week—both at home and away. Be honest now. It's not all broc-coli and skim milk. Look in your refrigerator and take note of all the stuff that's bad for you, bad for the environment, and bad for our furry and feathered friends. Not just the meat and the frozen pepper-oni pizzas, but the milk, the cheese, the carton of eggs, the jar of may-onnaise, and those frozen cheese pockets that made little Stephanie throw up.

Step 2. Eliminate the unnecessary.

Take all that bad stuff out of your refrigerator and throw it in the trash...No, just kidding. But at least consider not buying any more of it.

Now, think about all the bad things in your diet that nobody real-ly likes anyway—the boiled hot dogs you make only because they're fast, the Lard-O-Rama® breakfast scrapple, and the dry chickens' breasts you eat because you once thought they were healthy—and get rid of them from your diet. Remember the **Third Rule of Eating Vegetarian**:

The Third Rule of Eating Vegetarian

If it's both bad for you and unexciting, don't eat it.

Okay, now we're making progress.

Step 3. Use the meat substitutes.

Once you've used the *Third Rule of Eating Vegetarian* to eliminate all the animal products that are both boring and unhealthy from your diet, it should be easy to decide what you're going to eat for the next several days. To make it super easy, plan your meals *without giving a thought in the world to whether they're vegetarian.* Write it down.

Now, look at your list. Which dishes can you easily leave the meat out of? Do it. If the remaining dishes absolutely· need meat, never fear. You're still going to eat them. Just remember the *First Rule of Eating Vegetarian.* There's a vegetarian substitute for everything! But since those substitutes are sometimes hard to find (the *Second Rule of Eating Vegetarian*), I've got a shortcut for you. Just look in the very next exciting chapter of this book for ideas! Fix your regular diet using the meat substitutes, and you'll be surprised. You're going to like it!

Step 4. Use the dairy substitutes.

The same thing goes for dairy products. Just look in the chapter next to the next chapter of this book. We've got substitutes for everything from the cows' milk on your breakfast cereal to the chickens' eggs in your cookies. They taste great, and they're *much* better for you than something that came from a farm animal.

Step 5. Use a little creativity at restaurants.

One of the big problems you're going to have in figuring out a vegetarian diet for yourself is what to do when you go out to eat. Don't worry. Every decent restaurant since the dark ages has had at least one entrée for vegetarians on its menu. Order it. And never be shy about ordering something special ("Can I have the vegetarian special, without the cheese?"). Remember, you're the customer, and you're always right.

Step 6. Expand your diet with ethnic foods.

Instead of going to the chain restaurant out at the shopping mall, why not try your local "Mom and Pop" ethnic joint? Ethnic restaurants (unless they're Texan) will have lots of wonderful, creative vegetarian dishes that you've never tried before. If you're going to be a vegetarian you will soon learn to appreciate great flavors and foods from all over the world.

Step 7. Expand your diet from the veggie cookbooks.

Your local bookstore has lots of great vegetarian cookbooks on its shelves. Take advantage! These books have stuff ranging from extra-simple and fast meals, for dolts like me, to ultra-gourmet feasts you have to speak French to prepare. And remember, don't just look at individual recipes. When you read these books, try to get the big picture of the categories of dishes that are available, and how vegetarian chefs put together a great meal.

Steps 8-12. I wanted a 12-step program, but I couldn't think of anything to put here.

You'll come up with something. In the meantime, read the next few chapters, where I'll introduce you to some great vegetarian foods, including some stuff you've never heard of, and some other stuff you swore you'd never eat. I'll also give you some vegetarian food ideas that, hopefully, will make the mysterious eating habits of us strange vegetarians seem a little more accessible.

Chapter 2

Meat Substitutes—
It's nice to fool Mother Nature when this is what she really wants you to eat

I'd really like to be a vegetarian, but what would I do to fill that hole in the center of my plate—you know, the one where my burger used to be?

I'd really like to be a vegan, but what would I pour over my cereal? How could I ever bake again?

In this chapter, and in the next chapter on dairy substitutes, I'll answer these pressing questions and others, as we consider alternatives for everything from steaks on the grill to mayonnaise, and all without any animal products whatsoever!

Meat substitutes

The whole idea of meat substitutes may strike you wrong. It's kind of like money substitutes or sex substitutes. Sometimes you just need the real thing. Anyway, what can this book possibly have to offer that will substitute for a two-inch thick, 1400+ Calorie slab of governmentally-sanctioned USDA Prime, cooked just right so it's black on the outside, pink on the inside, and just brimming with those special meat juices? (What exactly *are* those meat juices, anyway?) There are several answers to this question.

Fooling Mother nature with three tried and true meat alternatives

First we're going to concentrate on three foods that will proudly provide an alternative for meat on anyone's barbecue grill or dining room table. Not surprisingly, all three of these foods are Asian, they've been around for thousands of years, and, of course, they probably weren't developed as "substitutes" for anything. Just for this chapter, though, we're going to think of them as meat substitutes because this is something you need, and this is something they do very well. You see, these three foods just happen to have many of the same properties that meat does in terms of their texture, calorie density, etc. So they do a great job of filling that all-important middle zone of your plate.

At this point pretend you hear Ed Sullivan's voice, but instead of George and Ringo, etc., he's introducing us to three great vegetarian foods and meat alternatives: **tofu, tempeh, and seitan.**

All right, stop your snickering!

Meat alternative #1
Tofu—the great unknown white blob

Yeah, you know tofu. It's the butt of all vegetarian jokes. It's got a worse public image than lawyers, if that's possible. (*Lawyer's wife: "You told me you wanted tofu." Lawyer: "I thought you were asking if I wanted to 'go sue'!"*)

Actually, tofu is *soybean curd*, whatever that may be. You've seen it on the menu when you go out for sweet and sour "pork" at the local Chinese joint. Of course, you never even *thought* of ordering it—except maybe to pull a joke on your friend Ernie while he's in the men's room.

You've also seen tofu at your local supermarket. It's in the plastic packages at the back of the produce section—just next to the eggroll skins. *Who buys that stuff?*, you once asked yourself, shaking your head. Certainly not you. It makes you kind of queasy just to be near it.

The fact is, though, that tofu's a great substitute for meat. (It's a great dairy substitute too, but more on that later.) Tofu can be purchased in varying degrees of firmness, so it's really versatile—just like you. And if that isn't enough versatility, it takes on a tougher—more meat-like—texture when it's cooked or dried, and an entirely new con-

sistency when it's frozen (tofu pops?) and thawed. Another good quality of tofu (and tempeh and seitan as well, for that matter) is that it
has very little taste of its own, but will readily absorb the flavors of
sauces and spices.

That's all well and good, you say, *but be more specific.* **What the
heck can I do with this stuff?**

Basically, you can do anything with tofu that you would do with
meat. The possibilities are endless. But here are a few ideas to get you
started:

- **Fried Tofu.** Fry tofu chunks up golden brown in a pan with
onions, garlic and your favorite sauce.

- **Marinated Tofu.** Marinate tofu in your favorite meat marinade.
Hint: if you bake the tofu in the marinade it will absorb the liquid and
get firmer in texture, so it's then easy to use in your favorite meat
recipe. If you're pressed for time (*i.e.,* lazy like me) you can buy baked
tofu at your favorite health food grocery.

- **Barbecued Tofu.** Barbecue slabs of tofu (marinated or not) on
the grill, keeping it moist with your favorite barbecue sauce. (See the
exciting barbecue section of this book for more details.)

- **A Cauldron of Tofu.** Use chunks of tofu instead of meat in just
about any kind of stew or soup. It will absorb the flavors of the other
ingredients.

- **Blackened Tofu.** Blacken slabs of tofu (especially soft tofu) just
like you would blacken fishes.

- **Tofu Jerky.** Make tofu jerky (everybody *loves* this stuff) by mar-
inating it in soy sauce, liquid smoke, vinegar and garlic, and then dehy-
drating it in your food dehydrator or a warm oven (it will take several hours).

- **Cold, Soft Tofu.** Eat soft tofu cold with your favorite oriental
sauce (or soy sauce), pickled ginger and wasabi (Japanese horserad-
ish). Okay, this is wonderful, but maybe you're not that daring yet.

If tofu sounds too good to be true, that's probably because it is. It
has almost **50% more iron than cow's liver, and more than twice the
calcium in cows' milk.** Asians have been crazy about this food for
ages, and maybe it's time the rest of the world caught up. Tofu isn't
perfect, though. Indeed, it's quite high in fat by vegetarian standards
and, because it's a processed food, it doesn't have a lot of dietary fiber.
So you won't want to make tofu your primary source of calories. It
sure is nice to have around, though!

> "The 'other' white meat? I spell it 'T-O-F-U!'"
> —Cynthia Grover

Get over your fear of tofu in seven easy steps

If you'd like to try tofu, but are a little afraid, don't worry. We know you're basically a good person, and don't really *want* to have an irrational fear of and/or loathing for a simple little cake made out of all-American soybeans. Remember, you aren't alone, and there's help out there. You may not find many tofuphobia (or is it "tofubia"?) support groups in your neighborhood, but with a little luck you can get through this crisis. Here's your 7-step plan:

1. **Find the tofu.** It will probably be banished to the bottom shelf of your smiling neighborhood grocer's most remote refrigerator case. Kind of like Siberia. You just might allow yourself to feel sorry for it.

2. **Touch the package.** In a mighty act of bravery reach in and grab a package. You'll probably want to start with the hard style, and remember to check the freshness date—this stuff spoils, you know.

3. **Compose yourself.** At this point your fears may start to overcome you. The tofu may seem cold and unnatural in your hand, and you may be battling an unsettled stomach. After all, this stuff looks like a hunk of gefiltefish that never saw the light of day, floating in some murky liquid. You may be tempted to rush over and buy that porterhouse steak on the spot, but remember, the dead cow looked a lot worse than this. Relax, take several deep breaths, and concentrate on something really gross—like what was in those cold cuts you had for lunch.

4. **Open the package.** When you get home open the package and throw all that murky liquid away. Let the tofu drain for a minute. Now, doesn't that look better? [Note: your tofu may have come in a paper wrapping without the water. That's okay too!]

5. **Touch the stuff.** This is the time you're actually going to reach out and touch your tofu. Go ahead, it won't bite. It feels moist and firm, doesn't it? Get someone to blindfold you and let you touch both tofu and hamburger. Which feels better?

6. **Eat some of it.** When you've handled your tofu for a couple of minutes you'll be ready for the big test. That's right, you're going to break off a piece and eat it. Stop wincing now. Act a little more mature, for Pete's sake. That's it, right on the tongue...Now swallow hard.

Second Part: Okay, maybe I'll think about vegetarianism.
But...what the heck would I eat?
145

7. **Taste?** Okay, what did it taste like? Not much of anything? Exactly! To paraphrase Bill Cosby, the air in your mouth has more flavor. That's why tofu is such a versatile little food. Now, don't you feel silly for being such a wuss about a food that doesn't taste bad at all? Aren't you glad you've gotten to know tofu?

Meat alternative #2
Tempeh— because man cannot live on tofu alone

Tempeh (pronounced "tem-pay", as in "the temporary agency doesn't pay very well") is practically the national food of Indonesia. It is a cake made from fermented whole soybeans, and sometimes other grains as well—yeah, it comes in flavors. Tempeh is firmer than tofu and lower in fat, and because it's a whole food you can actually see the grains in it. Just like tofu (and most meat, for that matter) it has a very neutral flavor and it goes well with just about anything.

Tempeh may or may not be in your favorite supermarket. Ask your friendly grocer about it, and if you get a blank stare just trot down to your equally friendly health food grocer, and he or she will get you fixed up. Buy lots. Although tempeh is perishable, it freezes extremely well.

Use tempeh just as you would tofu, as a substitute for meat in almost anything. I like to think of tempeh as the universal "chicken" substitute, maybe because a piece of tempeh has roughly the same color and texture as a chicken's breast. Try substituting tempeh for chickens in your favorite recipe and see what you think. Here are some other ideas you might try:

● **Tempeh Burgers.** Brown a slab of tempeh and use it as a burger. It's great with sautéed onions and your favorite condiments.

● **Tempeh Salad.** Instead of tuna salad or "chicken" salad, try tempeh salad. Make and use it the same way you always do, but use diced tempeh instead of those other grisly ingredients. Try using eggless mayonnaise too. (See the dairy substitutes in the next chapter.)

● **Barbecued Tempeh.** Of course tempeh barbecues really well, indoors and out. It makes great "sloppy Joes" too.

● **"Tempeh Italiano".** Use tempeh instead of "veal" and chickens in those Italian dishes you like so much. When it's covered with sauce you may not notice the difference (and if you do you may like the tempeh better).

Meat alternative #3
Seitan—proof that steaks and roasts can go vegetarian

If you've ever wondered if all meat "substitutes" have to be made from soybeans (is this some sort of kinky infatuation we vegetarians have?) the answer is no. Seitan isn't made from soybeans, and we vegetarians (along with millions of folks in Asia and other places) love it.

There must be a rule, though, that these things have strange names. Everyone wonders how to pronounce seitan. It isn't hard. The first syllable is like the word "say", and the second is "tahn", as in little *Tanya* Tucker.

However it may be pronounced, seitan is made from wheat gluten that has been cooked in a broth. That may not sound too tasty, but it is. It gives it a whole different texture and flavor than tofu or tempeh. I like to think of seitan as the universal "beef" substitute.

You mean seitan is a good substitute for ground beef?

No, no, we have other things for that (keep reading). Seitan is great for making the *big* things—steaks and roasts and the like. Really.

How might one come by (or, come to buy) this stuff?

There are three ways to get seitan. The traditional way is to make it yourself in a process that involves repeatedly kneading and rinsing dough. You'll find the recipe in many vegetarian cookbooks. Unless you're the kind of person who makes your own crackers and weaves your own suits, though, you may opt for something easier. You can buy a prepackaged mix at your favorite health food grocery. Just follow the directions on the box and you'll end up with a big chunk of seitan that looks like a "leg of lamb" (well, a small lamb anyway). If that's too much trouble, you can buy ready-made seitan. Look for it in your health food grocer's refrigerator case, right next to the tofu and tempeh.

Sure, you can take a slab of seitan and eat it as a burger, but there are more exciting things to do with it. Here are a few suggestions:

● **Seitan Steaks.** Brush slabs of seitan with a little olive oil and your favorite steak sauce and cook them on the grill or under the broiler. Serve them with a pitcher of martinis, and you'll have a dinner right out of the 1950s.

● **... and Steak Sandwiches.** Grill-up strips of seitan and onions, and serve them in a sandwich with steak sauce, mustard and lettuce. Fabulous.

● **Seitan Roast.** Take a big chunk of seitan, brush it with olive oil, and bake it until it's golden brown. (See the unbelievably exciting chapter on Holidays for details.)

Second Part: Okay, maybe I'll think about vegetarianism.
But...what the heck would I eat?

147

● **Seitan Strips.** Seitan strips better than the Chippendales. Use strips of seitan in stir-fry, soups, pepper steak—anywhere you'd use "beef".

● **"Seita-Fajitas".** Marinate and grill seitan strips and use them in fajitas, just like "beef".

Whether you want to be a vegetarian or not, seitan is a great food to discover. And under the right conditions, it can be a remarkable substitute for "beef". (Very healthy, high fiber "beef"—if that could exist!)

"This isn't beef?" meat-eaters have asked me.

"Would I give you 'beef'?" I respond.

Friends don't let friends eat meat.

Fooling Mother Nature—
the sequel (with subtitles in Italian):

All those other meat substitutes,
or "That's not meat, that's my supper!"

Even though tofu, tempeh and seitan make great substitutes for the meat items on your plate, they were never intended to be copy-cats of something you might pick up (like a disease) at your local burger joint. But of course there are gobs of products on the market that are intended for *just* that purpose, and many vegetarians and vegetarians-in-training find them especially helpful.

Burgers and things

If you're in a pinch for something to take to the family barbecue, need something quick to fill the inside of a sandwich, or want to fool your spouse by serving him or her a healthier breakfast sausage, the world's food producers won't let you down. There are about a million varieties of meatless hamburgers, hot dogs, cold cuts and breakfast "meats" out there, and some of them are quite good. You can find these products refrigerated, canned, frozen, dried and otherwise at both your favorite and less-than-favorite health food store and at your smiling neighborhood grocer's.

Make sure you read all the labels carefully, though. Some of these meat substitutes are loaded with chemicals, and several products that are specially labeled for their "no cholesterol" value are heavily dependent on animal ingredients such as egg whites. You're looking for the all vegetable varieties, hopefully made out of some pretty healthy stuff.

> "The last time I had a hamburger all I could taste was the blood."
>
> —Virginia Zimmerman
>
> (...who gave up eating hamburgers at age 78)

Textured vegetable protein

Textured vegetable protein, which usually goes by its monogram "TVP", is a highly-processed joint venture between the soybean plant and modern science. It isn't exactly macrobiotic but, depending on how pure one wants to maintain one's insides, that doesn't mean it can't have a place in the conscientious vegetarian's diet. TVP is probably best known as an ingredient in imitation "bacon" bits, but it has lots of disguises. TVP granules, for example, can be a dead ringer for ground "beef". You can dump them into various sauces and soups, and they're sure to please the "How do you make spaghetti sauce without hamburger?!" crowd.

Many years ago, when I was in vocational (law) school in Chicago, they had "vegetarian" meals in the dormitory. I was just a rookie, cub vegetarian at the time, trying to become a first-stringer, and it really irked me that sometimes the chef would throw some gratuitous meat into the "vegetarian" entrées. After this happened a few times, a couple of us went back to the kitchen to complain. The first woman we accosted with our grievance just laughed.

"That's not meat!" she said. Then she proceeded to show us all the packages of the high strength, industrial, textured vegetable protein in all shapes and sizes that the kitchen could use to emulate virtually any meat-eater's dead animal fantasy. Heck, they even made vegetarian chili *without the beans*!

But who needs a "meat substitute" anyway?

A meat substitute? What are you trying to do, imitate meat-eaters? Shouldn't vegetarians really be above all that?

Second Part: Okay, maybe I'll think about vegetarianism.
But...what the heck would I eat?

149

These are good questions that are asked all the time. But there are a number of good answers too.

First, I don't know any vegetarians who want to eat a meat substitute (*i.e.*, something that looks, tastes, washes down with beer, etc. just like meat) at **every meal**. That distinguishes vegetarians right there, because we all know *lots* of meat-eaters who insist on meat at every meal.

Second, maybe there's something in human nature that we just like eating **heavy, dense foods**, and that they serve well as the centerpiece around which to base a meal. And if it isn't something in human nature, then perhaps it's cultural. Remember, the vast majority of us vegetarians who grew up in Europe or America started out as meat-eaters.

There are better responses to those who criticize the use of meat substitutes, though. If 99% of the population around us eats meat, the odds are pretty good that some similar proportion of the cooks around us cook meat. There are **nine gazillion recipes** out there for meat dishes (it took me days to count them!), and for at least 8.95 gazillion of those, it's what they do with *non-meat* ingredients that makes them special. Why not take advantage of all that? If humans have developed 15 million ways to fix chickens' breasts, why not substitute tempeh and give a few million of those a try? **Most of the vegetarians I know aren't as proud as they are opportunistic, at least when it comes to food.**

One last reason for including meat substitutes in a vegetarian diet is that it's so much **fun** when you're dealing with meat-eaters all the time. I love the looks on meat-eaters' faces when I invite them over for barbecue, or when I offer them a taste of pepper steak without the steak, or "beef" fajitas without the "beef", or "beef" stroganoff without the "beef" or the stroganoff. It's fun to enhance dinner with a little gamesmanship, and if meat-eaters can be coaxed to try vegetarian foods by putting them in the context of something familiar, that's all the better.

Who says food is supposed to be stuffy? Pass the vegetarian "pork" rinds please.

Chapter 3

Dairy substitutes—
because Mother nature really wants to wean you

(Or: "Thanks for the mammary")

Most people—even most vegetarian people—eat dairy products and chickens' eggs, and don't give it a second thought. They can't imagine what dairy substitutes could do for them. If you're one of those people, please go back and re-read Chapters 4 and 5 of Part One. Then read this chapter just for grins. You may find that using the dairy substitutes listed here is pretty darned easy and painless, and may pay big dividends in terms of your health, and of course the health of all those cows and chickens.

Alternatives to cows' milk—the "motherless" milks

When people say "milk" in polite or impolite food conversation, it is naturally assumed that they're talking about the mammary secretions of a cow. How humans became such ubiquitous consumers of such a substance I won't speculate here, but suffice to say it doesn't have to be so. After all, every mammal has its own brand of milk that humans could consume if they wish (imagine "Elsie the Yak" on the label), and that includes *human milk* (just plain "Elsie" on the label), if you can conceive of such a radical idea.

Unlike baby mammals, grown up human beings don't really need a "complete food" on which to survive, but they *do* have a need in their various cooking and eating endeavors for milk-like substances— that is, liquids that contain sugars and emulsified fat. At least one of these liquids exists in nature outside the mammary glands of a mammal—coconut milk—and being the clever little creatures we are, we have easily developed lots of others.

Take a magical journey down to your local health food grocery and you'll find plenty of alternatives to cows' milk. There's:

- soy milk,
- rice milk,
- almond milk,
- oat milk,

and new varieties that seem to be coming out all the time. You'll find these various motherless milks *unrefrigerated*, in boxes on your grocer's shelf, and they'll keep for a long time before you open them (refrigerate after opening, please). Just like cows' milk they come in various fat concentrations—"2%", "1%", and fat-free, and just like the cows' milk people, the producers of these non-dairy milks don't tell the whole truth about their true fat content. (See page 53.) Try adopting a few of these poor motherless milks. Give them a home and a hot meal, and see which ones you like.

All plant-based milks have some real advantages over cows' milk:

1. **Health.** Of course, they're much healthier than cows' milk. Here are some reasons why:
- no cholesterol.
- lower in saturated fat (and no animal fat!).
- no concentrated animal protein.
- not allergenic like cows' milk.

2. **Compassion.** Human health is, of course, not the only issue. Motherless milks have an *even bigger* advantage over cows' milk in that they are much kinder. **When you use plant-based milks you're not promoting hideous violence against animals, and you're not taking the milk that a mother wanted to go to her babies.**

3. **Price?** Unfortunately, motherless milks, while not particularly expensive, are at a *disadvantage* to cows' milk when it comes to price. Is this because they are inherently more difficult to produce? Of course not. Raising cows to produce milk is slow, inefficient and expensive. It wastes energy and pollutes our environment. Producing milk directly from plants is relatively *much cheaper*. But it's that old "economies of scale" thing that turns the prices upside down. Everybody, it seems, wants to drink their milk from a cow, and only a tiny minority of people prefer to get it from a plant.

How come? It's that pesky "habit" thing again.

Second Part: Okay, maybe I'll think about vegetarianism.
But...what the heck would I eat?

153

Using motherless milks

There isn't much to say here, other than **you can use motherless milks just the same way you'd use cows' milk.** Remember, though, that none of the plant-based milk alternatives is going to taste exactly like cows' milk, so if you want to drink it plain it may take a little bit of getting used to. This should be no big deal. After all, if you'd grown up drinking soy milk, cows' milk would undoubtedly taste a little foreign the first time you tried it. (It might have a bit of that cow taste.) Some big-time cows' milk drinkers find rice milk to be a little more neutral tasting than soy milk, so if you're one of those milk mustache people, that might be a good place to start.

In most cooking you shouldn't be able to tell any taste difference at all between motherless milks and cows' milk. Keep in mind the fat content of the milks you are using, because they aren't all the same. Use higher fat content milks where you need more richness. (Obviously you knew that.) I haven't found a plant-based milk that has as much fat as *whole* cows' milk, but that's just as well.

But what about non-dairy coffee creamers? What about coconut milk?

Okay, where you need a *lot* of richness, these two high-fat alternatives are certainly available. Non-dairy coffee creamers, though, are highly processed foods filled with things like "mono & diglycerides", and "sodium stearoyl lactylate", so you might want to think about it before you start consuming them in large quantities. (Note too that many strange chemicals in our foods are derived from animal ingredients. Vegetarian groups often have lists of these available.) Coconut milk is wonderful stuff that is absolutely delicious in sauces and soups, but it has a distinctive coconut taste that doesn't go with everything, and it's high in saturated fat. You might want to save it for special occasions.

What would you recommend?

Since you asked, here are a few ways your humble author uses motherless milks (yeah right, as if he could cook):

- Milk for breakfast cereal—rice milk.
- General purpose cooking—soy milk.
- Cream sauces and soups—soy milk. For extra rich sauces and soups, coconut milk can't be beat.
- Coffee creamer—rice milk.

Speaking of coffees...

It's not widely known, but soy milk can be used to make perfectly wonderful cappuccino, café au lait, café latté, etc. (Also, of course, it's cholesterol-free and doesn't smell like cows.) Sophisticated coffee shops in big cities often have a soy milk option. Other places should be developing this option too. Be sure to ask.

What about ice cream...

Yes, we know. Ice cream is your absolute most favorite of most favorite foods. You couldn't live without it. Well, you don't have to—even if you decide to give up dairy products entirely. There are a wide variety of dairyless "ice creams" on the market, ranging from those that taste healthy to those that taste decadent. Some of them are made with tofu. (You remember good old tofu from the last chapter.) If you are into making your own ice cream, you can make truly *wonderful* stuff using coconut milk! (Coconut milk is awfully rich, so you may want to dilute it a bit with one of the other motherless milks.)

Need **hot fudge**? Don't fool with expensive ready-made stuff or complicated recipes. Just put your favorite vegan dark chocolate chips in a cup, *almost* cover them with soy milk, microwave for 30–40 seconds, and stir well. That's it. Guaranteed to be terrific.

...and Butter?

You've been eating a plant-based substitute for butter all your life. Good old margarine. Good old "oleo". Of course it doesn't taste exactly like butter, but it didn't take much getting used to, did it?

Is margarine vegan?

Actually, many brands *aren't*! Many brands contain whey, which is a cows' milk product. (You'll remember a certain arachnophobic young woman named Muffet who was fond of this stuff.) Anyway, you'll want to read the ingredients, and make sure the margarine you buy doesn't contain whey.

Margarine, of course, isn't at all good for you. It's full of saturated fat (or "trans" fat), just like butter. Try cooking with oil instead. And for most things you used to put butter on, try olive oil instead. It's much healthier, and many folks like the taste better too! (Let's see, bread with olive oil, baked potatoes with olive oil, pancakes with olive oil and maple syrup...Okay, maybe not pancakes.)

Second Part: Okay, maybe I'll think about vegetarianism.
But...what the heck would I eat?

155

Pass the cheese, please (pass right by it, that is)

Dairy cheese isn't very good for you. Well, that's an understatement. As we have already noted in exhausting detail, most dairy cheese is very high in cholesterol and saturated fat (cheddar cheese is 74% fat!), and has very little iron. If you're making this stuff a big part of your diet that's not good—even if you don't care about the ethical and environmental issues.

Fortunately, there are lots of different cheeses on the market that aren't made from cows' milk. Most of these are soy based, and they'll do just fine wherever you want cheese. Again, don't expect them to taste exactly like the dairy cheeses you are used to, but you shouldn't have much problem making the adjustment.

Are soy cheeses vegan?

Technically they *aren't*! Almost all of them contain "caseinate", which is a derivative of cows' milk and helps them to melt when heated. There *are* truly vegan cheeses out there, but you may have to look for them. It will be worth the effort—they can be quite wonderful.

Of course plant-based cheeses have the same advantages that plant-based milks do, for you and the cows and the Earth. They have the same disadvantages too, in that they are relatively more expensive and less available than their dairy counterparts. *It's a darned shame!* If everyone wanted vegan cheeses there would be scads and scads of wonderful varieties out there, and they could be made more cheaply than dairy cheeses, and we'd be better off and the cows would be better off and the Earth would be better off. But again, people insist on getting their cheese from the inside of a cow. Is this silly, or what?

Don't forget tofu!

In the right dishes tofu can make an outstanding substitute for cheese. Crumbled up, tofu has a texture and neutral taste similar to cottage cheese or ricotta. Tofu is legendary in lasagna, and also has a place in your favorite dips. Be creative.

Beating the chickens' eggs

People are creatures of habit, and nowhere is that more painfully obvious than in their ubiquitous use of chickens' eggs. Okay, if people *really* like the taste of these things scrambled or in omelets (and don't mind the ethics, the health issues, or the fact that eating reproductive matter is kind of gross), that's one thing. But cooking is another matter.

Years ago somebody discovered that chickens' eggs congeal with heat and can be used to bind baked goods and make various other concoctions sticky and thick. Ever since, humans have followed like lemmings (not to knock lemmings) and have put these little bombs of fat (61% of calories), cholesterol (212 mg. per egg. Wow!), and cruelty into everything they cook.

Is this necessary?

No!

The fact is that there are several vegetable products that are *perfectly fine* for binding baked goods or sticking bread crumbs to eggplant slices. In fact, they do just about *anything* short of an omelet or hollandaise sauce **just as well as chickens' eggs**, but without all the unsavory shortcomings. And when that banana bread or those chocolate chip cookies come out of the oven **you won't know the difference**.

I use a commercial egg replacer made out of potatoes and tapioca. (It's just a white powder which could easily be mistaken for various other legal and illegal substances.) Here's how it compares to chickens' eggs:

- No fat.
- No cholesterol.
- Stores on the shelf—no refrigeration needed.
- Keeps practically forever.
- Cheaper.
- Just as easy to use.

Given all these facts, **why do people still use chickens' eggs in cooking?**

It's one of the great mysteries of life.

Oh no, not tofu again!

Yes, it's true. Like the dreaded monster in a cheap Japanese horror movie, tofu just keeps coming back! This time it's as an alternative to chickens' eggs. No, tofu doesn't do "sunny side up", but crumbled and sautéed with spices, it does make a great breakfast substitute for **scrambled chickens' eggs**. It may not look or taste exactly the same (although you can buy "scrambled tofu helper" kinds of things at the natural foods grocery that make it come close), but it hits the old spot just the same. It won't take long before you don't miss your scrambled eggs at all.

Second Part: Okay, maybe I'll think about vegetarianism.
But...what the heck would I eat?

157

If you're a fan of **egg salad**, that can be made with chunks of tofu as well!

And mayonnaise. Can tofu do that too?

Made from a combination of chickens' eggs and oil, there aren't very many foods that are worse for you than mayonnaise. But fortunately there are things that can bind mayonnaise other than chickens' eggs. Indeed, you will find that there are plenty of different kinds of **eggless mayonnaise** available at your natural foods grocery. And yes...some of them are even made with tofu!

To sum up...

It shouldn't be "fake" anything

We vegetarians can't expect people to want to join us in our diets if we can only offer them "fake" substitutes for their favorite animal products. Maybe it's better to give all these "fake" meat and dairy products entirely new names. That way they can stand on their own as super-keen foods. For example, things that look like hot dogs but are made out of tofu wouldn't be called "meatless hot dogs", or even "tofu dogs", anymore. They might serve the same function as hot dogs (*i.e.,* providing a buffer between the sauerkraut and the bun), but we'll call them something else—"Sam", for example. After a while, if everything goes okay, everyone will think "Sam" and forget all about "hot dogs". There will be no reminder that Sam was originally intended to replace the "beastly" hot dog. It will stand on its own.

Imagine this conversation sometime in the future:

Mother *[taking a tray of cookies out of the oven]*: I baked you some chocolate chip cookies, Charlie.

Little Kid: Oh boy, cookies!

Mother: Did you know that back in the olden days when Grandma was your age people didn't use Lois in cookies. Instead they used eggs from chickens.

Little Kid: Really? What happened to the baby chickens?

Mother: Well, they weren't around yet. But people would break the eggs open and take all the thick liquid inside that might eventually become a baby chicken, and put it in their cookies.

Little Kid *[making a face]*: Gross!

Mother *[nodding]*: Aren't you glad you didn't live back when Grandma was a little girl?

Little Kid: Uh-huh....Mom?
Mother: Yes?
Little Kid: Can I have a big glass of Gertrude with my cookies?

Chapter 4

All foods great and small (mostly small)— more about foods, vegetarian (yeah!) and non-vegetarian (yuck!), and the people who eat them

T his is the chapter where I'm throwing in all the food leftovers—a couple more things of importance, and several more things of absolutely no importance at all—that you, the conscientious meat-eater considering a vegetarian diet, may want to "digest". I'll start off, though, by suggesting a few more vegan foods that you'll want to try to help you break out of that "cows and chickens every day of your life" food rut you've been in.

New foods to try #1—the vegetarian seafood diet

"You don't eat fish?" the meat-eater asks incredulously.

"No," answers the vegetarian. "But I **do** eat seafood."

"Huh?"

"Kelp, dulse, nori...There are all kinds of great vegetarian foods from the sea!"

Call them sea vegetables instead of that derogatory term sea*weed*, and use them in your soups and stir fry. Try lightly fried dulse instead of "bacon" to make a "DLT" sandwich. Really!

New foods to try #2—what else to put in a sandwich

Go into 99% of the sandwich shops, restaurants, and delis in the United States or Europe and the *only* vegetarian thing they'll have available to put between two slices of bread will be cheese—probably *American* cheese at that. This is ridiculous! There are lots of great vegan ways to stuff a sandwich:

- Commercially prepared vegetarian hamburgers, hot dogs, and burger mixes.
- Tempeh burgers and tempeh salad.
- Hummous (Middle-Eastern chick pea and sesame spread).
- Falafel (Middle-Eastern fried chick pea balls).

(You can get mixes for these last two from your fun-loving health-food purveyor.)

- Grilled vegetables.
- Reubens—vegan cheese broiled over vegan pastrami with egg-less mayo, mustard and sauerkraut. (Okay, so it sounds complicated and stupid. It's actually wonderful!)

Remember, whatever you choose to make a sandwich out of, take the time to do it right. Don't forget the whole wheat bread, lettuce, tomato, and onion, and some nice pickles. **You've spent your life eating crummy burgers served off a warming tray by a high-school kid standing next to a cardboard cutout of a clown. Isn't it time to do a little better for yourself?**

New foods to try #3—things to put on pasta

For the first two-thirds of your life, "pasta" meant spaghetti with heavy tomato sauce, swimming with ground "beef". When you got older and gained extraordinary wisdom you discovered that there were more exciting possibilities out there. You found fettucine Alfredo, but it's so packed with fat and cholesterol that restaurant waiters are trained to call the coronary care unit whenever they serve it. You know you can't live on that stuff, so now you're looking for healthier and more interesting possibilities, and you're ready to take the step up to pasta with vegan ingredients.

Lots of restaurants now have pasta sections on their menus (hey, pasta is cheap—these are high margin items). Many of the new pastas they serve are trendier, lighter, and sometimes even vegetarian. If something looks good, have them leave off the animals and the cheese.

Pasta is one of the mainstays of a vegetarian diet, and you should make it at home. Here are some things to put on it:

Vegetables

Start with:
- onions (or even better, leeks!) and garlic sautéed in olive oil.

Second Part: Okay, maybe I'll think about vegetarianism.
But...what the heck would I eat?

161

Add to the sauté pan in any combination you'd like:
- Tomatoes (fresh, canned or sun-dried).
- Eggplant (cook it first).
- Bell peppers (and/or chilies).
- Mushrooms (common or exotic, fresh or dried).
- Capers (a must!), Fennel, Parsley, Cilantro, and other flavorful things.
- Greens (try spinach or broccoli rabe!).

Try roasting or grilling the vegetables first for a totally different flavor.

Sauces

- Olive oil—with garlic, of course.
- Tomato (light)—just tomatoes and spices (fresh basil!).
- Tomato (heavy)—add tomato paste.
- Vegetable broth.
- "Cream"—add soy milk or, for a richer sauce, coconut milk to one of the above.
- Peanut or cold sesame sauces (find the recipes in Chinese cookbooks—great for summer picnics).
- Pesto (blended basil, pine nuts, garlic and olive oil—leave out the cheese and it's lighter but still has the flavor).

Other ingredients

- "Bacon" bits.
- Other meat substitutes.
- Lentils and beans.
- Nuts (try pine nuts!)—toasted to bring out the flavor.

But doesn't pasta have eggs in it?
Sometimes it does. Check the ingredients on the label. Why eat chickens' eggs in something that is just as good (and much healthier and kinder) without them? If you're making pasta at home—a good idea!—and your recipe calls for eggs, just leave them out and add water instead. It will come out just fine.

What about alternative kinds of pasta?
A splendid idea! Try whole wheat, spinach, buckwheat and flavored pastas. If you're making pasta at home try different grains and additions.

The whole idea with pastas, as it is with all vegetarian foods, is to experiment and try new things. You don't want to go to your grave never having tried spinach pasta with capers, pine nuts and roasted vegetables do you? Of course not!

*Some foods **not** to try...*

Foods that should be but aren't really vegetarian

(Depending on how fussy you are)

1. Marshmallows, Jell-O, some yogurts, gummy bears (*Oh no! Not gummy bears!*)—contain gelatin, made from animal hooves.

2. Hostess Twinkies, refried beans—may contain "beef" fat or lard.

3. Most cheese—contains rennet, taken from the lining of calves' stomachs.

Foods that should be but aren't really vegan

(Depending on how fussy you are)

1. Baked goods (*bads?*)—often contain chickens' eggs and/or whey.

2. Bread—sometimes contains cows' milk, whey and/or honey.

3. Soy cheese, many "non-dairy" or "lactose-free" foods—contain "casein" or "sodium caseinate" derived from cows' milk.

The Worst Vegetarian Foods Pageant

The lights go down in the Atlantic City Convention Hall. Spotlights pan back and forth across the stage. There is a drum roll, and then the first notes of a song from the golden-throated voice of Bert Whatshisname. This is the big one folks—the Worst Vegetarian Foods Pageant.

All right, I don't want to get carried away by this pageant thing. After all, it's not like we can have a swimsuit competition. But it is about time that someone said something about the subject of **lousy**

Second Part: Okay, maybe I'll think about vegetarianism. But...what the heck would I eat?

163

vegetarian food. You see, everyone knows that a vegetarian diet is healthier and better for the planet than the gruesome non-vegetarian alternative. And most of us vegetarians also know that, given its inherent diversity, vegetarian cooking is usually lots tastier too.

What never gets mentioned, though, are all the truly *bad* vegetarian foods out there. Having awards is one way to bring the subject out of the closet and alert potential innocent vegetarian victims. It's a story that has to be told.

Now, when I talk about bad vegetarian food I'm not referring to mistakes. We're not going to consider those eggrolls I once made where the onion somehow liquefied and soaked through the skins. And I'm not talking about the potato pancakes I didn't even taste because they were gray when I took them out of the pan. No, this pageant is for real planned food—stuff that's inherently lousy in its conception as well as its execution.

Let's have another drum roll and call Mr. Parks out for an encore—here are the winners!

Third runner up—
Mike's oriental goulash

You probably know someone like Mike. He's easy-going and friendly, with the kind of looks that ooze good health—a real vegetarian's vegetarian. The problem is Mike can't cook worth a darn. As a matter of fact he eats the same thing over and over—brown rice covered with steamed vegetables. On Sundays he might sprinkle some sprouts and a little wheat germ on top for diversity. Mike doesn't believe in spices. He doesn't really believe in cooking things very much either, and he chops his vegetables large enough that you'll have trouble fitting them in your mouth.

I've tried variations on Mike's theme cooked by many vegetarians (myself included) over the years. The experience is always pretty much the same—hours of chewing and a full stomach. You can almost feel the vitamins coursing into your bloodstream. Somehow, though, eating should be less work and more fun. Is there anything for dessert?

Second runner up—
Anything I cook outside my own kitchen

Many people must share this same frustration: I'm no great shakes even when I'm cooking in my own kitchen (I took cooking lessons from Mike), but ask me to fix food anywhere else and I'm a total wreck. That's too bad, because it's when I'm visiting non-vegetarian family or friends that I really want to show off that new vegetarian dish I've just discovered. So I usually end up bragging about it, and then when someone asks me to cook I turn into an obnoxious, brain-dead mass of Flubber.

"Where's your Chinese rice wine vinegar?" I ask frantically, halfway into fixing something. "Where are the knives? Do you have any pots other than these?? You expect me to use *steak knives*??? What do you mean, you *don't have any Chinese rice wine vinegar*???!!"

When I finish my tantrum I usually end up serving something with roughly the shape and texture of a deflated volleyball. "This is much better when it's fixed right," I say. My hosts smile politely and poke at the volleyball with their forks. They hate me. As soon as I leave they're out the door to Kentucky Fried Chickens.

First runner up—
Aunt Doreen's reunion food

(As you know, this is an important honor. If for any reason our winner is unable to serve, the first runner up will assume the duties of Worst Vegetarian Food.)

Everyone has an Aunt Doreen who insists on getting the family together for a reunion picnic every Labor Day. All the food (except Uncle Harry's honey chickens' wings) is prepared by six matronly women from the Midwest, and every year Aunt Doreen squeezes our cheeks as the food is laid out and says, "Look at all the vegetarian things you can eat!" Sure.

The problem here is that these six women, despite their best intentions, are deadly. To them no "vegetarian" dish is complete unless it contains one or more of the following: mayonnaise (and lots of it), marshmallows, canned mushroom soup, or Jell-O (flavor: red). The ideal "vegetarian" dish at Aunt Doreen's reunion might incorporate all of the above. This year, I'll eat before I go.

The worst vegetarian food—
Stuffed eggplant

There's a rite of passage in the vegetarian world that requires all new vegetarians to make a fancy dinner of stuffed eggplant for that

Second Part: Okay, maybe I'll think about vegetarianism.
But…what the heck would I eat?

165

special someone. If you want to try it, here's the recipe: Slice a large eggplant lengthwise and scoop out the middle. Chop the pulp, mix it with rice and vegetables, and stuff it back into the shell. Top with cheese (soy cheese, *please*) and bake for half an hour at 350°F.

Okay, so this is the scene. You've poured the wine and turned down the lights, and you've got your best Barry White album on the stereo (sexy, low voice). You bring this beautiful eggplant with a gold-en-brown topping to the table and serve it up. It looks just like the picture in the magazine. Everything is perfect until you start to eat.

The first thing you notice is that when you touch your beautiful dish with a fork, the tough slab of cheese slides right off the top. You put it back in place like a cheap toupee and hope your date didn't notice. Then you take a bite. You immediately realize that the fatal flaw with this meal is its disregard for two of the fundamental laws of vegetarian cuisine: (1) you often have to bake eggplant for three days to get it fully cooked; and (2) most people would rather eat their old furnace filters than uncooked eggplant.

You smile. Your date smiles. Neither of you will admit the meal is horrible. In the background Barry White is still singing on the stereo, oblivious to the disaster ("Oh baby, Oh baby…"). This is the worst night of your life.

No, it's not pretty when vegetarian food goes bad but, like I say, it's a story that had to be told. Now that it's out in the open, I can only hope that future generations of vegetarians learn from the experience and lead happier, tastier lives.

Thermonuclear war survival tactics

There's the old story about the group of Germans who were having a beer and talking. The conversation turned to the question of the place one would want to be at the moment the world ends. One German piped up, "Well, I'd want to be in Holland."

His colleagues gave him a horrified look. "Why Holland?" they asked in unison.

"Simple," came the answer. "In Holland everything happens ten years late."

If you don't get this joke, feel free to change the Germany/Holland relationship to New York/North Dakota, etc.

In the event of potentially dangerous, maybe even life threatening, thermonuclear war I know where I want to be, and that's under an eggplant. As we saw in the *Worst Vegetarian Foods Pageant*, eggplants are notoriously difficult to cook, and taste phenomenally bad when this is done incorrectly. It just so happens that one of the very best ways to cook eggplant is by leaving it whole and cooking it under the broiler in your favorite oven, turning as needed. A word of warning, however. Being the sly creatures they are, eggplants tend to sit under your broiler for lengthy periods of time looking totally uncooked. (Actually they look about as cool as a purple cucumber.) Even though this is deceptive and they are really cooking inside (the insides can then be scooped out and are seriously tasty!), it leaves no doubt in my mind that eggplants can provide really wonderful protection under adverse environmental conditions. So remember, you heard it here first. In the event of a pesky thermonuclear war, *run*, do not walk, to the largest eggplant you can find. No sense taking chances on anything less.

Chapter 5

Where might one acquire vegetarian foods?

Many people think of vegetarian foods as being mysterious sorts of things that can only be acquired through mail order or by visiting dingy little stores populated by hermits. While I have nothing against hermits, this perception of things is not entirely true. As a matter of fact, a great place to start buying foods for your new diet is your good-old familiar neighborhood supermarket.

The supermarket?

That's right. The modern supermarket represents the very best and the very worst aspects of our sophisticated free-market economy. Looking on the **bright side**, when in history have humans had such an expansive choice of thousands of food products from all over the world offered at extremely competitive prices 24 hours a day, seven days a week, in a well lit, climate-controlled environment? The vast array of vegetables, fruits, grains, pastas, etc. makes eating a good diet and being a vegetarian easier now than it's ever been before.

Of course, there's a **dark side** to all this too. Need I mention the pesticides used in growing most of those vegetarian foods, the tons of plastic covering everything in sight, the six gazillion types of high-fat, high-cholesterol processed foods, the Muzak system, or the tabloid pictures of the Royal Family in all the check-out lines? Oh yes, and lest we forget—the ties to the meat and dairy industry. Not that we could forget them, when there's a long wall lined with the carcasses of dead animals and another long wall devoted to the products of lactating cows.

Oh well, let's not get morbid. The point is to discover the wonderful things your local supermarket can do for you, and then use it to the max. Remember, even in those moments when your favorite store isn't inspiring you with new vegetarian foods, it can be inspirational in other ways. The smell of blood over by the meat case, or the gloppy mound of egg salad in the deli section are great advertisements for a vegetarian diet.

Ten exciting things to do at the supermarket

1. Buy one of the motherless milks. (Don't give up, your grocer has at least one version of this stuff.)

2. Visit the live lobsters. Tell them you're very sorry.

3. Tell the grocer you're very sorry about the lobsters.

4. Go to the produce section and buy a vegetable you've never tried before.

5. Check out the canned beans. Try "great northerns" in your favorite Italian dish, and black-eyed peas, garbanzos, or black beans in a salad.

6. When the lady giving out samples of breakfast sausage offers you one, tell her you wouldn't even *think* of eating such a thing.

7. Buy a bottle of "extra virgin" (just like you!) olive oil to use for cooking and on bread.

8. Go to the deli section and read the list of ingredients on a package of "head cheese".

9. Check out the health food aisle. There will be lots of different quickie food "mixes". Try one of the burger mixes for lunch.

10. Count the number of different kinds of bottled water. Add to that the number of different kinds of Coke. Divide by three. Add seven plus the number of open check-out lines. The number you come up with will be your age. Works every time.

Second Part: Okay, maybe I'll think about vegetarianism.
But...what the heck would I eat?

169

The "health food" grocery?

As you get more and more excited about the possibilities a vegetarian diet has to offer, you may find yourself becoming very familiar with the guy at the customer service counter of your supermarket. You'll be asking a lot of questions that a fellow catering to the general (*i.e.*, meat-eating) public may not be able to answer:

Are these vegetables "organic"?
I'm invited to a cook-out. Where can I get a vegetarian hot dog?
Where can I get a vegan hot dog?
Do you have any eggs without the cholesterol?
Where can I get eggs without the birds?
Do you have any yogurt without gelatin in it?
Where can I get yogurt without dairy in it?

Pretty soon it may become obvious that your search for a vegetarian diet has special needs that mainstream grocery stores just won't be able to meet. That's the time you'll want to get familiar with your local health food store. Don't be afraid, you'll find lots of people there who aren't hermits. As a matter of fact, in many urban areas health food groceries have become the trendy places to go on Sunday afternoons for folks who want to drink the newest gourmet coffee and munch on smoked Danish cheese while they read the *New York Times*.

Here are some of the basics that many vegetarians go to health food groceries to find:

● Organic fruits and vegetables.
● All those "substitutes" for the grisly things in the meat-eating world:
    1. Seitan.
    2. Tempeh.
    3. Egg replacer.
    4. Various fake meats, fake cheese, etc.
● Bulk items.
● Spices.
● Grains and flours.
● Legumes.

So, here's the bottom line on shopping for vegetarian food. If you live in New York City, you're going to have a wider selection of vegetarian foods available to you than if you're spending the winter at the Canadian Mountie post in Mooseknee, Saskatchewan. Nevertheless, between the possibilities offered by modern supermarkets and health food groceries almost anywhere *but* Mooseknee, you're not going to go hungry. You can spend years discovering new foods.

Forty years Of health food

In the beginning, health food was health food. Somehow you could trust it–and you certainly couldn't mistake it for regular food. Grocery stores sold regular food, but not health food. Health food stores sold health food, but not regular food. It was all very simple.

Health food stores in the old days were like those sweaty gyms where boxers train. They weren't very inviting, and you didn't go there unless you were a fanatic (or even serious) about your health.

All of that, of course, wasn't to last.

The change started taking place in the 1950s. Jack LaLanne was pushing fitness on television to every woman in America, and Bob Cummings was promoting a product called "Tiger's Milk". People started looking for their local health food store to check it out.

Pretty soon there were well known individuals selling products under their own names. For example, Joe Tanner *[Note: Name changed because I can't remember the real guy's name.]* marketed a whole line of products, and even published recipe booklets to give you ideas on how to use them.

Here's a sample dinner menu from one of Joe's booklets:

● Braised calf's liver with Joe Tanner's protein powder and Joe Tanner's special sea salt;

● Stewed tomatoes with Joe Tanner's protein powder and Joe Tanner's special sea salt;

● Apple crisp with Joe Tanner's protein powder and Joe Tanner's special sea salt.

There were other recipes, but you get the idea. Health food was starting to be a marketable commodity.

The ecology and back-to-the-earth movements of the late 1960s and early 1970s proved to be a real boon to the health food industry. Suddenly, everything health food stores sold was "organic", and you couldn't buy peanut butter without bringing your own container. This was also the period when every health food store in sight opened up a shoe department to sell Earth Shoes.

I was young and idealistic back in that era. I owned a pair or two of Earth Shoes, and I figured anything I bought at a health food store just *had* to be as good and wholesome as Ozzie Nelson himself.

Second Part: Okay, maybe I'll think about vegetarianism.
But...what the heck would I eat?

171

My thinking didn't change for years, until one day when I went into a new store in my home town. The owner of the store (we'll call him "Mr. Health") was a suntanned, athletic looking guy with bleached hair and a gold chain around his neck. He came up to me with a phony smile and said in a booming, confident voice: "Hi! How's your health today?" It was then that I realized snake oil salesmen were still around—some of them owned health food stores.

Maybe Mr. Health was a premonition of things to come, because the 1980s changed the face of the health food industry still one more time. It was the decade of the Yuppie, and health and fitness were back with a vengeance. Health food stores went high-tech. They replaced their old bulk foods barrels with fancy Lucite dispensers, and the food went uptown too. Fresh pastas, French roast coffee beans and (God forbid!) meats were on the shelves next to the wheat germ.

Health food stores aren't necessarily healthy anymore (as if they ever were), and it's hard to find one that reminds you of a sweaty gym. Most of them have merged with gourmet stores, and now they'd probably tell you they sell "specialty foods". The future promises more of the same—bigger, brighter, more stylish. This may not be a good trend. Who wants to get dressed up just to buy a pound of whole wheat flour?

And speaking of getting dressed up—where can you find a good pair of Earth Shoes these days?

Portrait of a vegetarian family

The Third Part:
So, if I actually decide to become a vegetarian, just what can I expect?

or...

leading the vegetarian life (a/k/a the good life)

By this point you know all the good reasons why you really should stop eating animal products, and you even have a pretty good idea of how to spruce up your diet if you do. But there are probably some nagging questions in the back of your mind. After all, you don't want to be associated with a bunch of weirdos.

In this final (yeah!) part of the book we're going to talk about day-to-day life as a vegetarian. There will be a few helpful hints and, of course, lots more worthless and extraneous ramblings that you should feel free to skip right over.

Mostly though, this part of the book is here to give you a heads-up on how the world looks when you're a vegetarian. It's pretty much the same old world. Some of it looks worse (remember, I warned you that vegetarianism can be inconvenient), but you probably won't be surprised to hear that most of it looks a whole lot better.

The benefits of barbecue (p. 174)

Chapter 1

The vegetarian cook

All the joys and trials of keeping meat at a distance

C ooking is special to all vegetarians, and in this chapter we'll explore some of the things that make vegetarian cooking both fun and frustrating. Let's start in your kitchen (what a surprise!), and then we can move outside and get that barbecue grill in shape.

The vegetarian kitchen, Part 1—
The spiritual advantages

T o a vegetarian, the kitchen is a very special place. In an otherwise insane world it is a refuge. Put simply, it's a place where the vegetarian doesn't have to worry. Food choices make sense, and there aren't shreds of "beef" and E. coli and salmonella bacteria lurking in unexpected places.

More importantly, the vegetarian kitchen nourishes the soul as well as the body. The constant media hype from the meat and dairy and fast-food industries is rendered meaningless here. This is the place that embodies the vegetarian ideals of nonviolence and respect for nature and reverence for one's own body. This is the sanctuary of life, the temple of...Okay, so I'm troweling it on a little thick. After all, it's only a *kitchen*. But you get the idea—it's an important place to us vegetarians.

Maintaining a vegetarian kitchen—*i.e.*, keeping it vegetarian—is important too. The farther we get from our meat-eating days, the more unappealing animal products get, and the more distance we want to keep from them.

The problem is with our meat-eating friends. They always want to bring stuff over. You see, they don't understand the following fundamental principle:

> To the meat-eater it's *food*. To the vegetarian it's *toxic biological waste*.

This problem is exacerbated by the fact that sometimes we vegetarians are too polite or too unassertive with our omnivorous friends. When that happens meat can make its way into our kitchens. We always regret it.

I remember a couple of these incidents many years ago when I was a rookie vegetarian. One fall, a friend of mine came to visit. She was coming down with some strange disease and insisted that the *only* way she could fight it off was to make some "chicken" soup—in *my* kitchen! *Holy smokes!* I objected! I pleaded! I gave in.

It was a tragic situation. She got sick anyway of course, and I still have memories of seeing my beloved soup pot in the sink the next morning, full of murky dishwater with animal fat floating on top of it. It wasn't a sight for weak stomachs.

Another breach of my vegetarian kitchen came a couple of years later when I had a big party and didn't set an ironclad rule that no dead animals would be allowed on the dance floor. One of my friends brought a big taco salad with ground "beef" in it. It was a very long party, and by three in the morning that salad had been sitting out for about eight hours. You could *actually see* the germs crawling across the top of it. (I swear I could hear their incessant germ-chatter, and I could make out their footprints! Maybe I was just partying a little too hard.) Anyway, my friends were standing around this thing, dipping chips in for a late night snack. Again, it wasn't a sight for the weak at heart. I wasn't as concerned about my poor kitchen as I was that one of my friends would instantly die of ptomaine poisoning at my party.

It only takes a few instances like this one to make even the most reticent of us vegetarians put our foot down and say **no more meat in our vegetarian kitchens**. We hope our meat-eating friends will understand. We have standards to maintain. We have a shrine to civilization to preserve...etc., etc.

What's this about "chicken" soup, anyway?

Who's the bozo who came up with the idea that "chicken" soup wards off and/or cures an assortment of horrible diseases like colds, flu, acne, and the plague? Of course, there's no scientific basis for this belief. Sure, when we're sick we all like comforting foods that remind us of Mom, but if we have to have a universal folk remedy can't we come up with something a little healthier and a lot less violent than soup made from chickens? We vegetarians vote for miso soup. It will steam up your glasses and make you feel warm inside without all those unpleasantries.

The vegetarian kitchen, Part 2—
The earthly advantages

L est anyone get the idea that we vegetarians spend all our time pondering the nature of reality and other metaphysical matters, let it be said here and now that there are some very down-to-earth, pragmatic advantages to having a vegetarian kitchen. These may not seem like a big deal at first, but they are.

Consider, for example, that meat-eaters must spend *many minutes* every day scraping hardened animal grease off not only their stoves and exhaust fans, but also most other surfaces in their kitchens. Vegetarians kitchens, of course, are much easier to clean. (This is especially true if one goes out to eat often.)

But the advantages of a vegetarian kitchen go way beyond ease of clean-up. Over time, maintaining a vegetarian kitchen will save you substantial amounts of time and money.

The little stuff...

Consider kitchen utensils. Housewares stores are full of literally thousands of different gadgets for the kitchen. (The object of such gadgets is to make people with kitchens spend all of their disposable income in $2 increments on things they don't need.) Many of these gadgets, however, are meat-related and *need not be purchased by the vegetarian.* There are basters, sewing sets to lace the stuffing into turkeys, and little flags that can be stuck into steaks that say "medium rare" and "well done". We vegetarians never buy any of these things. We also never buy a whole group of more substantial meat-related utensils either—like roasting pans, carving boards (the kind with spikes sticking up and blood troughs), and plates with cutesy pictures and words like "veal" written in French on them.

Over the years a vegetarian can save thousands of dollars by not having to buy these items—not to mention thousands of hours by not having to wash them, and enough kitchen storage to hold two carts of groceries and that old popcorn maker you used for making soup in your college dormitory room. Such a deal. And remember, when you open a bank account as a vegetarian you can choose the clock radio instead of the steak knives.

The big stuff...

Okay, you're saying. All this is well and good, but what about those "Big-Ticket" kitchen items? Well, here's where vegetarians *really* make out like politicians. Consider microwave ovens, for example. We vegetarians are more than happy with the cheapo models. We don't need the meat probes and the special browning options. (Of course some vegetarians are opposed to microwave ovens in general—considering them health hazards promoted by a subversive military-industrial establishment. These folks will save even more!) And when buying a range, your average vegetarian won't even be tempted by the $2000 yuppie signature models with the grill and rotisserie options that require two miles of piping to vent away the smoke. No, a more modest range (no broiler pan necessary, thanks) will meet our vegetarian needs quite well. (On second thought, maybe we *could* use that broiler pan—for doing seitan steaks.)

...and refrigerators

There is one problem, though, that vegetarians will find when shopping for Big-Ticket items for their kitchen. That problem is with refrigerators—more specifically *meat-keepers* in those refrigerators. The sad fact of the matter is that *it's difficult to find a refrigerator without a meat-keeper*, even if you're willing to slip the appliance salesperson a few bucks under the table!

Old refrigerators were better. They had meat-keepers too, but they were simple drawers that could easily be taken out. (I put mine in a back corner of the basement, and have fantasies that after several hundred years when everyone is vegetarian an archeologist will find it and wonder what it was used for.) In modern refrigerators meat-keepers are complicated contraptions constructed on the belief that if you maintain just the right temperature and humidity, meat will take an extra three days before it turns green.

Not only are modern meat-keepers harder to remove than they used to be, but many come with disgusting pictures of chickens and cows on them. These are no doubt to remind meat-eaters of how "natural" their diets are. Yeah, sure.

Part Three: So, If I Actually Decide to Become a Vegetarian,
Just What Can I Expect?

179

Refrigerator selection and use guidelines

If you must buy a refrigerator (it's probably a good idea if you don't have one), here are my vegetarian appliance-buying tips to guide you in the selection and use of your machine:

Avoid those pictures of cute farm animals. If you do some comparison shopping, you should be able to find a refrigerator with a meat keeper that says no more on it than "Fresh Meat". (An oxymoron, to be sure!)

The careful application of duct tape (the world's most useful substance) will permanently obscure the word "Meat" from the view of sensitive vegetarian refrigerator users.

Now you are left with a convenient temperature and humidity-controlled drawer labeled "Fresh" in which to store your fruits and vegetables and grains. This is appropriate, because everything we vegetarians eat is fresh. This is now a constant reminder of how fortunate we are not to be using this drawer for its intended grisly purpose.

The great vegetarian barbecue

Ah, it's summertime. Time to get out of the kitchen. Yes, It's time we all put on our Ray-Bans and head for the surf. Time for cruising up to the drive-in with Beach Boys music blaring from the radio. Time to engage in that great warm weather tradition—the vegetarian barbecue.

Okay, so maybe barbecuing isn't the thing most people think of in vegetarian summer activities. It *does* seem odd that health conscious vegetarians would ever want to coat their food with a possibly carcinogenic (and definitely not healthy) layer of soot. Nevertheless, we vegetarians *do* barbecue, and it's one of those things we just might do **even better than meat-eaters.**

Why we do it better

Okay, I still know what you're thinking: *Did he really say that? Is this moron trying to tell me I'm going to choose the taste of a bunch of vegetables over a thick, juicy 24 oz. Porterhouse steak marbled with fat and just off the grill? Is he trying to tell me they're better than Uncle Bert's ribs (well, not his actual ribs) with that special sauce that drips down everybody's chins? Is he trying to intimate that vegetarian barbecuing isn't going to involve some heavy sacrifice? This guy's brain dead. He's been eating tofu and seaweed too long.* **How can I get my money back on this book???**

Now, now. I know that was just a little joke about wanting your money back. Let's not jump to conclusions here. There are very good reasons (at least they sound good to *me*) why vegetarian barbecues are pretty darned wonderful. First, remember that the really good stuff about barbecuing—that great carcinogenic smoke flavor, the aroma, your Uncle Bert's special sauce—is all vegetarian. We're not going to do away with any of that. And what we're going to *add* is variety.

Think back on all the stuff you (or almost any other meat-eater you can name) have barbecued over the last couple of years. There were the hamburgers last summer at Cousin Madeline's cookout, and the hot-dogs you made for the kids but they didn't eat. Then there have been a couple of steaks along the way, and of course Bert's ribs. But the last time you made those ribs the fire must have been too hot, because they were kind of dried out. They sure didn't taste as good as they smelled.

I'll bet the only vegetable you've tried on the old grill has been baked potatoes. You wrapped them in aluminum foil and buried them in the coals. The only trouble was, you forgot they were there. You found them that October when you were putting the grill in the garage. By that time they were shriveled up and hard, like little shrunken heads. The tires on your car looked tastier.

All right, maybe I'm not being fair. Maybe you're a real gourmet barbecuer. Maybe you shell out big bucks for salmon steaks that you cook in one of those special "fish" barbecuers. Maybe you have Vince the Butcher cut you special four-inch thick tenderloins that you serve with herbed butter and a special Cabernet from a vineyard in Napa so small that only you know it exists.

The point is, though, that unless you're barbecuing foods from the vegetable kingdom, you're probably cooking one food at a time. Try as you might, you're not going to get much variety that way. I want to get you thinking in terms of half-a-dozen foods on the grill at once— foods that are good for you, easy to fix, much cheaper than meat, and tasty as all get out.

Think about it. Vegetarian barbecued meals have to be more creative than meat-eaters'. We never get into the old rut: hamburgers and hot-dogs and steaks and chickens, hamburgers and hot-dogs and steaks and chickens (sing *ad nauseum* to the tune of "lions and tigers and bears, oh my"). And our barbecued meals never suffer from the

Part Three: So, If I Actually Decide to Become a Vegetarian, Just What Can I Expect?

181

"Gee, Dad, how come this chicken's black on the outside and raw on the inside?" syndrome.

The overriding rule of barbecue

What you barbecue (as long as it's vegetarian) isn't nearly as important as *how you do it* (*i.e.*, get it cooked but don't burn it, use the right barbecue sauce, etc.) ...And how you do it isn't as important as *what you do with it afterwards* (*i.e.*, serve it hot, don't let it dry out, use the right condiments and side dishes, and don't keep your boss and her husband waiting for dinner so long that they get in a grumpy mood.)

What do vegetarians barbecue?

● **The fake meats**—You want hamburgers? You want hot-dogs? We've got 'em! No, they aren't made out of meat, but after you get all the good stuff on them (barbecue sauce, onion, lettuce, Kaiser bun, sauerkraut, carcinogenic smoke) who's going to know? The point is, they're just as tasty and just as much fun to barbecue as the "real" (pronounced, "beastly") thing.

● **The vegetarian meat alternatives**—Buried somewhere in the bowels of this book (all right, maybe not a good choice of words in a book about food—and actually it's in Part 2, Chapter 2) is lots of information on three terrific meat substitutes—tofu (I promise you're going to like it on the grill), tempeh, and seitan—that will make you forget there's no meat on your plate. You want ribs to put Bert's sauce on? Strips of tempeh are the thing for you. You want something to marinate? Tofu is perfect. You want steaks? Seitan's a dead ringer (actually, it's not as dead as the steaks). You can cut it nice and thick, just like you like it.

● **Vegetables**—Of course there are plenty of ideas for vegetables on the grill as well, some of which you may never have considered. Just about every vegetable there is barbecues great. (Well, you might want to cook your leafy greens indoors.) Just brush your vegetables with olive oil and/or your favorite barbecue sauce and go to town.

Here are some hints for cooking veggies on the grill...

1. Just like with stir-fry, cut up *lots* of different kinds and have them ready to go. Start the ones that take longest to cook first.

2. Use lighter barbecue sauces for vegetables, like teriyaki sauce. Go liberally on the vinegars (rice and/or balsamic), tamari, miso, etc.

3. Keep everything moist while it's cooking, and turn frequently.

4. Get a crosshatched (###) vegetable grate for your grill so little things don't fall through.

Here are some vegetables to try...

1. Leeks—separate them first, and don't let them burn!

2. Eggplant—slice it thin, and turn it often.

3. Peppers and chiles—try a variety.

4. Sweet potatoes, broccoli and zucchini and squashes.

I could go on, but you get the idea.

● **The Exotic**—Nothing says, for example, that garlic bread and pizza won't be great cooked over the coals. And what about burritos, and breaded artichoke hearts and...

And so, in conclusion...

Many years ago I used to eat meat, and I thought barbecuing was okay, but nothing to come out of my socks for. Becoming a vegetarian forced me to widen the old horizons and experiment with what could be done on a barbecue grill. What a difference! Now, all summer long I practically live for my next barbecue fix. I drool at the sight of charcoal briquettes, long-handled forks and shish-kabob skewers. I sniff charcoal lighter fluid. (Just kidding.)

Even though, as with most things (*ha!*), we vegetarians do barbecuing better, there's still a long way to go. We need more vegetarians to take up the cause, and to do it more often. Then maybe one day we can dispel barbecuing's image as an activity dominated by meat-eaters.

I have a vision of the suburban back yard of the future. A bunch of kids are playing on the swingset and some women are setting out potato salad and iced tea on the picnic table. Three paunchy, middle-aged men stand with utensils in their hands, staring blankly into a smoking grill.

"How do you fix your tofu, Ralph?" one asks. "Mine always comes out dry."

Chapter 2

Eating vegetarian away from home

Watch it, there's meat under that piece of cabbage!

As much as most vegetarians love to cook, we can't always eat at home. That's okay. By eating other people's cooking we get new ideas and try new things. (Vegetarians love to try new foods!) There's only a slight problem...Most other people aren't vegetarian.

In this chapter we'll explore the exciting world of eating out as a vegetarian. It's a world that can be a lot of fun once we get past our **two primary goals**:

- get enough to eat, and
- don't eat any unsavory things that once had a face.

We'll start with a look at restaurants, and move on from there.

Restaurant dining as a vegetarian—*Can you do that?*

Yes, contrary to popular belief, it *is* possible to eat out once you become a vegetarian. Vegan even. It's not only possible, but it can be a truly gratifying experience. There's always a thrill in finding a new restaurant with an array of creative vegetarian dishes. (Okay, so some of us get cheap thrills.) And at those established restaurants that we vegetarians frequent, well there's a certain satisfaction knowing that we are an important part of the clientele and that we keep the vegetarian items on the menu.

But here's the bad news...

It goes without saying that there is a negative side of the restaurant experience that looms large for the vegetarian too. Heck, out of the hundreds of thousands of restaurants in the world (millions, even) there can't be more than a thousand or two (outside of India) that serve *only* vegetarian food, and even fewer that are vegan. Wow, what a sorry track record! That means that for the most part, when we vegetarians want to eat out, we're stuck at the meat-slinging places with the rest of the masses. That's a scary proposition, because for every restaurant that holds some promise, there are at least five others out there with no redeeming social value at all. Dinner at one of these can mean an evening of anger, embarrassment, starvation, and worse.

In the interests of providing a public service, here are a few of the disasters that regularly befall the unwary, unwise, or just plain unlucky vegetarian diner:

1. There's nothing on this menu I can eat.

How can one begin to describe the sense of horror and panic that will be felt by the unsuspecting vegetarian, when he or she sits down with a group of friends at an unfamiliar restaurant, opens the menu, and finds **nothing there without meat in it!**

We're talking here about pasta and rice cooked in "chicken" broth. We're talking about foods fried in lard. We're talking about the only vegetable on the menu being frozen green beans boiled with the skin of a pig!

Under circumstances as primitive as these, we're stuck with the "old standbys"—an iceberg lettuce salad and a baked potato. Yes, the "old standbys" have saved many a vegetarian from starvation. I lived on them for what seemed like a month once, when I spent a few days in rural Texas.

2. I bet there's nothing on the menu I can eat.

This may be the only thing worse than #1 above. It usually happens when we are with a group of meat-eaters and we're starving. That's when everyone will decide to go to a restaurant with a name like "The Branding Iron" or "Ed's Steak Pit", or a slogan like "Home of the belly-busters!" Not only is the vegetarian likely to have a miserable meal, but he'll have to spend a couple of hours worrying about it beforehand.

3. Oh my god! There's meat in this!

Let's say a vegetarian finds something on the menu that looks all right. She breathes a sigh of relief and orders it. But she's still not out

Part Three: So, If I Actually Decide to Become a Vegetarian,
Just What Can I Expect?

185

of the woods. Restaurants seem to delight in slipping meat and other animal products into everything, especially when they aren't mentioned on the menu. This, of course, is common in Chinese restaurants where shreds of "beef" are often hidden under the bamboo shoots by sadistic Chinese chefs, and "pork" regularly invades the egg rolls. But no category of restaurants is immune. Maybe all chefs are sadistic.

4. Your new best friend—the waiter.

(Hi, I'm John, and I'll be your waiter this evening...)

Okay, you don't have to be a vegetarian to know how obnoxious it is to have your waiter come to the table, introduce himself like he's your son-in-law to be, and then come on to you with the demeanor of a vacuum cleaner salesman. But all this is even *more* obnoxious for vegetarians.

Let me tell you about our specials...

First of all, there's the traditional half-hour litany of all the chef's specials, spoken as if these represented the very pinnacle of gustatory achievement rather than (as we all know is true) merely high profit items that the restaurant is pushing. Well, the specials are **almost never** vegetarian. When the first word out of the waiter's mouth is "veal", who wants to sit around through "...with shallots and drawn butter" etc., etc.?

How about we start you off with an order of our house special—the calamari?

When the waiter wants to be your best friend and guide you through the restaurant's favorite (and most profitable) dining experience, it's no fun to have to reveal that you're an old stick-in-the-mud vegetarian who's going to order something unexciting (to the waiter) and cheap. The waiter may quickly turn cold and concentrate his energies on a more susceptible table. (See #6 below!)

5. The "Local Color" syndrome.

As a general matter it can be said that restaurants in big, sophisticated cities will be more likely to have satisfactory vegetarian items on their menus than restaurants in small, rural burgs. But while that can be said, the exceptions are legion. Vegetarians certainly can't rely on this rule of thumb. There's a simple rule we *can* rely on though to weed out huge numbers of undesirable restaurants, and here it is:

The Local Color Rule: avoid like the plague any restaurant that hints of having any measure of "Local Color".

Local Color restaurants include steak places in the American Midwest (or Argentina!) and "seafood" restaurants anywhere near a coast. This category also includes any restaurant that (1) has someone's first name followed by the word "grill" on the sign, or (2) has been in the "same location for 20 years", or (3) has red carpeting and black vinyl chairs. In short, if the "locals love it", a vegetarian probably won't.

No matter what "local color" restaurant we go into, we vegetarians get the same waitress. (Even in Argentina!) Her name is Marge, and she's worked there since the Coolidge administration. Marge is pretty saucy and prides herself on being a "colorful character". She thinks all vegetarians are communists.

Since we won't see anything vegetarian on the menu, we'll have to ask Marge what vegetables are available. She will curtly respond "we don't have any vegetables," and will do her best to make our evening miserable from that point on. She won't even smile when she brings us the "old standbys".

6. Everybody hates me.

As if all the hazards set forth above aren't enough for restaurant-going vegetarians, there is one more. By the end of the meal everyone will hate us.

The waitperson hates us...

Even if we're lucky enough not to get Marge for a waitress, whomever we do get may be just as bad. We really can't blame the waiters and waitresses. After all, they've been trained to think their restaurant's prime rib is the best thing that's ever happened to food. And even if the vegetarian isn't directly insulting the cuisine, he or she probably is *creating some additional work.*

...and fellow diners too.

Vegetarians eating with a group of omnivores shouldn't expect them to love us either. They'll be almost as embarrassed as we are when we ask if the soup-of-the-day is made with "chicken" stock, or if we can get the club sandwich without the "bacon", or the turkey, or the mayonnaise. While the vegetarian is desperately trying to find something (anything!) to eat, everyone else at the table will be wondering to themselves why a simple thing like ordering dinner has to be made into such a production.

Part Three: So, If I Actually Decide to Become a Vegetarian, Just What Can I Expect?

187

So, how do we make the bad news better?

I f you insist on eating meat, take pity on your vegetarian friends. Let them choose the restaurant once in a while. Consider that new ethnic joint, or maybe try the place by the college where all the students hang out. You just might learn something.

Of course the savvy vegetarian can also do some things to improve the odds that his or her dining experience will be more on the "pleasant" side and less on the "total disaster" side. Here are some suggestions, which stop just short of grabbing Marge by the collar and choking her into submission. They are based on the proposition that if we want better treatment from restaurants, we vegetarians at least have the obligation to let them know who we are and what we do and do not want to eat.

1. Ask about everything.

It's not enough to simply say "I'm a vegetarian" and expect good treatment from a restaurant. Restaurants share the popular belief that all vegetarians *surely* eat chickens, or at least fishes. Tell them we're "vegan" and their eyes will glaze over.

No, it's much better to announce our vegetarian lifestyle by asking pointed questions about *everything*. Even if something on the menu looks totally safe, *ask anyway*—we've got nothing to lose. If there's meat hidden in it somewhere we'll be forewarned, and if it *is* vegetarian at least they'll know we appreciate the fact. If our waitperson doesn't know what's in a menu item (they usually won't) we can send them back to the kitchen. After all, they have to do something to earn that fat tip we're going to leave, and this is how word gets back to the management.

2. Order something that isn't on the menu.

Imagine you're a street-smart vegetarian, and you've just asked your waiter, "What are you serving today that's vegetarian?" This question invariably brings a flustered response as the waiter flips through the menu and points out "seafood" dishes. (While he's doing this you wonder why he thought you asked the question. Did he think you couldn't read the menu yourself?) You quickly explain your dietary preferences, and then you smile calmly.

This is when it's time to play "challenge the chef", and see if the big kahuna in the white hat can actually cook something creative that isn't set in ink on paper. You lean close to the waiter, you flash a big wad of bills, and, using your incredibly realistic English-upper-crust accent you say: "I assume your chef can do something *truly spectacular* with vegetables?"

3. Call ahead.

Whenever vegetarians are unsure about a restaurant, we can call before we go and ask them about their vegetarian dishes. Remember, we've got *more bargaining power* when we're just *thinking* about their restaurant than when they've already got us seated and they know they can block the door with the salad bar if they have to. It's also a lot easier to be self-righteous, obnoxious, etc. about one's diet over the phone than in person. Nothing will get vegetarian items on restaurant menus faster than restaurateurs thinking they are losing business because they don't offer them.

4. Spam, scram, "thank you, ma'am."

Remember, one will catch more flies with molasses than with anti-freeze. (Or something like that. But why would one want to catch flies in the first place?) Anyway, all vegetarian comments don't have to be negative or create extra work for somebody. When we vegetarians find something good on a restaurant menu we should be lavish with our praise. Praise will get back to management faster than anything else.

We should tell Marge the food is great, and we should explain to her *why* it's so good. It would be okay to throw in a little white lie too—like maybe telling her she reminds us of Audrey Hepburn in *Breakfast at Tiffany's*. Marge will blush. She'll think vegetarians aren't so bad after all.

Isn't that what we really want?

Airline food: A contradiction in terms?

The **bad news** is that they don't really serve food as we know it on airplanes anymore—at least if you have to sit back in steerage (a/k/a "coach"). Instead of real meals they like to throw something in a bag or a box at you. They call it a "snack". On the few long trips these days that are billed as "lunch" or "dinner" flights, the meal comes on a little plastic tray and features specially miniaturized versions of entrées, salads, desserts and rolls. Teeny weenie little plastic dishes containing teeny weenie little vegetables, tiny parts of chickens, etc.

The actual process for making these miniaturized foods was developed by the Japanese transistor radio people in the 1960s and is now a secret highly guarded by the airlines. (Indeed, airline food may be even smaller than it looks, because they probably shrink the silverware too.)

The **even worse news** is that in addition to not getting much food on your flight, you can also count on there being meat somewhere on the menu. The airlines buy whole hog (no pun intended) into the Standard American Diet ("SAD") and assume that their passengers *must* have at least part of a deceased animal at every meal lest they keel over dead (or even worse—stop buying airline tickets).

There is some **good news** here though. Virtually all the airlines offer special vegetarian meals in place of their regular foul fare. Often we vegetarians can specify whether we want dairy (the "ovo-lacto" choice) or non-dairy (the "pure" choice—remember, that's because we're so pure at heart).

These vegetarian meals are sometimes quite good, and it's not uncommon for meat-eaters to look at what we vegetarians are being served and say: "Boy, that looks better than what I got." So, if you're a meat-eater who flies a lot, the vegetarian special meal is a good way to experiment with vegetarianism and get away from the tedium of eating your 20,000th (really!) chicken. You should try this.

Of course this story has to end with **more bad news**: Vegetarian meals can sometimes be hard to get. But do not despair, my dear meat-eater on the road to enlightenment (and any vegetarians who happen to be tagging along). You can drastically increase (1) your chances of getting a vegetarian meal, and (2) your resulting happiness in the old friendly skies, merely by being pushy and obnoxious. Here's what you have to do:

• Request your vegetarian meal when you make your reservation, *at least* a day in advance. Airline bureaucracies can't do anything in less than 24 hours. Call back again later, just to confirm that your meal made it into the computer. (Remember, if you aren't on the computer, you don't exist.)

• Mention your meal again when you check in for the flight, just so they'll remember to put it on the plane instead of leaving it in the kitchen. (This really happens!)

• Identify yourself to the stewards (sorry, I mean flight attendants) when you board the plane so they can find you and won't give your dinner away to someone else before they get to you. (Amazingly, this happens all the time!)

• If they do screw up your meal make a fuss. Demand that they turn the plane around and go back for it. This will help make traveling better for all of us in the future.

Remember, you are one of the special few who really cares about what goes into your mouth. You deserve better than airline food!

A modest proposal for the airlines folks

You airlines people must get really fed up (pun intended) with having to prepare and serve special meals to meet all the weird diets of all your weird passengers. Here's a little suggestion that will make your job easier, Mr./Ms. airline executive. Why not make the regular meals on your airline vegan? That way not only will you never have to worry about vegetarian special meals again, but you can probably forget about the low cholesterol, low fat, low salt, high fiber, lactose-free and Kosher special meals too. Wow, what an idea! You can serve everyone the same thing!! Think of all the money you'll save!!!

Chapter 3

Vegetarians and non-vegetarians coexisting in a flesh-eating world

"Now Billy, stop pulling your sister's hair. You're just going to have to learn to get along with each other!"

It's a flesh-eating world out there, and we vegetarians are just a small minority in all those herds of cows and people. Is that sometimes inconvenient? Sure. Are we sometimes discriminated against? You bet. But it can also work the other way around. We vegetarians know we are members of a special group, and sometimes we can get a little bit snooty about that too. Sorry.

In this chapter we'll consider all of this, as we explore some of the ways that vegetarians relate to meat-eaters and vice versa. We'll start by talking about the burdens and the ecstasies of being a little "different", and then we'll move on to the essential topics that I know are on your mind—topics like monks and major league baseball.

Vegetarians are weird

Yeah, any meat-eater will tell you that we vegetarians are weird. We take one of the most basic and necessary of human functions—eating—and we screw it all up. On top of that, we take one of the most fundamental ways that people interact and socialize with each other—eating—and we screw that up too.

If you're a meat-eater, you've been embarrassed by us. You've wondered about our sanity.

If you're a vegetarian, you know that life isn't always a slice of peach shortcake.

Here are **a couple of examples**:

● The gung-ho vegetarian does a good deed for a friend. The friend responds by baking chocolate chip cookies as a thank you. The vegetarian smiles nervously. "Gee, I'm sorry but these aren't on my diet. Butter and chickens' eggs, you know..." The friend is embarrassed. The vegetarian is embarrassed. Everyone looking on thinks, "This person is *weird.*"

● The rabid vegetarian takes an extended trip to the wilds of Texas, Alaska, Russia, etc. The vegetarian rejects all proffered native foods. The vegetarian starves to death. As they lower him/her into the ground, the mourners have one collective thought: "Boy, that person was *weird!*"

The toughness of weirdness

It's tough to be weird. It can get you down. It can make you feel sorry for yourself and angry at yourself for making life so difficult.

But there's another way we vegetarians can look at our predicament. We can substitute for the word "weird". We can substitute the word "individualistic". Yes, we can say to ourselves, "Everyone else might eat meat, but I'm not 'everyone'. Maybe it's because I have different ethical standards than most people. Maybe it's because I understand things that they don't. Whatever the reason, by golly I know I'm right doing what I do, and I'm not going to change. It's *everyone else* who needs to change."

The goodness of toughness

As much as we'd like everyone to join us in our vegetarianism, sometimes we're *glad* it's difficult to be a vegetarian in our society. It makes us feel good to know that we understand the concept that humans should be vegetarians, when most people don't. And it makes us feel good to know that we've stuck to our beliefs every day in situations which weren't easy.

Yeah, it's not always convenient to be a "weird" vegetarian in a meat-eating world. But we can use that to our advantage. Life wasn't easy for lots of folks whose ideas of what was right went against the social norms of their times—Susan B. Anthony, Martin Luther King Jr., Gandhi. They were called "weird" in their day too. But now that history has judged them, nobody can use that *other* five letter word beginning with a "w". Nobody can call them *wrong*.

In our own small way we vegetarians are in the same situation as those famous people with their famous causes. No, we're not heroes

Part Three: So, If I Actually Decide to Become a Vegetarian, Just What Can I Expect?

193

like they were, but that doesn't mean what we're doing isn't important, and it doesn't mean we can't celebrate that fact. For many of us, being vegetarian is the **single thing in our lives of which we are the most proud.**

Wait, are you equating vegetarianism with the great "causes" of history?

Absolutely. Years from now people will look back on eating animal products the way we now look back on slavery, the denial of the vote to women, and bell-bottomed pants. It will be seen as an idea who's time never should have come.

Woe is me! *Another* burden of being a vegetarian

As if being weird isn't enough, there's another hardship we plant-eaters have to endure. Sometimes it can be a terrible burden on us *individual* vegetarians to represent our minority to the rest of the world. Think about it. There's a stereotype here. We are expected to be healthy and vivacious all the time. And heaven forbid if we have any of those annoying personal vices, like drinking, smoking, or being a serial killer. That just wouldn't be fitting for a vegetarian. We have a standard to uphold.

Meat-eaters love to find chinks in our vegetarian armor. (Who could blame them?) At the observation of the most minor health imperfection (a cough, a sniffle, a broken neck), meat-eaters simply cannot resist teasing us vegetarians with the line: "If you ate some red meat once in a while you'd be healthier." We know they are being very witty, but every time we hear this line, there is a great temptation to scream.

Fortunately, most vegetarians acquit themselves pretty well in the "always being healthy" and "having no discernible vices" departments. Others of us, though (this group includes me), are lousy representatives of the vegetarian cause. Sure, we could be perfect if we wanted to. (Yeah, right!) But, heck, most of the time we just don't feel like it.

Wait, we want some stories!
You mean stories that illustrate the difficulties of vegetarians getting along with non-vegetarians?
Yeah, sure. As long as they're stories, we don't care.
Okay, here goes.

The monk story

When meat-eaters and vegetarians mix it up over their respective diets, it often starts with the meat-eaters asking the innocent question: "Hey, how come you follow that weird diet?"

But down deep, they really don't want to know. You see, they're really hoping we'll say something like this:

"Well, I'm a vegetarian because my great-great-grandfather met this monk on a mountaintop in Tibet in 1893, and ever since then my family has followed this exotic religion that requires us to dance naked on hot coals, meditate 16 hours a day, and give up meat."

The reason they want this answer is so they can smile politely and think:

"Thank goodness. The only monk my great-great-grandfather ever met on a mountaintop was a chipmunk, and I don't have to worry about any strange religions. Boy, it's great to be a normal person, and not weird like this guy...What's for dinner, anyway?"

Of course, most people know they can't expect to get the answer about the monk. The answer they *expect* to get goes something like this:

"Well, I gave up meat because I thought it might be better for me, ...but I've been sick lately, and now I'm not so sure."

Again, the meat-eater can smile and, without too much effort, think:

"Yeah, but I'm a pretty healthy guy myself. I avoid the really fatty meats and, hey, wasn't it just the other day that I had that thing (what was that thing, anyway?) that supposedly had oat bran in it?"

When people ask why we are vegetarians there's one kind of answer they really *don't* want. That's an answer that implies that being a vegetarian might somehow be a little more wholesome or a little more ethical than not being a vegetarian. Answers they *don't* want to hear deal with issues like world starvation, rainforests, and (heaven forbid!) animal rights. When a vegetarian gives a non-vegetarian an answer with one of those themes, the subject of their conversation will immediately change to the Super Bowl or the big sale at K-Mart.

There's a reason for this. The meat-eater may not know it, but when he asks why we're vegetarians he's subconsciously thinking:

"If it has anything to do with ethics I'd rather not know, because if I knew then I'd feel guilty, and if I felt guilty then I'd have to change my lifestyle, but I don't want to change my lifestyle, so I'd rather not know."

Give him an answer he doesn't like, and he has to think:

Part Three: So, If I Actually Decide to Become a Vegetarian, Just What Can I Expect?

195

"I didn't want to know but you told me anyway, so now I feel guilty, but since I don't want to change my lifestyle I'm going to take that guilt out on you, thank you very much."

Not a very good basis for a vegetarian/non-vegetarian relationship, is it?

So, are vegetarians something special?

As the monk story illustrates, sometimes vegetarian/omnivore relations break down because meat-eaters feel an implied criticism coming from vegetarians, even if we never say a word. (Of course, sometimes we *do* say way more than we should, and then it gets even worse.)

It shouldn't have to be this way.

Let's set the record straight. There are a lot of things that define who we all are, and our way of eating is just one of them. If you take everything together and put it under those new reading glasses you picked up at the drugstore, you'll find that we vegetarians are pretty much like everyone else—no more sensitive, compassionate, noble, vain, radical, smart, stupid, or better looking. (Okay, maybe just a *tiny bit* better looking.) Indeed, if one were to ask the average vegetarian to name someone he or she greatly admires, the odds are good the person named would be a meat-eater.

The only thing that really makes us vegetarians different from our meat-eating brethren is that we've discovered, usually through no great effort of our own, a simple change we can make in our lives that has truly remarkable consequences for ourselves and the world around us. But anyone can make the same discovery. **Heck, even a dork can become a vegetarian!**

While you're thinking about that, here's another story:

The "chicken" story

In the library at the office where I was working several years ago I noticed a small paper bag with a chicken's bones in it that someone had left beside a chair. I casually remarked to my secretary that there was a bag in the library with the decomposed body of an animal in it. A horrified look came across her face, and she immediately picked up the phone to call the maintenance department. They sent up two men (count 'em, *two*) to take care of the problem. As the men were laughing and walking off with the small paper bag, my secretary was not subtle in expressing her anger.

"That's someone's lunch!" she yelled, threatening to club me with a thick file. I attempted to defend myself by pointing out that *she* was the one who made a big deal out of it by calling the maintenance department. Then I tried to explain my viewpoint. Why would it be different, I asked, if someone hadn't been eating it for lunch? If it had just been your ordinary dead bird, without being dismembered, processed a million ways, cooked, and bitten with human teeth—why would it have been so much more offensive?

She didn't respond to that, but I guess to most meat-eaters it certainly would be different.

How come?

Minding my meat metaphors

We vegetarians (along with everyone else) have been deluged with cutesy little meat metaphors for years and have quietly put up with it. We've had everything from the butcher who backed into the meat grinder and got a "little behind" in his work to the classic "where's the beef?" And how many times has our intelligence been insulted with slogans like "our reputation is at steak" or "we won't give you a bum steer". Where's it all to stop? Well, I for one have had *enough*. It's time to speak out against this atrocity.

It seems that when meat metaphors work their way into modern conversation, more often than not meat is made out to be the good stuff. For example, to "beef up" something is to make it better, more substantive. The "meat of the matter" is what's important. On the other hand, references to vegetarian foods are often negative. Nobody wants to be referred to as "small potatoes", or as a "vegetable" or a "fruit". And being called "full of beans" is, of course, the ultimate insult (well, almost).

The same thing carries over to animals. Our culture seems to associate good attributes with carnivorous animals and bad ones with vegetarian animals—especially those that are eaten. Most people don't mind being referred to as "tigers", or "eagles", for example. But nobody wants to be called a "pig", a "chicken" or a "turkey".

I've got a "bone to pick" with anyone trying to get cute with meat. Maybe it's because I sometimes unwittingly use meat metaphors myself, and I resent having been so conditioned. Anyway, I think it's about time fruits and vegetables got equal billing, and I want to rally vegetarians everywhere in support of this cause.

Part Three: So, If I Actually Decide to Become a Vegetarian, Just What Can I Expect?

197

Fortunately, progress along these lines has already been made, and it has come from within the ranks of the American national pastime. Yes, it was baseball that broke the race barrier in professional sports, and baseball that is still the only sport to dress its 60-year-old coaches in team uniforms. (Wouldn't it be great if basketball tried this?) Now baseball "strikes" again. You see, when a manager gets angry and kicks dirt on the umpire's shoes, this is commonly referred to as a "beef". But it's *also* commonly referred to as a "rhubarb". This is important. Equating "beef" and "rhubarb" in baseball lingo gives us license to equate the two in other references.

For example, when the local football team drafts a huge offensive lineman we can refer to him as "rhubarby". We can use terms like "rhubarb up" and "where's the rhubarb?" You get the idea. Pretty soon we'll be going even farther. We'll be tossing out phrases like "bringing home the rhubarb" and "Merrill Lynch is rhubarbish on America."

All of this may sound pretty silly, but there's a serious point to be made. If we as a society eat meat we're going to think meat. It will carry over into our patterns of speech, and who knows what other areas of our lives. As a vegetarian I'd rather have us eating and thinking vegetarian foods. And anyway, I don't want my mind's limited storage space cluttered with meat slogans. I want to get back to the basics. I'm a simple fellow, I guess. Just a "rhubarb and potatoes" kind of guy.

The Meatball Sub (p. 201)

Chapter 4

The Great Vegetarian Dating Game

*If I become a vegetarian won't my love life be
ruined?*
Yeah...Maybe.

S o, you're single and you're thinking of becoming a vegetarian?
Congratulations! Here's something you should know. Your field of
potential mates will be reduced by 90%.

Oh, the joys of being a single vegetarian! The good news for you
single folks who decide to become vegetarian is that you'll be healthier because of it. Vegetarians are known for their good skin, trim bodies, etc. Not to mention their energy and stamina—assets that can make
you legendary in the romance game. The other good news for single
vegetarians is that you can date anyone you want: meat-eaters, semi-
vegetarians, or vegetarians. Each of these groups has a lot to offer in
the search for a potential mate. The bad news is that all three of these
groups present some real challenges as well.

With that in mind it's time to play The Great Vegetarian Dating
Game. Let's open that first door and see who we find.

Bachelor/Bachelorette no.1—*The meat-eater*

W hen you're a vegetarian the advantage to dating meat-eaters
should be obvious: just like cockroaches and dandelions, you'll
find them everywhere. The odds are good that the blonde at the bus
stop or the macho hunk you've been eyeing at the water cooler does-
n't share your vegetarian philosophy. But if you find them attractive
you'd like to be able to go out on a date without having to grill them
in advance about their eating preferences. Now, that's all well and
good until the problems arise. And they *will* arise.

The Big Confession

The first obstacle you will have to overcome is explaining to your meat-eating date why you are a vegetarian. Since you'll probably be eating on your first date, the chances are good The Big Confession will come early. If you want to make it to date number two, you'd better handle it well. The best advice is to do it in a way that minimizes the differences between the two of you, and makes it seem very acceptable that both of you are the way you are. This is no time to use your conversion tactics. As we'll see below, that comes later.

(I, of course, always took the coward's way out when dating meat-eaters. I would invite the woman in question over for dinner. That way I could control the food, and I didn't even have to point out that it was vegetarian. This little trick was usually good to delay The Big Confession until our next time together. Given my luck with women, I often didn't have to worry about when that would be.)

The Barbed Wire Fence

Let's say you make it past The Big Confession and find that you and your meat-eating friend are getting along just great. In fact, you are really starting to like each other. Uh-oh. That means you are just about to hit the next obstacle—The Barbed Wire Fence. This is when you and the meat-eater start to throw little barbs at one another about your respective diets. At first it will all be good-natured, and you might even see it as a sign that you are feeling more comfortable with each other. You'll have this conversation over dinner:

"Hey meathead, want to try a bite of my buckwheat noodles in miso broth?"

"No thanks, tofu face. I prefer to eat food."

As time goes on, however, both of you will get more serious about your barbs, and The Barbed Wire Fence will become more annoying. It will come to a head the night your date takes you to dinner at his or her parents' house. Afterwards you'll have this little discussion:

"You didn't eat any of my mother's chicken."

"Come on, you know I don't eat that—I'm a vegetarian."

"Well, it would have been the polite thing to do, you know. She was nice enough to invite you to dinner."

"I'll die before I'm that polite."

Part Three: So, If I Actually Decide to Become a Vegetarian,
Just What Can I Expect?

201

The Meatball Sub

With every romantic relationship come instances of aesthetic disappointment. There is the time, for example, when you find out that some of her best assets only exist thanks to the miracle of space-age plastics, or the day when you discover that he's been wearing the same jockey shorts for two months. Since the meat-eating culture is inherently un-aesthetic to many vegetarians, there is even more potential here for friction between you and your meat-eating date. For example, you may have trouble snuggling up to his leather jacket or her fur coat, or maybe you'll be grossed out the first time you find your date has left the remains of a Big Mac in your refrigerator.

My meat-eating girlfriend and I were crazy about each other, and we'd been getting along well until that fateful day when she had to have The Meatball Sub for lunch. Yuck! After she finished she looked up and said, "Kiss me!"

I looked at her, the grease still dripping down her chin, and hesitated. "I think I'll take a rain check," I said. I handed her a napkin, and our relationship was never the same again.

Of course The Big Confession, The Barbed Wire Fence, and The Meatball Sub are all manifestations of the same problem: vegetarians and meat-eaters have a major philosophical difference between them. Physical attraction can be wonderful, and maybe they'll even have a number of common interests, but these things can wear thin when two people disagree about something as basic as food. Most folks eat three meals a day. When a vegetarian is with a meat-eater that creates three golden opportunities to fight.

We hear a lot about "mixed" marriages of vegetarians and meat-eaters, and I've known several such couples myself. They are all wonderful people. They have to be. For many less tolerant vegetarian souls, though, looking for Mr./Miss/Ms. Right from the ranks of meat-eaters can be frustrating at best. At worst, it can keep them looking for a long, long time. Sure, Bachelor/Bachelorette No.1 is great for the vegetarian who needs someone with a good smile to take to his or her high school reunion. For more serious relationships, though, there must be other choices.

Bachelor/Bachelorette no.2—*The semi-vegetarian*

Undaunted by our experience with *inter-diet* dating, we continue to play The Great Vegetarian Dating Game. This time we'll meet

Bachelor/Bachelorette No.2—The semi-vegetarian. The prospective dates in this group are all those who have "just about given up red meat", or who feel they "really should be a vegetarian". In short, this is everyone sympathetic to the cause who hasn't yet changed his or her lifestyle to vegetarianism.

Theoretically, this group should provide an ideal hunting ground for the single vegetarian. There are plenty of people around who fall into the semi-vegetarian category, and because they are already sympathetic to vegetarianism the potential for fireworks (of the bad kind) may not be as great as with a confirmed meat-eater. Unfortunately, things are never as easy as they seem.

The Prickly Hedge

If The Barbed Wire Fence describes the obstacle between vegetarians and meat-eaters, then between vegetarians and semi-vegetarians it's more like The Prickly Hedge—not as high or as sharp, but potentially even more deadly to a long-term relationship. The reason is that the semi-vegetarian will be receptive to the vegetarian's lifestyle, but the committed vegetarian won't be able to return that receptivity. It will always be the vegetarian's inflexible diet, for example, that dictates mutual food choices. And the barbs, however subtle and unintended they may be, are likely to continue from vegetarian to semi-vegetarian. The semi-vegetarian who, for whatever reason, isn't ready to convert is likely to feel oppressed in this situation. Not the best thing on which to base a relationship.

The Phony Conversion

What about the semi-vegetarian who falls in love and decides to convert to vegetarianism? Well, that's great if he or she is really ready for the conversion—go straight to Bachelor/Bachelorette no.3. But if the conversion is prompted more out of guilt, or a desire to please the vegetarian, it isn't likely to last long. It may just lead to more feelings of oppression (and the overwhelming desire on the part of the semi-vegetarian to end the relationship so he or she can finally get a decent—i.e., "beastly"—meal again)!

The Big Tease

Let's not forget the feelings of the vegetarian in all this. If you are dating a semi-vegetarian you will likely be very excited by the possi-

Part Three: So, If I Actually Decide to Become a Vegetarian,
Just What Can I Expect?

203

bility of converting him or her to a vegetarian lifestyle. If it doesn't work out, The Big Tease can be emotionally devastating. You might even be tempted to go back to Bachelor/Bachelorette no.1. At least with a confirmed meat-eater you knew where you stood from the beginning.

Bachelor/Bachelorette no.3—*The vegetarian*

W hen he or she has been going out with meat-eaters and even semi-vegetarians, your average veggie might be amazed at how easy it is to date a fellow vegetarian:

"I just love Tom's Tasty Tofu Emporium."

"Really? Gee, that's my favorite restaurant too!"

Then again, sometimes it won't be so easy, and both parties will end up asking themselves: did I expect too much? Do vegetarians really do it better? Does the heart really lie just behind the stomach?

Under Every Stone

There is a problem most veggies will encounter right away in trying to date a fellow vegetarian—finding one. Let's face it, we don't meet that many real vegetarians in our day-to-day lives, and those we do meet may not exactly be the Greek gods or goddesses of our dreams. Vegetarian and related organizations can help a lot in the search. (Sometimes having a "cause" can do wonders for a person's social life!) But don't count on this. In most cases you can expect the hunt to be a lot of work, and don't expect success overnight. While there may indeed be a vegetarian Under Every Stone, it's turning those stones over that's the hard part.

The three points of disagreement

I f you are persistent and a little lucky you will eventually find a vegetarian you actually want to date (and even more important, who wants to date you). Now, since you won't have all the problems you encountered with meat-eaters and semi-vegetarians, you and Bachelor/Bachelorette no.3 have it made, right? Wrong.

Vegetarians are such a diverse group that you can't rule out the possibility of serious compatibility problems arising. Indeed, after years of painstaking research (note the emphasis on *pains*taking), I've isolated **three potential areas of disagreement between vegetarian couples**:

1. their reasons for being vegetarian
2. their diets
3. everything else.

An example might be beneficial. Suppose you've got an evening scheduled with your new vegetarian friend. Both of you are really looking forward to it. The problem is that your date is planning on eating a raw vegetable salad and being in bed (and asleep!) by 10. It seems that he or she has to get up early to train for the Boston Marathon. You, on the other hand, envisioned staying up late over coffee, smoking cigarettes and planning your next animal rights march. You've got problems already, and you don't even know yet if you both like John Wayne films.

When it's all said and done a vegetarian will probably encounter many of the same problems whether he or she is dating another vegetarian, a semi-vegetarian, or a meat-eater. In The Great Vegetarian Dating Game what really counts, of course, are the individuals involved. With a little persistence and some measure of tolerance any vegetarian should be able to find Mr./Miss/Ms. Right, whether he or she is Bachelor/Bachelorette nos. 1, 2, or 3. So just keep playing The Great Vegetarian Dating Game and happiness awaits you.

Well...maybe if you're real lucky.

Chapter 5

Dealing with relatives—
Your parents, your significant other, your vegetarian kids, and your pets

Oh boy! You're going to be One Big, Happy Family!

O h, your relatives are going to love it if you become a vegetarian. If that happens they'll have a constant reminder of their own crummy diets—right in their own house, or at least at every family gathering. With you as a vegetarian they'll have to think about what you can and can't eat every time they cook. And of course they can have the pleasure of watching you stay healthy and slim while their waists and thighs expand like the National Debt. Oh yeah, they're going to love that all right.

In this chapter we're going to discuss how you can continue to get along, more or less, with all those other folks in your house after you make that big decision to become a vegetarian. Yes, there are parents to deal with, and husbands and wives to deal with, not to mention all those other extraneous people who hang around your refrigerator. Then we're going to talk about raising kids as vegetarians. (They'll want to follow in your footsteps, and that's great!) Finally, because they are relatives too, we'll talk about your pets. They may or may not want in on the action.

Dealing with parents

P arents are always especially pleased when their kids decide to give up meat. They'll sit across from you at the dinner table and look at you like you've just been drop-shipped to their house from Mars. You'll be able to read it in their eyes: "Why was my child taken away from me, and why was I left instead with this alien worshipper of the Devil?"

Parents' attitudes are understandable. They feel that if you reject the way they've taught you to eat, you're rejecting them. They don't have the benefit of your worldly understanding. (It may be best to buy them a copy of this book—I could use the royalties.) If you become a vegetarian your parents could be frightened for you, and perhaps even a little frightened *of* you.

Here's something that may be able to help. Cut it out and put it on the refrigerator:

A few words to concerned parents of vegetarian kids

Y our child has just come home and announced that he or she will not be eating the flesh of animals any more. *Holy Smokes!!!* Once you overcome your shock and have an extended conversation with the kid in question (during which voices may be raised, tears shed, etc.), you'll have a right to be worried. After all, this is new to you.

As a public service to foster domestic tranquillity, we address below the most common concerns of parents the world over who have faced this difficult problem:

The doctor says my kid may not be getting enough protein and vitamins and nutrients!

There are hundreds of millions of vegetarians in the world. As explained in agonizing detail earlier in this book, unless your child lives on a steady diet of Cokes and French fries (a distinct possibility), his or her vegetarian diet will be *much* healthier than the previous meat-based diet (which probably consisted of Cokes and hamburgers). Be glad your child has finally expressed an interest in his or her diet and health. This is what you've been asking for for years! ("Eat your vegetables!")

As for protein, as we've discovered, it's virtually impossible *not* to get enough of it on a vegetarian diet. A dietitian can't design a varied vegetarian diet that doesn't supply enough protein! On the other hand, *too much* protein is a real problem in our culture—causing diseases like osteoporosis (it takes calcium from the body) and maybe worse.

Your doctor's warnings come from supposition, not scientific fact. Ask him or her to cite just *one* example from either personal experience or the medical literature of a vegetarian (who wasn't otherwise starving to death) suffering from too little protein. Ask him or her for other *real world* examples of dietary deficiencies caused by vegetarianism.

Part Three: So, If I Actually Decide to Become a Vegetarian,
Just What Can I Expect?

207

On the other hand, you probably know a dozen people *person-ally* who have suffered from heart disease, cancer and stroke—diseases that have been shown in scads of scientific studies to be associated with meat-eating.

This vegetarian thing is just a fad.

Actually, on the time line of human history it's *meat-eating that's the fad*. Humans and their ancestors have historically been gatherers and foragers, and we have only made meat a substantial part of our diets in relatively recent times. Anyway, those of us who feel strongly about the health, environmental and ethical ramifications of meat-eating aren't about to change our minds because this diet may not be trendy some day.

By the way, there are lots of us vegetarians, and we have quite a tradition. Ask Gandhi, George Bernard Shaw, Pythagoras, and a few hundred other household names from history if their deep commitment to vegetarianism was just a fad.

I worry that my kid is being brainwashed by vegetarian and animal rights groups!

Don't take this the wrong way, but maybe *you've* been brain-washed. Maybe you're stuck in your thinking because of meat-eating habits learned in childhood and passed down from previous genera-tions that didn't have either the food choices or the knowledge of nutrition that we now have. (By the way, your great-grandfather's gen-eration ate a lot *less* meat than your generation does!) Maybe you've also been influenced by advertising from the meat and dairy indus-tries that either contained misinformation (the infamous "Four Food Groups") or was just plain silly ("Beef Gives Strength").

Vegetarians are weirdos and radicals!

Name calling is the last refuge of those who have run out of cred-ible arguments to support their position. If you think vegetarians are wrong, why not study the matter and try to get the facts to refute what they say? Go ahead. You might be surprised at what you learn.

I can't always cook a separate special meal for my child.

Why not let the kid do the cooking? Vegetarians all learn to cook eventually. Even if your child is very young, it's a good time to start, and the learning process could be quality time together for you both. In any event, it wouldn't hurt the rest of the family to eat vegetarian once in a while, would it?

My child is rejecting me!

Hardly. Your child is thinking for him- or herself, and making his or her decisions for a wealth of good reasons. (As found in the rest of this book!) This isn't a rejection of you or your values. Rather, it shows individuality, and demonstrates a lot more character than blindly going along with the rest of the pack. (Sounds like you did a pretty good job of raising this kid!) Rather than focusing on your child, consider why you're so uncomfortable thinking about giving up meat. What are you afraid of? Is it worth the risk of alienating your child?

Kids always think they're smarter than their parents.

Yeah, and they eventually learn that they aren't. But that doesn't mean that they can't sometimes have a good idea or two. Vegetarianism is one of them.

What about those *other* relatives?

With non-parental relatives things aren't so frightening (on both sides), and that usually makes it a lot easier on the vegetarian. Brothers and sisters and aunts and uncles and cousins might roll their eyes a little, but what can they really say? In secret they'll be delighted if you become a vegetarian. After all, it's good gossip to have a nonconformist in the family. It takes some of the pressure off them.

Cooking for relatives

What to tell your husband, kid, significant other, mooching cousin, etc. when you put a bean burger on the table instead of the rib-eye steak he or she was expecting.

- "It's done medium-rare, just the way you like it."
- "The steak is actually *inside* the beans."
- "The dishwasher's been doing a lousy job of getting the blood stains off the plates, so we had to make the change."
- "The cat had first pick and ate all the steak."
- "We saved $2.50 on the meal, and another $25,000 on future cardiac surgery. We can buy a new car."
- "Close your eyes; you won't know the difference."
- "Put some steak sauce on it; you won't know the difference."
- "I love you too much to feed you meat."
- "The steer ran away before I could cut off its head."
- "The steer's in the back yard waiting for you. Here, you'd better take your steak knife and several napkins."

Will this lead to War or Peace?

When Russian author (and vegetarian) Leo Tolstoy's sister came to visit and demanded meat at family meals, legend has it that he put a live chicken and a knife on the table, telling her that if she wanted flesh, she'd have to kill it herself.

Kids: Having that kid in a flesh-eating world

Years ago a woman came to me with a problem that related to vegetarianism and kids. Her sister had been a long-time vegetarian and was now pregnant. Her obstetrician had refused to continue to care for her unless she started eating meat. (The doctor probably had good intentions but was, well, a dim-wit.) The poor woman was trying to incorporate meat into her diet, and it was making her sick.

As I say, this was back in the dark ages before a lot had been written about vegetarianism and childbearing. I sent my friend what information I could, but have to surmise that the end of the story turned out bleakly.

Today we're luckier and our doctors are smarter. There is lots of good information available on childbearing and vegetarianism. I've seen lots of happy, healthy babies (come to think of it, none that weren't) born to vegetarian couples.

Think about it. The human body has no metabolic requirement for meat or dairy products. *Why should you eat something that's unhealthy for you just because you're pregnant?*

Little kids and little calves love vegetarians.

K ids are natural vegetarians. The reason is simple—when they are young they have no preconceived notions about what they should and shouldn't be eating. Moreover, kids love animals. Kids are naturally sensitive to the pain of others. They have to be *taught* to be insensitive. Kids don't like to kill things, and they have to be taught that too. (What a terrible thing to be teaching children!) Vegetarian writer Harvey Diamond has a great line: "You put a baby in a crib with an apple and a rabbit. If it eats the rabbit and plays with the apple, I'll buy you a new car."

When kids are confronted with meat, though, they have a problem. Many children may have a hard time justifying their feelings about animals, and the way they love their own pets, with the fact that the meat they eat comes from animals too.

When I was young I thought there must be some missing explanation that I just wasn't getting. I figured there had to be some way that we could eat animals, but that they wouldn't be hurt. Maybe they just shaved those steaks off the sides of cows, I thought, and they grew back good as new. My mother told me that animals used for food were "raised to be eaten." That made me feel better for a while, but when I actually thought about it, that didn't make any sense either.

Many years later, after I became a vegetarian, I talked with another child who must have been going through a similar period of doubt. He was the younger brother of one of my friends, and he was probably about eight years old at the time. I asked him what his favorite food was. "Veal," he said without hesitation. I asked him if he knew where veal came from. "Sure," he said. "It comes from baby calves." Then he thought about what he'd just said for a second and his eyes got wide. He looked up at me and asked in an obviously troubled voice that was almost a whisper, "Do they have to kill the calves for that?"

Yes, they have to kill the calves, and the way they go about it isn't very pleasant either. Shielding kids from the whole truth about what they're eating isn't good for the calves and it isn't good for the kids.

The upshot of all this is that kids will gladly follow you into vegetarianism. They'll think it's a wonderful idea. And if you think they're

Part Three: So, If I Actually Decide to Become a Vegetarian,
Just What Can I Expect?

211

not sophisticated enough to see beyond the temptations that the Ronald McDonalds of the world present them with, then you underestimate kids. Kids know what's important.

4H x 3

How many kids in 4H Clubs and similar farm organizations want to kill the animals they so carefully raise? Here are three possibilities of what could happen when little Jimmy first learns what is to be the fate of Patches, the pig he's raised from a baby:

The world as we know it scenario:

Jimmy *[in tears]*: You can't let them take Patches, Dad! He's my best friend, and they're going to kill him!

Dad: I'm sorry son, but it's a cruel world. You're just going to have to understand that and learn to accept it.

Jimmy: But why does it have to be that way, Dad?

Dad: It just does, that's all. Now your mother has fixed pork chops for dinner. Let's go eat.

The Hollywood adaptation:

[In this version the part of Jimmy is played by Mickey Rooney, and the part of Dad is played by Gregory Peck.]

Jimmy *[in tears]*: You can't let them take Patches, Dad! He's my best friend, and they're going to kill him!

Dad: Now, now son. Don't you worry. That was Mr. Rockefeller on the phone from that big fancy farm down the street. He's agreed to take Patches and let him live out his life in a beautiful field with lots of other rich pigs!

Jimmy: Can we visit him?

Dad *[smiling]*: Sure son, anytime you want. Now, let's go get some of those pork chops.

The vegetarian scenario:

Jimmy *[in tears]*: You can't let them take Patches, Dad! He's my best friend, and they're going to kill him!

Dad: Son, they're only going to kill Patches because people want to eat him.

Jimmy *[horrified]*: Why would anyone eat a wonderful animal like Patches?

Dad: Would you give up eating "bacon" and "pork" and "ham" to save Patches?

Jimmy: Of course!

Dad: If everyone felt that way, then Patches and all the other pigs could be saved.

Jimmy *[leery]*: It sounds too easy. What's the catch?

Kids who get the chance to grow up as vegetarians are to be envied. They learn good eating habits early and, unlike the kids in the 4H Club, they're in on a big secret: there's no universal law that says you have to kill your friends just because they happen to be cows, pigs or sheep.

Only half-a-cow

When I was five years old, I was told my grandparents had just bought "half-a-cow". Now, if you're a little kid and you get news like that, all kinds of things go through your head. I had visions of being a farm kid—out in the fields tending to the cow. It would be like a pet that I could ride and show off to my friends. I guess I did wonder how it could be only "half" a cow, but to a five-year-old that was a mere technicality that could easily be overlooked.

Just when I'd gotten all excited about my grandparents' new cow, I was informed that it wasn't a *live* cow, but rather was half of a dead one that had been purchased to be eaten. This was, of course, a major disappointment—after all, you can't ride a dead cow. But I still had morbid fascination at the thought. I remember opening my grandparents' freezer and expecting to see something resembling a large dismembered animal. Again I was disappointed. All the freezer contained were perhaps 100 packages, all carefully wrapped in white paper and tied with string.

Half-a-cow, I thought. Big deal. At least maybe I could save the string.

Real kids/fake foods

Several years ago some friends of mine lived in Loma Linda, California with their seven-year-old son. Loma Linda is the home of Loma Linda University, operated by the Seventh Day Adventist Church. Since the Church espouses vegetarianism, the town of Loma

Part Three: So, If I Actually Decide to Become a Vegetarian, Just What Can I Expect?

213

Linda has become somewhat of a Mecca for vegetarian foods. My friends are meat-eaters, but they were curious about the diet of so many of their neighbors. One day they decided to go whole hog (to use an especially inappropriate phrase) in making a vegetarian dinner. They went to the local health food store and bought a selection of meats without the meat, ice cream without the cream, etc., and then came home and put together a vegan version of their standard dinner.

After eating they asked their son how the fake versions of some of his favorite foods compared with the real thing. "Pretty good," he said, "...but was the cauliflower fake too?"

Are you sure that's what you mean???

One night at dinner the six-year-old nephew of a friend of mine announced that he had decided it wasn't right to eat meat, and that he was going to change his diet.

"That's right," he said to his parents. "From now on I'm only eating vegetarians."

Things to think about #4096

Eating animal products is the *only* thing we both:
1. encourage our kids to do, and
2. shield them from knowing the details and consequences of.

Pets (a/k/a companion animals)

What to feed your pet

Every morning millions of vegetarians around the world get out of bed, poke at their faces in the mirror, and are suddenly overcome by the question, "What do I feed my cat?" No, actually it's more agonizing than that. It's more like, "WHAT DO I FEED MY CAT??!!??"

For meat-eaters the answer to this question is easy. "Fluffy Feast," they'll tell you. The only question is "canned" or "dried". For vegetarians, though, it's a whole different story. We go through life priding ourselves on the fact that animals don't have to suffer for our food. How then can we justify keeping the slaughterhouses open just so we can feed our "companion animals"?

Vegetarians deal with this dilemma in many different ways. Some claim that their pets are perfectly happy on a vegetarian diet. (Usually easier for dogs than for cats, who will require taurine supplements to their food.) Others claim that their animal buddies are natural carnivores (especially cats) and that feeding them anything but meat is unnatural and cruel. (Just the opposite of humans!)

In some cases, the cute little animal buddies themselves make the decision:

Vegetarian Human: "Scooter, you've been such a good little kitty, I've made you a nice bowl of gruel."

Scooter *[baring teeth, claws extended three inches into human's neck]*: "Give me meat, you moron, or I take out your thyroid right here!"

Vegetarians who end up feeding meat to their pets often feel guilty. Even more often they copy meat-eaters by exercising a good deal of denial and rationalization. In an effort to ameliorate this situation, I offer the following suggestions for guilt-free (well, not really) ways to feed your pet.

1. Road kill

Every community has its own "Road Kill Café". Yes, that 3-mile strip of U.S. 47 that runs between the dump and the woods serves up a bounty of deceased small animals every day. There's really not much you can do to save these unfortunate creatures, so you may as well use their poor, lifeless bodies to nourish your dog Boris. And what pet *wouldn't* enjoy a succulent (albeit bruised) loin of squirrel or possum? Mmmm! Make sure your rabies shots are up to date, Boris. And careful to eat around the tire tracks.

2. Animals you don't have to kill to eat

Delicacies that fall into this category are Rocky Mountain Oysters (if you have to ask, you don't want to know) and stone crab claws (the fisherpersons tear the claws off the live crabs, and they supposedly grow back to be harvested again). Occasionally meat-eaters suggest that these things should be great fare for us "ethical" vegetarians. Sure. Anyway, if you are willing to pay big bucks for these "foods", your pet should be happy.

3. Carnivorous fishes

Ben Franklin was supposedly darned close to being a vegetarian. The only exception he'd make was to eat carnivorous fish. That way

Part Three: So, If I Actually Decide to Become a Vegetarian, Just What Can I Expect?

215

he figured that with every meal he was saving the lives of lots of other little fishes.

You could use this same questionable reasoning and decide to feed carnivorous fishes to your cat Sandy Claws. On the other hand, using this reasoning an ethical vegetarian might decide to *eat* Sandy Claws!

4. Surgery

They say that surgeons are a pet's best friend (sung to the tune of "Diamonds Are a Girl's Best Friend"), and with good reason. What cat or dog could resist a juicy appendix or spleen, still warm from the body cavity? Yes, your pet will dance for joy when you make the trip to the old bio-waste cans behind Memorial General part of your daily routine.

Well, there you have it—a series of suggestions sure to please any cat, dog, or other carnivorous friend, non-human or human. To show you his gratitude we're sure little Morris will want to jump up on your lap and contentedly purr...just before he shreds your sofa.

Cats are strange

I love cats. You love cats. Everyone loves cats—everyone, that is, except all those people who *hate* cats.

Yes, the relationship between cats and human beings is ambivalent to say the least. **At our best** we dote on them as pets, buy them expensive food in little cans, and even freeze dry them when they die so we can keep them around. **At our worst** we curse their shedding, let them live overpopulated and homeless on the streets of our cities, and worse. But more about that later.

Perhaps one reason for the love/hate relationship we have with cats is that they're smart enough that we can attribute all kinds of human traits to them, but inevitably, since they're cats, they let us down. Imagine, for example, that you've just brought home a new electronic gadget, and your cats gather around to watch you unpack it.

"It's got dual power supplies and discreet circuitry," you tell them, taking the gadget out of the box and proudly holding it up. The cats really don't care about that, of course. What *does* fascinate them, though, is the plastic wrapping and the box half filled with Styrofoam peanuts.

Oh cats. Even though they bathe all the time, they're always covered with cat hair. And they have such strange taste in food. Every time our cats bring some poor bird home in their mouths we are reminded that these are vicious carnivores. **If they were our size and we were their size they would eat us.**

Back to the wild!, you might think. How can we humans ever expect to get along with heathens who prefer catnip to watercress, cottage cheese to truffles?

"Care for a glass of Bordeaux?" you ask. "Perhaps a '61 Chateau Haut Brion?"

"Not interested," replies the cat. "But if you don't mind, I *would* like to bat the cork around the kitchen floor."

I suppose one reason cats were originally domesticated was precisely *because* they don't enjoy the same foods humans do. That way they could be trusted to protect the stores of grain from rodents. We've come a long way since then. Cats still have an economic value to humans, but in a much more hideous way—as laboratory animals for medical experimentation.

Someone, it seems, came up with the notion that cats' brains are very similar to human brains in the way they function. That has led to a plethora of gruesome experiments in which living cats' heads are opened up and electrodes are implanted in their brains.

The thought of all this is repulsive beyond belief, but it also makes me doubt the wisdom of these "researchers". I mean, just how much can they expect to learn from studying the brains of animals who think it's fun to chew on houseplants and then systematically throw up on the carpet in five different rooms?

Sure cats and humans have some similarities, but we know what those similarities are without the grisly research: along with all the other animals of the Earth, we share an innate need for physical and emotional comfort, freedom, dignity and peace.

Cats are strange, all right. And humans are even stranger.

They eat dogs, don't they?

(...or, dog food—Korean style)

When the Olympics were held in Seoul, South Korea in 1988 there was a big effort to suppress the local dog restaurants for a couple of weeks. The South Korean government figured (and they were certainly right) that caged dogs in the back of restaurants waiting to be woked might offend some Western sensibilities and make the country look bad.

Part Three: So, If I Actually Decide to Become a Vegetarian,
Just What Can I Expect?

217

How come???

1. **Dogs are very smart and cute, and to eat them would be wrong.**

No, this can't be the answer, because pigs are just as smart and cute and we eat them.

2. **Dogs are affectionate pets whom we admire on TV with June Lockhart, and with whom little children bond. We therefore treat them well.**

This can't be the answer either, because, even though we don't eat them, we do hideous medical and military experiments on dogs, and put them to death by the thousands in our laboratories and dog pounds.

3. **Little children don't know about pigs because there isn't a live one in the house, and they don't know what happens in the laboratories. If we had dogs on our dinner plates they'd start asking embarrassing questions.**

Bingo.

**If cats were our size and
we were their size (p. 216)**

Chapter 6

A vegetarian for the holidays

There's Columbus Day, Arbor Day, and Groundhog Day. And every Thursday in my neighborhood it's Garbage Day. Yes, there's a holiday for everyone— even vegetarians!

Let's say it's the holiday season (Thanksgiving, Christmas, Hanukkah, New Year's, whatever) and you're a vegetarian. There is no in-between. You're either going to have:

1. A miserable time during which you'll starve and feel like a social outcast, or

2. The best holiday ever.

The difference, like so many other things in your life, will depend on one factor: **whether you have control of the food.**

The food, you say?

Yes, the food. For most folks holidays center around food, and food centers around dead birds and/or other animals in the center of the dining room table, This is bad news for vegetarians. Holidays also center around *tradition*, which means everyone is likely to get all out of joint at even the *suggestion* of doing something differently. This is more bad news for vegetarians.

So the end result of all of this is that if you leave the holiday food to somebody else, you, the conscientious vegetarian, are going to be left with precious little to eat. You're also going to feel like a total dork when everyone else is wolfing down a turkey and stuffing, and Uncle Ralph is giving you the evil eyeball because you're sitting there at the table with a plate of peas.

Fortunately, there's an easy way around this problem. That's right, all you have to do is take control of the food. With just a little effort (a lot *less* effort than stuffing and cooking some poor bird) you can whip up your family's **very traditional holiday meal**, and you can make it **totally vegan**. What's more, *everyone's going to love it*—even Uncle Ralph.

A vegan turkey???

Okay, so you can't make a vegan turkey. But you can come up with a main dish just as tasty and just as festive. As for everything else—well those deadbeat, meat-eating relatives of yours probably won't even know the difference. And if they do, it's because your vegan feast will be *even better* than what they're used to.

Here's your menu:

● **Seitan Roast**— Proudly starring in the leading role of the turkey is a huge seitan roast. Just boil up a big chunk of seitan using the directions on the mix. When it's done, brush it with olive oil, and bake to a golden brown. The kids will "ooh" and "aah" when it comes out of the oven, and Aunt Sue will take pictures. Just for show you'll put it on the carving board (the one with the spikes and the blood trough) and let Uncle Ralph "do the honors".

● **Stuffing**— Read the ingredients on the stuffing mixes at the store 'til you find one that's vegan. (Many, for some unknown reason, have whey in them.) Then make it with olive oil, sautéed onions, celery, garlic, fresh sage, parsley, and your favorite nuts.

● **Mashed Potatoes**— You can't live without these. Whip them up smooth with soy milk, olive oil and/or margarine. Leave the skins on for more flavor, color and nutrition.

● **Gravy**— Make it from a quick mix available at your friendly, neighborhood health food store, or from scratch using a recipe from your favorite vegetarian cookbook. Be sure to add onions and a little sherry.

● **Roasted Vegetables**— Cook them in a hot oven, keeping them moist with a mixture of water, olive oil, wine, miso, seasoned vinegar, garlic, and your favorite spices.

● **Cranberry Sauce**— Out of the can or made from scratch. (I make mine using whole cranberries, cardamom seeds, lemon peel, etc. A dash of Triple Sec adds a nice touch too.)

● **Pumpkin Pie**— You'll follow the traditional recipe on the can, but you'll use soy milk and egg replacer instead of those bizarre dairy ingredients. A dollop of almond or pecan butter mixed in will give it a special flavor and richness. Make the crust whole wheat, with soy milk and oil.

Part Three: So, If I Actually Decide to Become a Vegetarian, Just What Can I Expect?

221

Well, there you have it—your basic totally vegan holiday meal. It's ultra-traditional, with just a couple of special touches to make it interesting. This is a holiday meal the most jaded meat-eater is sure to love, even if it does have less fat, more fiber and scads better nutrition than what they're used to (not to mention no cholesterol!).

So, how come this is going to be the best holiday ever?

Everybody learns something when the traditional holiday meal goes vegetarian. Here's what your family just might learn.

● **Vegetarian food can be very festive.** And tasty and filling too! People will still be rolling on the floor and moaning after dinner—just like they did when you were serving meat.

● **A dead animal doesn't make the holiday.** What's important is not what kind of dead animal is on the table. Rather, it's the opportunity to be together to share love and fellowship.

● **Vegetarians like football, just like other folks.** (Well, you have to do *something* after dinner.)

● **Guilt doesn't have to come to the party.** No one will have to look at a dead turkey or other animal on the table and feel sorry, ever again.

● **Violence doesn't have to come to the party.** Admit it now. You've always been aware of the irony involved in giving thanks for the bounty of life by taking life away from another. You've always been aware of a certain inconsistency in violently killing an animal and then drinking a toast to "Peace On Earth" over its dead body.

● **Your kids will have better traditions.** When I was a kid the thought that we invariably killed an animal for our Thanksgiving and other holiday celebrations was always in the back of my mind, always making a joyous occasion just a little less so. It doesn't have to be that way. When there's no killing and no guilt, your kids will have something *better* to build upon. Along with all the other holiday traditions, now there will be something new—a message of reverence for the Earth and for all of its life—that is part of the holiday celebration itself and can be passed from generation to generation.

How could your holidays be better than that?

Something to remember,
the last Thursday in November:

"Turkeys give thanks for vegetarians!"

Chapter 7

Moving beyond vegetarianism

*Warning! This is the part about how vegetarianism
just might affect lots of other stuff you do in life.*

There's an old Chinese proverb that tells us that happiness is a *journey*, not a destination. Think of vegetarianism the same way. It's a rare person who makes the transition to vegetarianism and then stays the same the rest of his or her life. Rather, once you take that fateful step and hang around town as a vegetarian you'll find yourself learning more every day, and you'll find your perspective on things—even the everyday things you've always taken for granted—changing. It's kind of like being on mind-altering drugs, only better. Legal too.

Your health and the environment

Just by becoming a vegetarian you'll be taking a huge step to improve your health and the health of the Earth. But when this much progress comes so easily, it's only natural to sit up and take notice. *Gosh, Darn!* you'll say to yourself. *That was great! What else can I do?*

This is where the journey part comes in. While it's certainly not mandatory to keep their membership cards, most vegetarians find that they develop life-long interests in learning more about maintaining their health and maintaining the environment. They eat salads, they recycle. Beware—this could happen to you.

Animal rights

The transition to vegetarianism makes most people aware of other animal rights issues too. Since these issues are *so* important to *so many* vegetarians, the rest of this chapter will be devoted to them.

223

So, why are vegetarianism and other animal rights issues related?
Two reasons:

Mindset...

Remember when I said earlier that eating animals is the A#1,
super-primo, meanest thing we humans do to them? Well that's true.
But the very fact that we're willing to go so far as to *eat* animals makes
all the other mean, exploitive things we can think of seem very reasonable in comparison. On the other hand, once we vegetarians say
Enough already! I'm not going to eat these creatures anymore!, then
we are in a frame of mind to consider what else we might be doing
that's mean, and question whether we really wouldn't feel better if we
stopped doing those things as well.

So, it's a question of *mindset.* **The mindset for eating meat is one
of animal exploitation; the mindset for vegetarianism is one of animal liberation.**

> **Remember this:** The people who hunt, and the peo-
> ple who test their cosmetics in rabbits' eyes, and the
> people who club baby seals to death for fur coats all
> want you to keep eating meat. It gives them some-
> thing to point to if you ever question their actions.

...and money

There's another way that meat-eating and other forms of animal
exploitation are often related too—economically. The dairy farmer
needs the extra profit he gets from selling baby calves to the "veal"
folks. In turn, the "veal" folks need the extra profit they get from selling "calfskin" to the leather folks. You get the idea.

With that being said, let's look at some of the animal rights issues
that are on most vegetarians' minds.

not nice things we do to animals #1...

A saga of cowskins, shoes and sofas

There comes a time in every vegetarian's life when he or she has
to think about leather. I resisted this little discussion with myself
for a long time, rationalizing that when I die I'll be happy if my fami-

Part Three: So, If I Actually Decide to Become a Vegetarian,
Just What Can I Expect?

225

ly, friends and undertakers make a nice pair of shoes or a sofa out of what's left. It's meat that causes the killing, I reasoned, and once the cow's dead, leather is a benign industry.

Of course this isn't true. Leather is right there with the meat and dairy industries, helping to expand the dead animal market and make the whole bizarre scene profitable. All of this finally sunk into my cone-shaped head, and I eventually got the message that wearing the remains of dead carcasses on our bodies isn't much to be proud of. It's a visible statement to the world of our beliefs.

How vegetarians cover their feet

I remember when I bought my first pair of non-leather dress shoes. They were unstylish things, made out of some kind of vinyl that went from black to a milky color when they were flexed. These shoes were also quite shiny when they were new, as plastic tends to be.

The people at work showed me no mercy.

"New shoes? They look like something you wore to the prom."

"They look like something you'd see on a dead body at the funeral home."

People were wearing sunglasses to protect themselves from the glare.

I was actually *proud* of those shoes. They were so uncomfortable (warm in the summer, cool in the winter, etc.) and so ugly they always reminded me of the sacrifices I was making for my principles. My feet sweated. I got blisters. Young children and their pets and dolls laughed at me. It was like a scene from *Buster Brown in Hell*. If I'd been any more proud my feet would have fallen off.

Non-leather dress shoes have come a long way since then. The modern ones look virtually identical to their leather counterparts. They're stylish, durable, they breathe, and best of all they're cheap. Really, I'm not kidding.

One pair of non-leather shoes I bought looked just like those fancy Italian calfskin jobs, with all the special tooling and little doo-dads. (Well, they *are* imported, just not from Italy.) I knew I was on to something when I wore them into the office and people noticed them and actually thought they were nice. My friend Dave, who's a commercial real estate broker and dresses really well, cornered me one day:

"Hey, I bet those are Allen-Edmonds shoes, aren't they?" *[Note: commercial names may be altered slightly to avoid lawsuits.]*

"No," I answered.

"Well, I was going to tell you, if you like Allen-Edmonds, I've got this catalog where you can get great discounts. They're usually over $200 a pair, you know."

"Yeah..." I pretended I was thinking about it. "But I got these at the mall for $17.99."

"*What?*"

"They're plastic, Dave. I'll get you a pair if you like."

Dave didn't say a whole lot about my shoes after that.

I had another experience in the men's room at the Chicago airport. I was washing my hands, and the guy at the shoe shine stand looked decidedly *un*busy.

"Shine?" he asked.

"No thanks," I said. "They're plastic."

"Huh?"

"Plastic."

He shook his head.

"The shoes are plastic, man. You don't shine 'em, you just hose 'em off."

These advanced generation non-leather shoes are the greatest things since pneumatic tires. Not only are they cheap to buy and practically maintenance-free, but when you can fool the shoe shine guys in Chicago, you know you've got a winner.

Tips for jocks #27

Lots of running and athletic shoes are now being made with synthetic leathers and suedes. These materials are light, strong, and durable. (From personal experience I can attest to the fact that the soles of the shoes will wear out before these fabrics will.) Look for them.

Where do you go for non-leather shoes and accessories?

Discount stores are always a good bet. But for higher quality and an even better selection of shoes, belts, purses, wallets, etc. there are specialty stores and catalogs that cater to vegetarians.

Part Three: So, If I Actually Decide to Become a Vegetarian, Just What Can I Expect?

227

What's another option for belts?

I go to the department stores where they have their selection of inexpensive (a/k/a, "cheap") dress pants. A lot of these pants come complete with color coordinated belts which, it just so happens, are always made out of plastic.

These pants/belts combinations are intended for those of us with no discernible taste in clothing—those of us who always relied on our mothers to make sure we matched. They're high on the old hokey scale. That's okay with me though. I'm not proud. I can get a belt for just the right price and, what the heck, they throw in the pants for free.

Leather jackets...

- Are not particularly warm.
- Are not particularly comfortable.
- Are not particularly good in rain and snow.
- Are worn to make a fashion statement.

What is that fashion statement?

not nice things we do to animals #2...

Wearing furs

The world has come a long way since Fred Flintstone

- Things made out of animal fur are (pick several):
  1. Warm
  2. Soft
  3. Comfortable
  4. Pretty
- Ironically, these adjectives are the *very antithesis* of what went into making these things from the bodies of living creatures (pick four):
  1. Violence
  2. Cruelty
  3. Pain
  4. Gore

Long ago there was a time when owning a fur meant a woman had arrived. She was successful or (sadly, more often) the man in her life was successful. There was a time when a woman could wear a fur and not realize the animal cruelty that went into it.

That time has now passed. For many years now we've been inundated with scads (and double scads) of publicity about fur (anti-fur demonstrations, pictures of animals in leghold traps, fur store "going-out-of-business" sales, etc.). These days any woman (or man) this side of Mars who has an IQ larger than her or his shoe size and who continues to wear fur has a reason—a reason that goes well beyond wanting a comfortable coat, or even showing the world how rich she or he is.

> **Wearing fur is now a statement. It says: "I want the world to know that I don't care about these creatures—that their worst pain is not as important to me as my ego."**

Just like any other situation where an individual has to show superiority, domination and/or control over someone else in order to raise him or herself up (racism, child abuse, kicking a dog), wearing fur is the product of insecurity and lack of self esteem.

But wait! The fur in my coat was raised on a farm. (And anyway, didn't Liberace once say that minks were such disgusting creatures they deserved to be made into coats?)

This reminds me of the perhaps true story of the businessmen from the Soviet Union who, many years ago when their country was still open for business, came to the United States to study American agriculture. They were visiting a pet food company and were shown a room filled with cats who were being used to taste test the company's new food formulas. The Americans were very proud of their research in this area, and the Soviets were very impressed. One of them went up to his American host and said, "This is great, but we have just one question...What do you do with the pelts?"

This also reminds me of the totally fallacious story of my Uncle Harry and his "cat and rat" farm. The idea was that he would feed the rats to the cats, skin the cats and sell the pelts, and then grind up what was left of the cats and feed it back to the rats. It was a veritable perpetual motion machine, and my fictitious Uncle Harry got very rich.

All this aside, to say that "my fur is okay because it was raised on a farm" is only big time rationalization. All it means is that, instead of dying a slow painful death in a leghold trap, the animals in your coat never even had the chance to live in the wild. Instead, they led a very short, very miserable life crowded onto a "farm", and were killed, at a very young age, by an electrical shock to the one place on their bodies where the fur wouldn't be damaged. (This is a family book, so I won't go into detail.)

This isn't something you would do personally, is it? Then why would you pay someone else to do it?

> "Killing an animal to make a coat is a sin. It wasn't meant to be, and we have no right doing it. A [person] gains status when she refuses to see anything killed to be put on her back."
> —**Doris Day** (obviously many years after she starred in *That Touch of Mink*)

Technical Note: Killing other creatures and wearing their skins isn't the worst thing we do to animals. (It doesn't even come close to meat-eating in that regard.) But it just may be the worst *symbol* of how we treat animals.

> "Fur looks great on the original owner, and terrible on everyone else."
> —**Susan Zimmerman**
>
> "Custom will reconcile people to any atrocity; and fashion will drive them to acquire any custom."
> —**George Bernard Shaw**

not nice things we do to animals #3...

Animal testing

(No, this has nothing to do with seeing if the animals work.)

E veryone has heard the joke that we shouldn't test on animals because they get nervous and give the wrong answers. For most vegetarians, though, using animals for the "advancement of science" is serious stuff. It's the biggest animal rights issue next to eating meat.

Here's the critical question: Should we as a society experiment on animals:

1. with abandon,
2. only to the extent "necessary", or
3. not at all?

The way that we, as a culture, have answered this question so far (option #1) reveals much about our weaknesses and much about our selfishness—traits we humans don't like to admit.

Vivisection

I first heard the word as a young child when I saw an advertisement for an anti-vivisection group. I remember asking my mother what vivisection was, and why there was an organization against it. The answer—the dissection of animals while still alive—horrified me. I just couldn't imagine that anyone would do such a thing. I still can't.

The word "vivisection" has come a long way since its origins. It is now synonymous with a rogue's gallery of gruesome practices perpetrated on tens of millions of animals each year in medical laboratories, schools, and military installations around the world—not to mention the back rooms of your local consumer products or cosmetics company. Most of the victims of animal "research" are rats and mice—animals that don't garner much of the sympathy vote. But of course, there are many thousands of dogs, cats and non-human primates (about 50,000 primates each year in the United States) mixed in for good measure.

Why we need animal testing.

Proponents of animal testing tell us that the practice is necessary to advance medicine and science for the betterment of humans *and* animals, and to make sure that the products we use every day are safe.

Part Three: So, If I Actually Decide to Become a Vegetarian,
Just What Can I Expect?

231

They point to advances like the polio vaccine that, they claim, could only have been developed in conjunction with animal testing. They tell us that, while they are improving the welfare of laboratory animals and working diligently to reduce animal testing to the extent possible, the elimination of animal testing entirely would be a huge step backwards for both science and human welfare.

Why we don't need animal testing.

Opponents of animal testing tell us that there are alternatives that make animal testing obsolete. These include:
- "In-vitro" testing on cell cultures rather than live animals;
- The use of microorganisms rather than larger animals for certain toxicity tests (*i.e.,* who could love an ameba-230?);
- Computer simulation of chemical reactions and organic systems;
- Better data collection and distribution systems that can at least eliminate redundant testing.

They point to the many products on the market that command a premium price by proudly advertising the fact that they were not tested on animals.

Opponents of animal testing also promote the fact that animals are different from human beings in significant ways, and that the use of procedures and results from animal tests on human beings can have disastrous results. They point to drugs like DES and thalidomide, and to silicone for breast implants (all of which tested safe in animals) as examples of this. They note that HIV—the AIDS virus—may well have been spread to human beings as a result of animal testing.

So, what's *really* wrong with animal testing?

Arguing over whether animal tests are ultimately beneficial or detrimental to humankind misses the point. Both sides seem to agree that causing animal suffering is wrong. Where they disagree is on the question of *whether the ends justify the means.*

When anti-vivisectionists tell us that we can't learn anything from animal testing they are wrong. If only to the extent that animal testing tells us more about animals—how they function, how they react to outside stimuli, how they die—it serves to advance human knowledge, for whatever that is worth. Perhaps the knowledge we gain is substantial. Maybe so. But the problem lies in the tremendous *price* we pay for that knowledge. The price is of course paid by the unimaginable suffering of those killed, and by the grief that many of us humans feel. More than anything, perhaps, the price is paid by the *compromise to human morality* that is required.

> **If supposedly good ends justify what everyone agrees are bad means, what other atrocities are we prepared to condone in the quest for "scientific" knowledge?**

If we can learn a lot about human disease, for example, by testing on animals, certainly we can learn *even more* by testing on humans. *Lots* more. We could use the aged, the retarded, people in prison or others who, just like animals, are in no position to object. There is no doubt that we could speed up the pace of medical progress dramatically, perhaps saving countless lives. **If we could save the lives of three million children by sacrificing 30 children in the laboratory, wouldn't that be worth it?**

As a society we answer this question "no", not because of a cost-benefit analysis of the ends vs. the means, but because we consider it immoral to experiment on children, *whatever* the possible benefit.

One could say the same thing about testing on animals. Consider this proposition: Experimenting on animals isn't worth it. It's a bad deal for all of us. The knowledge it gives us (that we couldn't get from other sources) is *paltry* compared to the degradation of the human species that results from our moral compromise and our selfish behavior. Just as with experimenting on children, it shouldn't be an option a civilized society would even consider. We can find better ways to make our products safe and to further medicine and science.

My friend Peter Cohn sums it up the best when he says that **animal testing may advance human knowledge, but it does so at the expense of human character.**

Yeah, this certainly makes sense #27

In the United States we kill sixty to ninety thousand animals a day in our research laboratories. A *large* part of this is for medical research on diseases that are caused or aggravated by eating the fifteen thousand animals a *minute* we kill in our slaughterhouses. Is something wrong here? Might we be better off if we eliminated the killing altogether?

Part Three: So, If I Actually Decide to Become a Vegetarian,
Just What Can I Expect?

233

Things we don't understand about floorwax

There are lots of cosmetic and consumer products companies that test on animals, right? Sure, many of the biggest companies in the business, with products you see at your local store every day. Well, if these companies *really* believe what they are doing is ethical, and *really* believe animal testing makes their products safer and better, shouldn't they advertise the fact? Shouldn't they jump at the chance to proclaim it on their product labels? Something like: "For your protection Philmont Products proudly tests Squeekie-Kleen on laboratory rats!" But we never see labels like this. Instead companies seem to want to cover up their actions, as if they feel they have something to hide. How come?

"Animal rights extremists"?

"I think it's extreme to torture and kill something. I don't think it's extreme to be against it."
—Susan Zimmerman

Perhaps the term should be "animal experimentation extremists"?

"I abhor vivisection. It should at least be curbed. Better, it should be abolished. I know of no achievement through vivisection, no scientific discovery, that could not have been obtained without such barbarism and cruelty. The whole thing is evil."
— Dr. Charles Mayo, founder of the Mayo Clinic

---

not nice things we do to animals #4...

Hunting: hunters and vegetarians getting along?!

This is where I have the opportunity to say how we vegetarians think hunting and hunters are disgusting. Well, I'll take half of that opportunity. Ethical vegetarians obviously feel that hunting is a vicious and cruel practice. (Killing an animal may provide an adrenaline rush, or temporarily boost a fragile ego, but that doesn't come close to making it a "sport".) And there are certainly plenty of times when hunters and vegetarians disagree vehemently when it comes to personal lifestyle, social and political policies and whom their daughters should marry. But that doesn't mean that your average vegetarian can't get along just fine with your average hunter (or at least the one who isn't thrilled by picking off prairie dogs with a bunch of drunken guys in the back of a pickup truck). As a matter of fact, **vegetarians often get along *better* with hunters than with other assorted flesh-eating folks.** Here are some reasons why:

● Even though they approach the subject from radically different perspectives, there is some genuine common ground between hunters and vegetarians when it comes to **respect for wildlife** and maintenance of wildlife habitats. (Neither group may admit it though!)

● Some vegetarians have grudging respect for the fact that hunters make a **conscious decision about what they are going to eat** and don't expect society to isolate them from the killing of their dinner.

● **Hunting is *far less cruel* than factory farming.** For the most part hunted animals have good lives until the time of their death. So, in a very real sense, **hunters who eat what they kill subject animals to *less* suffering than members of the general meat-eating public.** (If you are a meat-eater and you've ever criticized hunters as being less moral than yourself for shooting Bambi, think about this.)

● One would hope that most hunters have come to terms with what they do, and **they don't feel guilty** about meat-eating to the extent that non-hunters do. Therefore, they tend to be much **less defensive** than non-hunters in their dealings with vegetarians.

Before we get carried away with too much brotherly love and understanding, let's remember that no vegetarian is going to feel comfortable pumping lead into birds or gutting an elk, and it's going to be the rare hunter who gets excited about the latest brand of low-fat tofu to hit the supermarket. That's okay. Both groups can agree to view each other as being filled with strange, misguided souls.

not nice things we do to animals #5-3678...

Holy Smokes! There are so many other things too!

Now, I don't want to flog a dead horse here (to use the popular animal rights vernacular), but if you want to consider our society's track record with animals, then leather and furs and laboratories and hunting are only the beginning. Let's take a quick look.

Part Three: So, If I Actually Decide to Become a Vegetarian,
Just What Can I Expect?

235

Hey, so many "fun" things involve animals!

Think, for a moment, of all the things that humans do to animals for their own pleasure (that's the humans' pleasure, not the animals'). Sure, there are the obvious things like rodeos and bullfights. But think about sports, too. In a world with digital timers and instant replays on huge televisions, we still use old fashioned animal-skin balls and gloves. Then there are the myriad of "prank" and summer festival activities (frog jumping, greased pigs, roadside petting zoos, and the like). Pick up your local paper today and you're likely to read about one.

Living in a society where billions of animals are killed each year to give us pleasure at the dinner table, most of us haven't given these other things a second thought. Maybe we should start.

Hey, there are animals in everything *!*

The production of many of the products we use every day, unfortunately, involves animal cruelty. There's wool, silk (they boil the worms, you know), and down, of course, but it goes beyond that.

We as a society have gotten used to throwing animal products into just about everything. It's easy and cheap, and we do it without thinking. Unfortunately, it's also cruel, and the irony is that there are always non-animal alternatives readily available. Here are just a few of the places animal products may show up around your home:

- drug and vitamin capsule casings
- lipstick
- soap
- face cream
- nutritional supplements
- bone china
- cigarette papers
- stamp adhesives
- shampoo
- photographic film

Hey, you're saying, *this is just like Native Americans using the earlobes and toenails of buffaloes! It would be impossible to avoid everything that might involve cruelty or have an animal by-product in it!* Unfortunately, that's probably true. We vegetarians do what we can and hope for the best. We have to remember that what drives it all is the meat industry, and when that starts to go downhill it may provoke all these other industries to find some less gruesome ingredients for their products too.

Treat them like dogs

Ever notice that in many chronicles of human rights abuse there are often implicit references to the way we treat animals? Just consider how often phrases like "butcher", or "treated like dogs" come up. Perhaps when we ponder the sad way we treat our fellow human beings, we should also consider the way we treat animals. Is it right to "butcher" them and to treat them "like dogs"?

Maybe human rights abuses wouldn't be so prevalent in this world if we didn't have so many animal rights abuses to serve as our models.

> "The animals of the world exist for their own reasons. They were not made for humans any more than black people were made for white, or women created for men."
> —**Alice Walker** (author of *The Color Purple*)
>
> "Until he extends the circle of compassion to all living things, man will not himself find peace."
> —**Albert Schweitzer**

Chapter 8

The flesh-eating past and the vegetarian future

T his is it! The absolute *last* chapter of the *last* part of this book! I promise. If you're one of the three people who started at the beginning and has made it this far, I have just two things to say: congratulations, and hi Mom and Dad.

Uh-oh, you are thinking, *If this is the last chapter, that means I have to make a decision on whether to be a vegetarian real soon, huh?*

Yes, you do. Even if you stop reading right now and hide this book in the furnace room, you're going to have to decide.

I can't put it off for a few days, can I?

Sorry. Not to decide is to decide. Remember, if you just sit there and eat whatever Mom or your significant other puts in front of you, that's a decision, and it's *you* who has decided.

To help you in making this momentous choice, in this last chapter we're going to look forward to the bright and wonderful vegetarian future (imagine the sounds of birds singing here). Yes, it's true— our collective future, if indeed we are to *have* a future, is in vegetarianism. Every day, as new scientific discoveries are made about diet and our health, flesh-eating gets a little deader (pun intended) and vegetarianism makes more sense. Every day, as human empathy and justice evolves, flesh-eating gets a little deader and vegetarianism makes more sense. And every day, as our good old Earth gets a little more crowded, and feeding everyone without killing the planet becomes more of a priority, flesh-eating gets a little deader and vegetarianism makes more sense.

But before we look at how groovy the future will be, let's look at the past. Your past? Yeah, and long past too.

The role of tradition

Tradition is what gets us all misty-eyed when we think about our parents and grandparents, or the history of our favorite baseball team. It's the embodiment of our values, and the glue that holds our society together through the generations. Heck, it's the stuff Zero Mostel sang about in *Fiddler On The Roof!* With all that going for it, tradition must be pretty wonderful, right?

Well, most of the time. Unfortunately, **tradition is probably the biggest enemy to vegetarianism and many of the other sane things on this Earth!** Here's why...

We are all creatures of habit and will cling to things that are familiar, even if those things are nonsensical or conflict with other values we may have. It doesn't really matter how it all gets started. Just like an untrue rumor, *if an action is repeated often enough it develops a certain credibility.* With the glossy patina of age, it becomes "tradition".

Think of all the ridiculous things in our society that are perpetuated by tradition. Here are some examples:

● For years we have had a whole class of people called "cheerleaders" who go to sporting events in miniature pleated skirts, with funny things called "pompoms" on both hands.

● Women in our society regularly wear uncomfortable shoes with spiked heels, and paint their fingernails red and their eyelids blue.

● Men in our society wear odd paraphernalia called "ties", which appear to have no purpose other than constricting unimportant things like arteries and windpipes.

The reason for all this nonsense is unknown. But then again, **it doesn't need a reason—it's tradition.**

Along with the frivolous aspects of tradition are some pretty serious ones. It can be a convenient excuse used to justify otherwise unacceptable behavior. This is what I call the "my Daddy did it, and by golly I'm going to do it too" syndrome. Among the evils it's responsible for are bigotry, racism, sexism, and those fuzzy dice people hang from their rear-view mirrors.

Those of us who are vegetarians and who love animals often find the "my Daddy did it" syndrome particularly disconcerting. It is the rationalization for barbaric behavior all over the world, from shark's-fin soup in Asia, to genitally mutilating girls in Africa, to Thanksgiving turkey in North America. Tradition is the excuse given when all others fail to explain why sons of fishermen must continue to fish when populations of fishes are threatened or sons of loggers must continue to log when our forests are dwindling. Tradition justifies the ritualistic torture of animals as part of "religious" ceremonies in the Caribbean, and under the auspices of "bullfights" in Spain and Mexico.

Let's say it again, just for emphasis (yes, that would be the traditional thing to do):

If behavior cannot otherwise be justified, we defend it by saying it is "tradition".

Eating meat and dairy products is so *economically and environmentally wasteful,* so *unhealthy,* and so *downright unnatural* that its continued viability must in large part be due to tradition. Just like bigotry, racism and sexism, repetition over the years has given it a credibility that we vegetarians have barely been able to dent. That's too bad. Tradition should never be used as a source of comfort for those who cannot otherwise defend their actions to themselves or others.

Needed: more vegetarian traditions

A tradition like meat-eating seems so deeply rooted in our society that maybe the only way to fight it is with tradition itself. Maybe we vegetarians need to start some silly tradition of our own—like eating millet burgers on Groundhog Day, for example. If we did that for, say, 50 years, everyone would start to think it was the natural thing to do and would follow along. Of course, people will need to hear about it. It's tough to start a good tradition without lots of publicity. If we could just get some well known celebrities to join us that would help...Too bad Zero Mostel isn't available.

Hey, it's time to stop reliving the past. Let's look ahead for once!

The great vegetarian future

What would happen if tomorrow morning everyone on Earth decided to stop eating meat and other animal products?

Here are the bad things that would happen...

1. People would miss the taste of meat.

But not for long. Pretty soon they'd realize that the tastes and textures they liked about meat can be easily duplicated in the vegetarian world. And being vegetarian would expose them to a diversity of new foods they never knew existed. It wouldn't take long before most people would be repelled by even the thought of eating the animal flesh, cows' milk and chickens' eggs they once *thought* they couldn't give up. Folks would be as happy with their new vegetarian diets as...well, they'd be as happy as we vegetarians are right now! But then, that's one of the good things.

2. People associated with the meat industry would lose their jobs. So would many people in the health care and weight loss industries.

But not for long. With a hugely wasteful and destructive industry out of our economy, tremendous resources would be made available for more productive endeavors, and lots of people would be hired to fill new jobs. But then, that's one of the good things, too.

3. Sports would be less bizarre.

Since they wouldn't grow up on a fluid designed to add hundreds of pounds to a farm animal in its first year of life (cows' milk), and since they wouldn't stuff themselves with high-protein, high-fat foods, the next generation of basketball centers and offensive linemen might not be as huge (or as *offensive*). But on the other hand, with steaks off the training table and everyone eating a much healthier diet, we could expect the *overall* level of athletic competition in the world to increase significantly. Darn it, that's *another* good thing.

Here are some of the good things that would happen

1. People would get healthier.

With animal products out of their diets, people would find themselves eating healthier despite themselves—getting just the right amount of protein, dramatically less fat and more fiber. As a result, rates of diet related diseases (heart disease, many types of cancer, osteoporosis, diabetes, etc.) would fall off a cliff.

2. We'd spend less money on health care.

With a healthier population, the cost of medical care in the developed world would decline precipitously. The United States, for example, presently spends $800 billion a year on health care. If this declined by only an eighth (an outrageously conservative estimate given that some of our most costly diseases—eg cancer and heart disease—are meat related), we'd have an additional $100 billion every year to put into schools, housing, factories, bridges, and other more productive areas of our economy. Healthier people would be more productive people too!

3. We'd discover new foods.

Just think how exciting it would be to take all the great chefs in the world, unchain them from having to find new ways to fix the same old four foods over and over again, and let them use their creativity with the diversity that the vegetable kingdom has to offer. Yum! And with the inefficiencies of animal agriculture out of the way, just think how cheap those foods would be, too.

4. Obesity would be a rarity.

Less fat in means less fat on. There just aren't very many fat vegetarians in the world. All those people who thought they'd never lose weight would suddenly find that it's easy.

5. Our governments would save money.

National, state and local governments spend billions of dollars a year subsidizing animal agriculture. Programs to kill "varmints" and provide water, drainage, fencing, and topsoil conservation for ranchers could be eliminated or drastically scaled back. So could government purchases of dairy products (to artificially shore up prices) that end up going bad in government-funded warehouses. Again, all this money could be spent on schools, housing and factories, creating jobs and benefiting our economy.

6. We'd save resources.

Remember, feeding crops to farm animals is inherently inefficient—five to 12 times less efficient than feeding those crops directly to human beings. Animal agriculture is our biggest user of water and land, and meat-eating is the biggest threat to the health of our rain-forests and oceans. If it were to make a quick exit from our culture, not only could these things be saved, but we'd have more topsoil, more fossil fuels and lots more wildlife habitat to go around. We could raise more food too, so we don't have to decide who gets fed and who goes hungry.

7. We'd reduce pollution.

Huge sources of water, air and land pollution would magically vanish.

8. Our attitude toward animals would change.

If we stopped killing and exploiting animals for food, it just might make us think about the other nasty things we do to them. (Of course it would!) We'd certainly stop exploiting animals for their skin and fur. And then we might start to question the ethics in our laboratories and at some of our entertainment and sporting events. Eventually, we might just find ourselves with a whole new attitude of non-violence and respect toward our non-human friends. Not only would such a shift in thinking eliminate untold suffering, but it would help maintain the biodiversity of our planet and insure a better world for our children and grandchildren.

9. Our attitude toward people would change.

Just think what substituting non-violence for violence as an every-day part of our lives might accomplish. Remember:

Human rights is just a subset of animal rights.

If we aren't willing to kill and exploit animals, we won't be willing to kill and exploit people either, will we? It just makes sense. And when we start giving animals—the lowest members of our social totem pole—more respect, we can't help but give our fellow human beings more respect as well. Does this mean no more war, no more discrimination, and a new generation of children being brought up to believe the Golden Rule is actually something to live by? Maybe.

Imagine you win a contest and you get to be God for a day...(Wow, what luck! How come *I* never get to be God?) After you indulge your

Part Three: So, If I Actually Decide to Become a Vegetarian,
Just What Can I Expect?

243

fantasies with that hot number and the red Ferrari (or maybe Tom Cruise on a tropical island) and you get down to work, isn't this the kind of world you'd create?

If everyone on Earth decided to stop eating meat and animal products tomorrow morning it wouldn't solve all the problems of the world. There would still be plenty to go around. But it *would* result in some pretty amazing changes on this old planet of ours. Take another look at the list above and really think about it. What other change in human behavior as simple and painless as changing what we buy in the supermarket could produce such a wonderful cost/benefit ratio for our Earth and its inhabitants?

A vegetarian world

If you think a vegetarian world might be a nice place to live in, there's bad news and good news. The bad news is that it isn't likely to happen in our lifetimes. The good news is that it will happen one day. That's right, it will—assuming we don't all destroy each other in the interim. We humans are pretty amazing creatures. Harry S. Truman once said, "the combined thought and action of the whole people of any race, creed or nationality, will always point in the right direction." Given all the facts and the opportunity to make some mistakes along the way, we'll eventually come to the right choice every time. And there's no doubt that vegetarianism is the right choice.

If you like the idea of vegetarianism there's more good news too. You don't have to wait for everyone else. Every time you sit down for a meal you can get the benefits of vegetarianism for yourself, and you can give those benefits to the animals and human beings and the natural environment of the Earth around you. This isn't just theoretical—it's something you can measure every time you eat.

Sure, it sounds corny to say that every individual act makes a difference, but I'll say it anyway. There is a story of a beach littered with starfish and a man who was throwing them back into the sea. Someone came up to him and questioned what he was doing, saying, "there are thousands of them, how can your meager actions possibly make any difference?" The man smiled, and as he picked up another starfish to throw it back into the ocean he said, "It makes a difference to this one."

So it is with the food on your plate. So it is with vegetarianism.

Time for a decision

In the end, then, vegetarianism is at the same time a very social thing and a very personal thing. It's a physically and spiritually linked network of individuals with a vision of a better world, but it all depends on individual behavior.

That's where you come in. Now it's time for *you* to decide.

But this is an easy decision! Of course I want to be a vegetarian!

Really?

Sure! Where do I sign up?

Well, congratulations and welcome! There will be someone by this afternoon to deliver your special certificate and teach you the secret handshake. (You can send your dues—$1,000 in small, unmarked bills—directly to me.)

Seriously, isn't it nice to have the decision behind you? Wasn't it **a lot easier** than you ever imagined? Isn't it great **not to have to worry** quite as much about all the things meat-eaters worry about? Aren't the **Three Great Reasons to be a vegetarian** really terrific? Don't you **feel good** about yourself and the world around you?

Do one more thing for me.... Now that you're a vegetarian you have to start taking advantage. Tonight, gather up the people you really love and treat yourself to a huge, no-holds-barred, gourmet vegetarian meal. Whether you go out or fix it yourself, don't be shy about the food—stuff yourself to the gills (remember, you can do that now). Then, when the evening gets mellow, take a glass of whatever beverage you prefer and drink a toast (heck, drink *several* toasts) to the new vegetarian you. You deserve it. Life just got a lot better.

SOME VEGETARIAN RESOURCES

M y editor warned me that no self-respecting reader will take anything *I* have to say seriously, and that I'd better lead you to the people who *really* know what they're talking about. That's okay with me! Finishing this book should just be the beginning anyway. There are gazillions of other books out there about vegetarianism, health and animal rights, gazillions of Internet pages to visit, and gazillions of wonderful people in wonderful organizations who can give you support and information.

At the risk of being out of date in the next three minutes, here are some resources I used in writing this book, along with a few other items of interest. If you want to, you can make a whole career out of learning about vegetarianism. Good luck!

Vegetarian Books

General
Akers, Keith. *Vegetarian Sourcebook: The Nutrition, Ecology and Ethics of a Natural Foods Diet.* Denver: Vegetarian Press, 1993.

Lappé, Frances Moore. *Diet for a Small Planet/20th Anniversary Edition.* New York: Ballantine, 1992.

Marcus, Erik. *Vegan: A New Ethics of Eating.* Ithaca, NY: McBooks, 1997.

Robbins, John. *Diet for a New America.* Walpole, NH: Stillpoint Publishing, 1987.

Wasserman, Debra and Mangels, Reed. *Vegan Handbook.* Baltimore: Vegetarian Resource Group, 1996.

Vegetarianism and Health
Barnard, Neal D. *Food for Life: How the New Four Food Groups Can Save Your Life.* New York: Crown, 1994.

Diamond, Harvey. *Fit for Life.* New York: Warner, 1987.

Diamond, Harvey and Diamond, Marilyn. *Living Health.* New York: Warner, 1987.

Eisman, George. *A Basic Course In Vegetarian and Vegan Nutrition.* Burdett, NY: Diet-Ethics Publishers, 1993.

Elliot, Rose. *Vegetarian Mother & Baby Book.* New York: Pantheon, 1986.

Klaper, Michael. *Pregnancy, Children and the Vegan Diet.* Paia, Maui Hawaii: Gentle World, 1988

Klaper, Michael. *Vegan Nutrition: Pure and Simple.* Paia, Maui, Hawaii: Gentle World, 1987.

McDougall, John A. and McDougall, Mary A. *The McDougall Plan.* Piscataway, NJ: New Century, 1983.

Ornish, Dean. *Dr. Dean Ornish's Program for Reversing Heart Disease: The Only System Scientifically Proven to Reverse Heart Disease Without Drugs or Surgery.* New York: Ivy, 1996.

Vegetarianism and Philosophy

Adams, Carol J. *The Sexual Politics of Meat: A Feminist-Vegetarian Critical Theory.* New York: Continuum, 1990.

Adams, Carol J. *Neither Man nor Beast: Feminism and the Defense of Animals.* New York: Continuum, 1994.

Aronson, Kristin. *To Eat Flesh They Are Willing, Are Their Spirits Weak?.* New York: Pythagorean, 1996.

Berry, Rynn. *Famous Vegetarians and Their Favorite Recipes.* New York: Pythagorean, 1995.

Berry, Rynn. *Food for the Gods: Vegetarianism and the World's Religions.* New York: Pythagorean, 1998.

Clark, Stephen R. L. *Animals and Their Moral Standing.* New York: Routledge, 1997.

Fiddes, Nick. *Meat: A Natural Symbol.* New York: Routledge, 1991.

Linzey, Andrew. *Animal Theology.* Urbana: U. Illinois, 1995.

Mason, Jim. *An Unnatural Order.* New York: Continuum, 1993.

Noske, Barbara. *Beyond Boundaries: Animals and Humans.* Montreal: Black Rose Books, 1997.

Patterson, Charles. *Animal Rights.* Hillside, NJ: Eslow, 1993.

Pluhar, Evelyn. *Beyond Prejudice: The Moral Significance of Human and Nonhuman Animals.* Durham, NC: Duke University Press, 1995.

Regan, Tom. *The Case for Animal Rights.* Berkeley: University of California Press, 1983.

Singer, Peter. *Animal Liberation* (rev. ed.). New York: Avon, 1990.

Vegetarianism and Farm Animals

Coe, Sue. *Dead Meat.* New York: Four Walls Eight Windows, 1996.

Davis, Karen. *Prisoned Chickens, Poisoned Eggs.* Summertown, TN: The Book Publishing Company, 1996.

Eisnitz, Gail. *Slaughterhouse.* Amherst, NY: Prometheus, 1997.

Lyman, Howard. *Mad Cowboy.* New York: Scribner, 1998.

Mason, Jim and Peter Singer. *Animal Factories.* New York: Crown, 1990.

Rampton, Sheldon and Stauber, John. *Mad Cow USA: Could the Nightmare Happen Here?* Monroe, ME: Common Courage, 1997.

Vegetarian Cookbooks

Diamond, Marilyn. *The American Vegetarian Cookbook From the Fit For Life Kitchen*. New York: Warner, 1990.

Hurd, Frank J., and Hurd, Rosalie. *Ten Talents*. Collegedale, TN: The College Press, 1968.

Nashimoto, Miyoko. *The Now and Zen Epicure*. Summertown, TN: Book Publishing Company, 1991.

PETA, *Cooking with PETA: Great Vegan Recipes for a Compassionate Kitchen*. Summertown, TN: Book Publishing Company, 1997.

Pickarski, Ron. *Friendly Foods*. Berkeley, CA: Ten Speed Press, 1991.

Pickarski, Ron. *Eco-Cuisine*. Berkeley, CA: Ten Speed Press, 1995.

Raymond, Jennifer. *The Peaceful Palate: Fine Vegetarian Cuisine*. Summertown, TN: Book Publishing Company, 1996.

Wagner, Lindsay and Spade, Ariane. *The High Road to Health—A Vegetarian Cookbook*. New York: Prentice Hall, 1990.

Wasserman, Debra, and Mangels, Reed. *Simply Vegan* (2d ed.). Baltimore: Vegetarian Resource Group, 1995.

Vegetarian Organizations

American Vegan Society, P.O. Box H, Malaga, NJ 08328

International Vegetarian Union, P.O. Box 38.130, 28080 Madrid, Spain, www.ivu.org/

North American Vegetarian Society, P.O. Box 72, Dolgeville, NY 13329, www.cyberveg.org/navs/

The Vegetarian Resource Group, P.O. Box 1463, Baltimore, MD 21203, www.vrg.org

The Vegetarian Society of the United Kingdom, Parkdale, Dunham Road, Altrincham, Cheshire WA14 4QG, www.vegsoc./index1.html

The Vegetarian Youth Network, P.O. Box 1141, New Paltz, NY 12561. www.geocities.com/Rainforest/Vines/4482/

Vegan Action, P.O. Box 4353, Berkeley, CA 94703-0353, www.vegan.org/

Vegan Outreach, 211 Indian Drive, Pittsburgh, PA 15238. www,vegsource.com/vo/mainsite/main.html

Vegan Standards and Certification Project Inc., 91 Joralemon Street, Suite 4, Brooklyn, NY 11201, www.veganstandards.org/

Vegetarian Union of North America, P.O. Box 9710, Washington, DC 20016

The Vivavegie Society, P.O. Box 294, New York, NY 10012, www.earthbase/org/vivavegie

Organizations Supporting Vegetarianism

American Anti-Vivisection Society, 801 Old York Road #204, Jenkintown, PA 19046-1685, www.aavs.org/

Animal Place, 3448 Laguna Creek Trail, Vacaville, CA 95688-9724, www.envirolink.org/arrs/animal place/ap www.htm

Doris Day Animal League, 227 Massachusetts Avenue, NE, Suite 100, Washington, DC 20002, www.ddal.org

EarthSave International, 620B Distillery Commons, Louisville, KY 40206, earthsave.vegsource.com/index.html

Farm Animal Reform Movement (FARM), P.O. Box 30654, Bethesda, MD 20824, envirolink.org/arrs/farm

Farm Sanctuary, P.O. Box 150, Watkins Glen, NY 14891, www.farmsanctuary.org

Friends of Animals, 777 Post Road, Suite 205, Darien, CT 06820, envirolink.org/arrs/foa

Humane Society of the United States, 2100 L Street, NW, Washington, DC 20037, www.hsus.org

People for the Ethical Treatment of Animals, 501 Front Street, Norfolk, VA 23510, envirolink.org/arrs/peta/index.html

Physicians' Committee for Responsible Medicine, 5100 Wisconsin Avenue, Suite 404, Washington, DC 20016, www.pcrm.org/

The Fund for Animals, 200 West 57th Street, New York, NY 10019, envirolink.org/arrs/fund/

United Poultry Concerns, Inc., P.O. Box 59367, Potomac, MD 20859. www.envirolink.org/arrs/animal place/ap

Vegetarian and Related Publications

The Animals' Agenda, 3201 Elliott Street, Baltimore, MD 21224, www.animalsagenda.org

Satya: A magazine of vegetarianism, environmentalism and animal advocacy, P.O. Box 138, New York, NY 10012, www.montelis.com/satya/

Vegetarian Journal, The Vegetarian Resource Group, P.O. Box 1463, Baltimore, MD 21203, www.vrg.org

Vegetarian Times, P.O. Box 446, Mt. Morris, Ill. 61054-9894, www.vegetariantimes.com/

The Vivavine, P.O. Box 294, New York, NY 10012, www.earthbase/org/vivavegie

Vegetarian Conferences

American Vegan Society—annual conference in the United States sponsored by the American Vegan Society (see above)

European Vegetarian Congress—periodic conference sponsored by the International Vegetarian Union (see above).

Vegetarian Summerfest—annual conference in the United States sponsored by the North American Vegetarian Society (see above).

World Vegetarian Congress—periodic conference sponsored by the International Vegetarian Union (see above).

Some Other Resources

Bloch, Abby and Thomson, Cynthia A. "Position of The American Dietetic Association: Phytochemicals and Functional Foods." Chicago: 1994.

Havala, Suzanne and Dwyer, Johanna. "Position of The American Dietetic Association: Vegetarian Diets." Chicago: 1992.

National Research Council, Commission on Life Sciences, Food and Nutrition Board. *Recommended Dietary Allowances,* 10th ed. Washington, DC: National Academy Press, 1989.

Shanklin, Carol W. and Hoover, Linda. "Position of The American Dietetic Association: Health Implications of Dietary Fiber." Chicago: 1992.

The China-Cornell-Oxford Project on Nutrition, Health and Environment at Cornell University, Division of Nutritional Sciences, Cornell University, Savage Hall, Ithaca, NY 14853-6301. www.human.cornell.edu/DNS/ChinaProject/

United States Department of Agriculture, Agricultural Research Service, Nutrient Data Laboratory. "USDA Nutrient Database for Standard Reference, Release 11," and interim amendments thereto, Washington, DC: 1997. www.nal.usda.gov/fnic/foodcomp/

United States Department of Agriculture, National Agricultural Statistics Service, *USDA Economics and Statistics System.* Washington, DC: 1997.

United States Department of Agriculture, Office of Communications *Agricultural Fact Book* 1996. Washington, DC: 1997.

United States Department of Agriculture, United States Department of Health and Human Services. "Nutrition And Your Health: Dietary Guidelines For Americans, 4th ed." Washington DC: 1995.

United States Food and Drug Administration. "Daily Values for Food Labels". Washington, DC: 1997.

Mark Warren Reinhardt, once a perfectly contented meat-eater himself, has been a vegetarian for 20-odd years (some of them very odd). He is a former Director of the Vegetarian Society of Colorado and author of many articles on vegetarianism, including his popular vegetarian column *On or Off the Mark*. Mr. Reinhardt holds degrees in engineering and law from Duke, Harvard, and the University of Chicago, and was named *Time Magazine*'s Man-of-the-Year in 1966 (no kidding!).* He lives in Denver.

* All right, so what if that was the year they gave the award to everyone in America under the age of 25?

CONTINUUM BOOKS

ON VEGETARIANISM
AND ANIMAL RIGHTS

Carol J. Adams
The Sexual Politics of Meat
A Feminist Vegetarian Critical Theory

"[L]ikely to both inspire and enrage readers across the political spectrum."—**Library Journal**

"New ground—whole acres of it—is broken by Adams."—**The Washington Post**

"Original provocative...makes a major contribution to the debate on animal rights."—**Publishers Weekly**

"A monumentally important book. It holds the promise of helping change social customs. Neither the feminist movement nor the animal rights movements will ever be quite the same."—**Tom Regan**

"It's a consciousness-raising and conscience challenging book."
—**Andrea Dworkin**

"You thought you'd heard it all by now, but you were wrong."—**National Review**

"Adams' observations are telling, most are seductively sprung, and overall, the argument is both thoughtful and thought-provoking—and not without elegance."—**Kirkus Reviews**

"A dynamic contribution toward creating a feminist/animal rights theory."—**The Animals' Agenda**

"Read this powerful new book and you may well become a vegetarian."—**Ms.**

"The impact of a book like this is immeasurable."—**New Directions for Women**

256 pp   0-8264-0513-4 $16.95 pbk

Carol J. Adams
Neither Man nor Beast
Feminism and the Defense of Animals

"[Adams'] thinking is brilliant and original, and this volume belongs in every women's studies, theology, and environmental ethics collection."—**Choice**

"[Adams] advocates an activism that reveals the truth about animal suffering and about women's lives.... Recommended."—Library Journal

"[This book] very usefully brings together Adams' thinking on animal defense as it has developed since the publication of her first book *The Sexual Politics of Meat.*"—**The Animals' Agenda**

"This work of unflinching intelligence makes connections crucial to any kind of survival with integrity. Buy it. Read it. Be challenges and changed forever."—**ROBIN MORGAN**

"A collection of compelling new reflections on animal rights, vegetarianism, and ecofeminism."—**Feminist Bookstore News**

"Carol Adams does for women and animals what the authors of *Our Bodies, Ourselves* did for women's health. She provides a strong feminist foundation upon which a movement can be built and analysis can be deepened. She proves insightfully that 'the unexamined meal is not worth eating.' Her visionary construction of an animal- and women-friendly future deserves widespread attention and adherence."—**MARY E. HUNT**

"For anyone wanting to enlarge their understanding of and feelings for animals, nature and ourselves, *Neither Man nor Beast* is one selection that must be read."—**The AV**

"Carol Adams looks unsparingly at the way our culture has conditioned us to accept as normal the staggering cruelty inflicted daily on millions of animals. From theology to nutrition, from reproductive rights to pornographic images, she shows how assumed male superiority to women and other animals pervades our lives."—**JANE TOMPKINS**

272 pp 0-8264-0803-6 $15.95 pbk

Carol J. Adams, Editor
Ecofeminism and the Sacred

Includes articles by Karen Warren, Rosemary Radford Ruether, Stephanie Kaza, Catherine Keller and others.

"An outstanding introduction to the issues and problems of ecofeminist spirituality."—**Choice**

"This multicultural anthology is a thoughtful contribution to an evolving body of analysis and action."—**Ms.**

352 pp 0-8264-0667-X $15.95 pbk

Josephine Donovan and Carol J. Adams, Editors
Beyond Animal Rights
A Feminist Caring Ethic for the Treatment of Animals

Writings by Marti Kheel, Deane Curtin, Brian Luke, Kenneth Shapiro, and Rita C. Manning.

"An important and challenging collection."—**Feminists for Animal Rights Newsletter**

"A valuable addition to the genre."—**Publishers Weekly**

228 pp 0-8264-0836-2 $24.95 hbd

Jim Mason
An Unnatural Order
Why We Are Destroying the Planet and Each Other

"Clever and subversive."—**Kirkus Reviews**

"An eloquent, important plea for a total rethinking of our relationship to the animal world. Mason analyzes the West's 'dominionist' world view, which exalts humans as overlords and owners of other life.... His powerfully argued manifesto will change many readers' attitudes towards hamburgers, animal experimentation, hunting, and circuses."
—**Publishers Weekly**

"A wonderful and important book."—**JOHN ROBBINS**

352 pp 0-8264-1028-6 $17.95 pbk

Michael Tobias
World War III
Population and the Biosphere at the End of the Millennium
New Continuum Edition

This compelling call for the earth to wake up to the environmental crisis threatening us all, explores the issues of environmental resources and human population growth. Tobias argues that these problems are only going to increase in urgency, and we need all the resources we can to combat or possibly avert the coming disasters.

"[Reads] like a volcano erupting."—**Psychology Today**

300 pp 0-8264-1085-5 $19.95 pbk

WESTFIELD PUBLIC LIBRARY

7 8292 000135578

613.262
Reinhardt, Mark Warren
Perfectly Contented Meat-Eater's
Guide to Vegetarianism

WESTFIELD PUBLIC LIBRARY
333 West Hoover Street
Westfield, IN 46074

Westfield Public Library
Westfield, IN 46074

$1.00 Fine for Removing
the Bar Code Label!!

DEMCO